G000272679

ENTERTAINING
THE
PERSIAN WAY

SHIRIN SIMMONS

ENTERTAINING THE PERSIAN WAY

LENNARD PUBLISHING

1988

Lennard Publishing
a division of Lennard Books Ltd

Lennard House
92 Hastings Street
Luton, Beds LU1 5BH

British Library in Publication Data is available for this title
ISBN 1 85291 026 7

Editor: Jeni Wright
First published 1988
© Shirin Simmons 1988

This book is copyright under the Berne Convention.
No reproduction without permission. All rights reserved.

Phototypeset by Goodfellow & Egan, Cambridge

Cover design by Pocknell and Co.

Printed and bound in Great Britain by
Butler & Tanner Ltd, Frome and London

Contents

Spinach and Mortadella hors d'oeuvre/Pishghazay-e-esfenaj va kalbas
Aubergine Starter/Kashk-o-Badimjan
Gherkin hors d'oeuvre/Pishghazay-e-khiyar
Meatballs in Walnut and Yoghurt Sauce/Kaleh joosh

Meat and Vegetable Main Courses
Aubergine in Yoghurt and Saffron Sauce/Borani-e-badimjan
Savoury Meat Cakes/Kotlet-e-shirin torsh
Stuffed Shoulder of Lamb/Shaneh-e-bareh
Meatball Surprise/Koofteh tabrizi
Roast and Fruit Pot/Tass kabab
Complete Meal-in-a-bowl/Ash-e-sholeh ghalamkar
Mung Bean Meal-in-a-bowl/Ash-e-mash
Grape Meal-in-a-bowl/Ash-e-ab-e-ghooreh
Golden Meal-in-a-bowl/Ash-e-lapeh
Yoghurt Meal-in-a-bow/Ashe-me-mast
Pomegranate Meal-in-a-bowl/Ash-e-anar
Courgette Khoresh with split Yellow Lentils/Khoresh-e-kadu
Mince and Potato Khoresh/Khoresh-e-kimeh ba sib zamini
Quince Khoresh/Khoresh-e-beh
Rhubarb Khoresh/Khoresh-e-rivas
Stuffed mashed potatoes/Kotlet-e-sibzamini
Lentil Cutlets/Kotlet-e-adas
Aubergines in Grape Juice/Khoresh-e-badimjamba ab-e-angoor
Dill and Broad Bean Khoresh/Koresh-e-shevid
Okra Khoresh/Koresh-e-bamya
Carrot Khoresh/Khoresh-e-havij
Dill and Coriander Khoresh/Khoresh-e-shevid va geshnez
Garden Pea Pilaf/Polov-e-lubia sabs
Lime Pilaf/Ghymeh polov
Crispy Yoghurt Rice with Lamb or Chicken/Tahchin-e-bareh ya-morgh
Berberry Pilaf/Zereshk polov
Crispy Potato Rice/Polov-e-sadeh ba sibzamini
Lentil and Crispy Potato Rice/Addas polov ba sib zamini
Aubergine and Tomato Dish/Shekam pareh
Spinach and Rice Mould/Tahchin-e-esfenaj

Chicken Main Courses
Olivier Salad/Salad-e-olivier
Roast Chicken in Honey and Cinnamon/Morgh-ba-darchin va asal
Stuffed Chicken with Apricots and Prunes/Morgh-e-porshodeh ba miveh va agil
Chicken in Pomegranate Puree/Khoresh-e-fesenjan
Chicken in Plum and Herb Sauce/Khoresh-e-naana jaafary
Chicken in Orange, Saffron and Nut Sauce/Morgh ba zaafaran va agil
Chicken in Plum and Lentil Sauce/Khoresh-e-alu
Chicken Drumsticks with Orange Sauce/Ran-e-morgh ba abe-porteghal

Side Dishes
Stuffed Courgettes/Dolmeh-e-kadu
Stuffed Onions/Dolmeh-e-piaz
Stuffed Vine Leaves/Dolmeh-e-barg-e-mov

INTRODUCTION

Who I Am

I was born in Yazd in central Persia, which is the name by which I still think of my country, although nowadays it is referred to as Iran. Most of my recipes are traditional and are accompanied by short stories of my childhood and a little of the folklore of the country. There is an old Persian saying, *mehman afarideh-e-khoda ast* – 'God is the creator of guests' – and I felt that in writing this cookery book I would in a way be inviting a very wide circle of 'unknown friends' to share my food.

Being the youngest member of a well-known Zoroastrian family, I was spoilt by my father Khodadad and mother Homayoun, and by my three older brothers and sister. My grandfather, Kayomars Vafadar, a prominent member of the community in Yazd, headed our closely knit and loving family.

Meals at home were as varied in style as the individual flavours of each dish. Usually we ate in the dining room seated around a large walnut table, which at other times was used for ping-pong! On very hot days we would eat in the cool cellar. Rather than move the heavy furniture, we ate *sofreh*-style: sitting around on various cushions, leaning against bolsters and eating from dishes laid out on the *sofreh*, which is a traditional cloth.

As a teenager I came to England with my sister; I qualified as a nurse and also took up an art course and one on beauty therapy. It was at that time that I first experienced a change in diet – roast beef and Yorkshire pudding and fish and chips! I married an Englishman, and a lot of our friends have been surprised when tasting my traditional cooking. Persian food *is* different, but it is not such a shock to Western tastebuds as, say, Indian food, which is very often hotly spiced.

It is a cuisine that offers tantalizing variety, and of course, its character owes an immense amount to the progress of Persian history.

The Persian Empire was perhaps at its peak during the reign of Cyrus the Great (c.550 BC), and its cuisine was influenced by the conquest of vast areas of the Middle East, stretching from Palestine, Cappadocia (Turkey) and Assyria almost to the Indus. However, it is generally considered that it was not until well into the Sassanid dynasty (c.AD 600) that Persian cuisine reached its apogee. Banquets were extravagant at that time, and dishes such as *dolmeh* and *kebabs*, and poultry and meat marinated in yoghurt were popular, just as they are today. Naturally, the Arab invasion (c.AD 636) had – and still has – an important influence on the day-to-day eating habits of the diverse population of this vast country.

The official religion at the time of Cyrus the Great was that of Zoroastrianism, an ancient monotheistic religion based on the sayings and teachings of the prophet Zoroaster. However, the conquest of Persia by the Arabs, and the resultant compulsory conversion to Islam forced many people to flee to India, where they established the Parsee community. The remaining population was made up of Jews, Christians and, in more recent times, a few Bahaists. The result is a culture that has benefited from the co-existance of diverse religions and traditions.

Persia is a country of extremes: lush, fertile areas in the north bordering the Caspian Sea and in the south-west Khorasan area, and arid desert and mountainous terrain in the central and eastern provinces. Although only a little over ten per cent of the land is under cultivation, wheat, barley, rice and sugar beet are all produced, together with rice in the western part of the Caspian lowlands and tea in the eastern Caspian. Apples, pears, quinces and plums are more temperate crops and their production is concentrated in the provinces of Azarbaijan and Khorasan, with pistachios, almonds and walnuts.

Climate, of course, has an important influence on food, both on availability and needs. Temperatures are very high in the south around the Persian Gulf, the Arabian Sea and through the Straits of Hormuz joining the Indian Ocean, but winters are severe in the north and north-west areas such as Azarbaijan, Tehran and some central regions, Esfahan and Yazd. Throughout Persia, however, the four seasons are defined below (the calendar being different from that used in the West).

Even with the great range of climate, religion, culture and other influences, Persian food has become a blend which does not differ greatly from region to region, apart from such small things as, for example, the substitution of almonds for walnuts. The most noticeable specialities are those enjoyed during celebrations and festivals which reflect individual traditions – Muslim Ramazan, Jewish Passover, Christian Christmas and Easter, and Zoroastrian New Year.

Cooking equipment also differs very little from one area to another. Traditional items include the essential *sikh* or skewer (called *shish* in the West), *tabeh*, a handleless flat pan for making HUSHVA NAN, and *gooshtkoob*, a meat tenderiser used in ABGOOSHT. Modern kitchen equipment such as electric choppers, blenders, grinders and food processors are now widely used, replacing the old traditional methods my mother used, and of course making Persian food quicker and easier. One of the main advantages of Persian cooking is that there is no complicated blending of spices, and the vast majority of ingredients can be obtained from most supermarkets and/or the garden.

'Modern' ingredients were already finding their way into my mother's kitchen, but now even more convenience foods have developed, and I make no apology for using such things as packet dried yeast and commercially dried herbs. At home we often used pomegranate purée, for example, but to be practical I suggest substituting tamarind here as it can be bought very easily and will save time and trouble.

Like my mother, and no doubt you too, I cook with a pinch of this and a dash of that, with lots of feeling, looking and tasting. For this book, however, I have meticulously measured every item, to ensure greater accuracy and to give you confidence when cooking Persian food for the first time.

The chapters in this book cover different traditions of Persian entertaining, bearing in mind that you are unlikely to be changing your basic diet. The first chapter is designed to be a gentle introduction to traditional Persian dishes which are easy to prepare and will blend well with the food of other cultures. It is not suggested that you cook your way consecutively through the book, but rather browse through it first and then try various dishes from different chapters. I hope that having let me introduce you to the taste of Persian food, you will soon adapt my recipes to suit yourself and put your own style of creativity on them. This will help perpetuate the development and spread of interest and enjoyment of *Entertaining the Persian Way*.

Persian Seasons

SPRING: 21st March (1st FARVARDIN) to 22nd June (31st KHORDADD)
SUMMER: 22nd June (1st TIR) to 22nd September (31st SHAHRIVAR)
AUTUMN: 23rd September (1st MEHR) to 21st December (30th AZAR)
WINTER: 22nd December (1st DEY) to 21st March (1st FARVARDIN)

1

Introducing Persian Dishes

As everywhere else in the world, each Persian household had its own favourite combination of dishes and individual ways of serving them. More often than not, the dining table would be laid with a selection of different dishes from which to taste, and everyone would choose for themselves, usually selecting one or two of the dishes. Whether one sat at the table or on a rug depended on the occasion and the size of the gathering. In summertime, cellars were often used for family and informal meals because they were so cool, and they were hung with rugs and paintings. Heavy, magnificently coloured and patterned carpets and rugs were laid on the ice-cold marble floor, and we would sit on these, leaning against long, ornate bolsters which lined the walls. In wintertime, with temperatures invariably several degrees below zero, we would eat in the dining room, upstairs in the main part of the house.

If this is the first time you have tried Persian food, you may prefer to try a single dish at first, and to serve it as part of an otherwise familiar meal. Cooking being a creative art you will no doubt have your own ideas, but at the end of this first chapter I have included suggestions for incorporating Persian dishes into everyday meals. These are only guidelines, and you will find that Persian food blends happily with most cuisines, so that menu-making is never a problem.

Abgooshtha

Abgoosht is one of the most traditional of Persian dishes and a good dish to start with as it is so economical and easy to prepare. It is best described as a cross between a soup and a thin stew, and it is so nourishing and substantial that it can be served as a complete meal with NAN (138) or your own choice of bread, followed by something light such as a ham or poultry salad and then cheese or a milk pudding. The basis for most *abgooshtha* is lean stewing meat – either lamb or beef – but if you prefer not to use red meat then chicken portions may be used instead. Traditionally, the bones are left in the meat for greater flavour and succulence, but if you prefer to use cubed, boneless meat or chicken then by all means do so.

The following recipe for ABGOOSHT-E-ALU VA NAANA was one of my father's favourites, especially in summer. Even though it is served hot, it is very refreshing. If any of the children showed signs of starting a cold this would be part of the next meal because daddy (*baba*) believed in the mint for curing coughs and the plums for purifying the blood and lowering the temperature. In fact, it was such a favourite with us all that we would sometimes pretend to have a cold or cough just to be sure of the 'treatment'. Healthy though it is, you certainly don't need to be ailing to enjoy it!

Plum and mint soup

Abgoosht-e-alu va naana

The plums look better in *abgoosht* if left whole, but if you would rather remove the stones before serving, simply press the plums against the side of the pan and you will find the stones will slip out easily. Sugar is often added to this *abgoosht*, but as it is not to everyone's taste it is best to offer this separately at the table so that everyone can help themselves. The amount of sugar needed will depend on the sweetness of the plums; greengages and damsons can be used instead of plums, in which case you will probably find more sugar is required because of their sourness.

2 oz/60 g brown lentils
1½ lb/685 g stewing lamb or beef, washed and cut into large serving pieces
1 lb/455 g red plums, washed
4 oz/115 g mixed fresh mint and parsley, finely chopped, or 2 teaspoons each dried
1 medium onion, peeled and finely chopped
1 teaspoon turmeric
salt and pepper

Pick over the lentils, removing any particles of stone and grit, then wash thoroughly in a sieve under cold running water. Place in a bowl, cover with plenty of lukewarm water and leave to soak for at least 5 hours, preferably overnight. This helps them to cook evenly and in less time.

Put the meat in a large, heavy saucepan. Cover with about 2 pints/ 1.2 litres cold water and place over moderate heat until the froth rises. Immediately remove the pan from the heat to prevent boiling over, spoon off and discard the froth. Return the pan to the heat and bring back to the boil, then reduce the heat to the lowest possible simmer. Cover the pan and cook for 1–2 hours until the meat is tender. (The cooking time will vary according to the type, cut and quality of the meat used.)

Uncover the pan and add the plums, herbs, onion, turmeric and salt and pepper to taste. Drain the lentils, mix into the ingredients in the pan and bring back to boil. Reduce the heat, cover the pan again and simmer for a further 30 minutes or until the lentils are cooked. Check the level of the cooking liquid occasionally during this time and add more water if the *abgoosht* seems dry.

Serve hot in soup bowls with NAN (page 138) or other bread. Alternatively, place a side plate of plain rice next to each individual serving of *abgoosht* so that guests can spoon solid ingredients on to the rice. Soup and rice are then eaten separately, with a spoon.

WATER

Before running water was introduced into the houses in Yazd, water was stored in giant covered reservoirs which had many stairs leading down to them. People had to go down the steep steps every day to fetch water from several brass taps installed in the walls. The water buildings were kept spotlessly clean and could be seen in every few streets, donated to the public by a wealthy member of the community, or by the government. In addition to these there were also small entrances to some hundreds of steps leading deep down into the earth where there was clean running water with stones installed on either side for washing clothes. Often a light of some sort was needed as it was completely dark down there, away from the daylight. Some of the old houses in Yazd had the luxury of having their own steps down to water. Ours was one such house and I remember how relaxing and refreshing it was to go down to have a dip in the clear running stream.

Mung and Blackeyed Bean Soup

Abgoosht-e-mash va-lubia
chesham siyah

In this traditional *abgoosht* recipe the solid ingredients are removed from the soup liquid and pounded. The soup is then served as a first course and the pounded meat (*goosht-e-koobideh*) follows as the main course.

1 oz/30 g mung beans
1 oz/30 g brown lentils
2 oz/60 g black-eyed beans
1 lb/455 g lean stewing lamb or beef, washed and cut into large serving pieces
1 medium or 2 small potatoes, peeled and quartered
1 medium onion, peeled and quartered
¼ teaspoon turmeric
salt and pepper

Prepare and soak the pulses as for the lentils in the recipe for PLUM AND MINT SOUP (above).

Put the meat in a large, heavy saucepan. Cover with about 2 pints/1.2 litres cold water and place over moderate heat until the froth rises. Immediately remove the pan from the heat to prevent boiling over, spoon off and discard the froth. Drain the pulses and add to the meat, return the pan to the heat and bring back to boil. Reduce the heat to the lowest possible simmer, cover the pan and cook for 1–2 hours until the meat is tender. (The cooking time will vary according to the type, cut and quality of the meat used.)

Uncover the pan and add the potatoes, onion, turmeric and salt and pepper to taste. Stir well and bring back to the boil, then reduce the heat, cover the pan again and simmer for a further 30 minutes or until the potatoes are cooked. Check the level of the cooking liquid occasionally and add more water (about 6 fl oz/175 ml) if the *abgoosht* seems dry.

With a ladle, transfer the solid ingredients from the pan to a heavy bowl. Keep the soup liquid hot in the pan over very low heat. Pound the solid ingredients with a tenderiser or potato masher, discarding any bones from the meat. Add 2–3 tablespoons of the hot soup liquid to the pounded mixture (*goosht-e-koobideh*) if you prefer a creamier consistency.

Serve the soup hot as a starter, followed by the *goosht-e-koobideh*. Alternatively, the two may be served together, with *goosht-e-koobideh* on individual side plates. NAN (page 138) and homemade plain yoghurt are the traditional accompaniments.

LEARNING BY ONE'S MISTAKES

In winter a wide variety of dishes were made with beetroot. I learnt one of my first basic cookery lessons when, cold and hungry, I arrived home from school in the snow. My mother had left out a plate of sparkling, ruby-red, diced home-cooked beetroot and a bowl of freshly set yoghurt. It looked temptingly appetising, so I decided to surprise mother and the rest of the family by mixing the two together and cooking them – so that there would be a nice hot dish to welcome them on such a cold day.

Unfortunately, I just poured both the ingredients into a large saucepan over high heat and within moments I had a curdled mess. My mother was very understanding and explained to me that yoghurt and beetroot are always served cold as a salad or starter. But at the same time she also told me that if I ever wanted to cook yoghurt again I should add a little flour or lightly beaten egg white to the yoghurt before putting it on the stove. This was a trick she had learned to prevent hot yoghurt curdling – and it certainly works.

Yoghurt and Beetroot

Mast-o-laboo

This is one of the simplest and cheapest of dishes, and yet it makes a most attractive starter for a plain meal such as grilled fish followed by a dessert of stewed fruit. Be sure to use only plain boiled or steamed beetroot, not the kind that has been pickled in vinegar. To crush dried mint, simply rub it between the palms of your hands.

8 fl oz/225 ml plain yoghurt
2 medium or 4 small freshly cooked beetroot (about 8 oz/230 g), peeled and rinsed
a little finely chopped fresh mint or crushed dried mint, to garnish

Put the yoghurt in a fairly large bowl. Dice the beetroot small, and stir gently into the yoghurt.

Spoon into 4 individual dishes and sprinkle with the mint.

Serve as a salad or starter. At room temperature in winter, chilled in summer.

THE MAGIC OF THE GHERKIN

For three months every year we would spend our holidays halfway up a mountain in Manshad, more than a mile from the nearest village. A stream gushed down to a nearby reservoir, which provided water for the small juicy gherkins that grew on the terraces.

We would get up early and walk up the mountain paths to the loganberry tree and cut the hard little stems with sharp scissors, usually returning home with our clothes dotted with the pink and red stains of the juice. We would stop on the way back to pick some of the little gherkins for MAST-O-KHIAR. Gherkins always make me think of those summer holidays on the mountains, in particular of the time that my brother showed us a bottle containing a very large cucumber which was much fatter than the bottle's neck. It puzzled me, until I realised that he had actually grown it in the bottle by placing the bottle on the ground beside the plant with the barely formed shoot inside. When the cucumber was fully grown he cut it free and filled the bottle with alcohol to preserve it.

MEMORIES OF HEALTHY AND TASTY YOGHURT

My sister was a nurse in a Tehran hospital, and it was not easy for her to be at home during the day, so I often took time off from work to give my mother a hand looking after my baby niece Jaleh. Fortunately I, too, had previously qualified as a nurse, so I was not too bad at handling the baby. She was very difficult to please as far as food was concerned, but I soon got to know her little ways and how to satisfy and feed her. I have vivid memories of holding her in my arms, wrapped in her little white blanket, walking along the terrace even on cold winter days, and spooning nourishing homemade yoghurt (*mast*) into her mouth. She loved it – so we were both happy. Later when my sister's son Farshad came

along he also loved being fed with *mast*. They are both grown up now, but we still all enjoy such dishes as MAST-O-KHIAR.

Yoghurt and Cucumber

Mast-o-khiar

This starter was served all year round and so dried mint was invariably used. Even if fresh mint is available, somehow it doesn't seem to have the subtlety of flavour to go with yoghurt and cucumber and so I find it better to always use dried mint. An attractive way to serve MAST-O-KHIAR is in individual bowls with the initial of each person sprinkled on top in mint.

8 fl oz/225 ml plain yoghurt
½ medium cucumber, peeled and very finely chopped
1 garlic clove, peeled and crushed
¼ teaspoon crushed dried mint

Put the yoghurt in a fairly large bowl, add the cucumber and garlic and stir well to mix. Add the tip of the spoon of mint and stir again, then spoon into 4 individual dishes. Sprinkle with the remaining mint, then chill well in the refrigerator before serving.

Serve chilled.

BAGH

A *bagh* is a plot of land surrounded by walls with a wooden door entrance; it was the most popular form of land ownership in Persia and virtually everyone in Yazd had their own *bagh*, usually handed down from one generation to the next. Our *bagh* was from my grandfather. It was built on a terrace and was very large. The 'bagh season' would start in spring and go on until September – or until the first snow was on the ground. Opening the wooden door to our *bagh* one passed straight away into an atmosphere of peace and tranquillity: ripened apricots and mulberries on the ground, panoramic views of fruit trees and roses, vegetables and pulses growing closely together in rows with brilliant coloured flowers. And the long narrow channel of running water, which we had to pay for by the minute!

PERSIAN CHEESE

When I was a child, a woman used to come to our door selling a basic Persian cheese (PANIR) and her own freshly made yoghurt from a deep pottery jar (*koozeh*). Although many years have passed since then I can still remember their taste and their natural freshness.

PANIR (page 151) is an all-year, all-occasion cheese. At its most elegant, for entertaining, it is served with style. In the hot summer months it makes a delicious morning snack eaten with fresh fruit such as melon and grapes or slices of cucumber and a bowl of honey or golden syrup. As a salad it is refreshingly tasty and satisfying combined with sliced cucumber, spring onions, mint and tarragon.

Cheese and Herb Starter

Salad-e-panir va-sabsi

Spring onion tassels make an unusual and attractive garnish for this salad. Cut off and discard the green parts of spring onions. Make lengthways cuts at both ends of the white parts, taking care that the cuts do not meet in the centre. Soak in iced water for about 20 minutes, until the ends curl up.

12 oz/345 g PANIR
2 fl oz/50 ml olive oil
1 garlic clove, peeled and crushed
3 oz/90 g mixed fresh mint, tarragon and parsley, finely chopped
3 oz/90 g nuts (preferably walnuts) coarsely chopped
GARNISH
2 oz/60 g sultanas
few spring onion tassels

Put the diced PANIR in a large bowl. Pour on the olive oil and gently toss a few times to mix. Add the garlic to the bowl with the chopped herbs and nuts. Toss again several times, then transfer to one large serving dish or individual dishes. Arrange the sultanas and spring onion tassels over the salad as a garnish.

Serve as soon as possible, at room temperature, with NAN (page 138).

ASH

This dish is not yet widely known in the West, but it is marvellously warming, economical and nourishing. Made from pulses and grains such as beans, peas, barley, rice and wheat, cooked with meat and sometimes fruit, it is a complete meal in a bowl. I find it excellent on cold winter evenings, garnished with HOT MINT (page 150) and eaten with bread. For vegetarians the meat can simply be omitted, yet it still provides a most nutritious one-course meal.

MORE GUESTS – MORE WATER

In the holiday region of Deh-bala in Yazd I used to wake up with the sun flickering through the vine arching over the balcony. The only sound would be the song of the nightingale and the flowing water of the stream from the high mountains that ran at the bottom of the deep bank which was only a few feet from the back door.

My middle brother, Khodabakhsh, was very good at carving walking sticks from the long, thick, fresh branches. He would cover the whole stick with beautifully worked flowers and birds so that they were almost too precious to dig into the steep rocky mountainside. He gave one to each of us; mine was the smallest and, I felt, the best. I was only about seven years old and I used to carry my walking stick proudly with me wherever I went.

In front of the house there was a green and fertile orchard with low growing fruit interspersed with various herbs, the scent of which was delightful. I was always keen to know what we were having for lunch so that I could be the first to pick the required herbs, and I was always tempted to use my little stick to shake the fruit from the trees. Too often I was scolded – for knocking off the unripe fruit!

I also used to help with the cooking, and the meal would be served under the arch of vines. It was an easy-going, simple life there. We had only a few neighbours, but they would often drop in during the morning and stay for lunch – my mother welcomingly saying, 'It's all right, I'll just add a little water to the pan and there will be enough for everyone.' That is in fact one of the advantages of a dish such as ASH-E-PORTEGHAL . . .

Orange Meal-in-a-bowl

Ash-e-Porteghal

The Persian name for the meatballs in this dish is *koofteh rizeh*. Even though the lentils used are the split variety, it is still essential to soak them before cooking. If they are not soaked they will not cook evenly.

2 oz/60 g split yellow lentils
8 oz/230 g minced lean lamb or beef
2 medium onions, peeled
2 fl oz/50 ml oil
8 oz/230 g fresh spinach leaves, stalks removed, washed and coarsely chopped
½ oz/15 g rice flour
¼ pint/150 ml fresh orange juice
salt and pepper

Prepare and soak the lentils as in the recipe for PLUM and MINT SOUP (page 11).

Put the meat in a bowl. Grate 2 oz/60 g of the onion to a juice over the meat. Knead with your hands for about 5 minutes until the meat binds together. Form into smooth balls the size of hazelnuts.

Finely chop the remaining onion. Heat the oil in a 4 pint/2.25 litre casserole or heavy saucepan, add the chopped onion and fry gently until golden. Add the meatballs to the onion and fry over gentle heat for 4–5 minutes until browned on all sides. Drain the lentils and add to the pan, stirring gently for an additional minute to help seal. Add the spinach and 8 fl oz/225 ml cold water, stir carefully to mix and bring to the boil. Reduce the heat to the lowest possible simmer, cover the pan tightly and cook for 45 minutes or until the lentils are tender.

Mix the rice flour to a paste in a bowl with 3 fl oz/85 ml cold water, then stir into the ingredients in the pan. Simmer gently, uncovered, for 4–5 minutes, stirring occasionally to keep the mixture smooth. Add the orange juice and salt and pepper to taste. Simmer for a further 2 minutes only – if cooked longer the orange flavour will evaporate.

Serve hot.

RICE

The two most common types of rice in Persia are *domsiah* and *sadri*, but these are not easy to obtain abroad except in Persian shops; basmati rice is the nearest equivalent in scent, flavour and texture and it is widely available in both supermarkets and Indian grocers. It is the rice I recommend for most Persian dishes, although sometimes short grain or round rice is more suitable, in which case I have specified it in individual recipes. There are various names for the many different ways of cooking rice. *Chelou* is plain rice, *polov* is rice mixed with other ingredients such as vegetables or meat. *Kateh* is cooked with one part rice and approximately two parts water and a little butter, oil or margarine so that all the liquid is absorbed into the rice.

Although most basmati rice is cleaned before packing it is advisable to place it on a white plate before cooking and to check that there are no odd pieces of grit or other bits that may have got through. In all the rice recipes in this book I refer to this as cleaning before washing. After cleaning, wash off excess starch by placing the rice in several changes of cold water and rinsing it well until the water is clear. Never use hot water for washing rice as it is likely to soften and break the grains. Drain the rice after rinsing, then soak in a bowl of lukewarm water for five hours or overnight – this ensures that each grain cooks evenly, as when soaking pulses. To keep each grain separate the secret is to cook in a large enough saucepan for the rice to expand without being pressed against the sides. Always use a non-stick or heavy aluminium pan with a well-fitting lid.

The Persian way of cooking rice is unique: first the rice is parboiled, then it is drained of all water and the cooking is finished off over dry heat in a heavy saucepan with an insulated lid. This method, called *dam* in Persian (meaning 'to brew'), allows the rice to cook in its own steam, producing separate grains with a fluffy texture and a crisp layer underneath. It is a far healthier method than boiling or steaming, in that excess starch is removed with the discarded water after parboiling.

When Persian rice is served it is turned out onto a serving plate so that the crisp layer is uppermost. Called *tahdig* (*tah* meaning 'bottom' and *dig* meaning 'pan'), this is considered the best part of the rice, especially by children. I remember my sister and brothers could never wait for dinner to be served and would often sneak into the kitchen to eat the crispy *tahdig* from the bottom of the pan, before it got to the table!

TO COOK PLAIN RICH (CHELOU) THE PERSIAN WAY

To serve with a main course, 12oz/345 g basmati rice and 3 oz butter is sufficient for 4 people.

First clean, wash and soak the rice as in the general instructions above, then 'insulate' the lid of a 4 pint/2.25 litre heavy-based saucepan. Lay a clean tea towel flat on a work surface, place the saucepan lid on top and wrap in the tea towel, bringing all the ends to the centre over the handle. Secure the ends with a safety pin. Fill the saucepan about one-third to one-half full with cold water (no more or it will boil over), add 2 teaspoons salt and bring to the boil. Drain the soaked rice, add it to the water and bring back to the boil. Immediately lower the heat to simmer gently and parboil for 4 minutes Drain in a sieve and rinse under cold running water to remove any scum. (Do not rinse under hot water as this is likely to spoil the texture of the rice.) Thoroughly wash the pan to remove all scum then, using both hands, sprinkle the rice into the clean pan (this allows air to get between the grains). Cut the butter and dot all over the rice. Fit the insulated lid on tightly, place the pan over high heat for 1 minute, then reduce to very low and cook for 15–30 minutes without lifting the lid. The lower the heat

the longer the rice takes to cook and the crispier the bottom layer becomes, although you can raise the heat towards the end of cooking to make it crispier still.

𝓛𝓸𝓿𝓮

Lentil and Sultana Pilaf

Adas Polov

With both lentils and rice cooked together, this pilaf makes a most nutritious meal. For vegetarians, simply omit the minced meat: the combination of lentils and rice provides first-class protein which has the same nutritional value as meat.

2 oz/60 g brown lentils
11 oz/315 g basmati rice
12 oz/345 g lean minced lamb or beef
2 medium onions, peeled
salt and pepper
25 ml/1 fl oz oil
2 oz/60 g sultanas
1 teaspoon ground cinnamon
2 oz/60 g butter or margarine

Prepare and soak the lentils as in the recipe for PLUM AND MINT SOUP (page 11). Clean, wash and soak the rice according to the general instructions above.

Put the meat in a bowl. Grate 4 oz/ 115 g of the onions to a juice over the meat. Add a little salt and pepper, then knead with your hands for about 5 minutes until the meat binds together. Form into smooth balls the size of hazelnuts.

Finely chop the remaining onion. Heat the oil in a heavy saucepan, add the chopped onion and fry gently until golden. Add the meatballs to the onion and fry over gentle heat for 4-5 minutes until browned on all sides. Stir in the sultanas and immediately remove the pan from the heat. Set aside to cool.

Put the lentils and their soaking water in a separate saucepan and bring to the boil. Lower the heat and simmer for 20 minutes until the lentils are cooked but not too soft. Drain and rinse under cold running water.

Drain the rice, then parboil, drain and rinse according to the general instructions above. Using both hands, sprinkle half of the parboiled rice into the rinsed-out pan. Sprinkle on the cooked lentils. Cover with the cooled meat and sultana mixture and its oil, sprinkle over the cinnamon, then top with the remaining rice. Cut the butter or margarine into small pieces and dot them all over the rice. Wrap the lid of the pan in a tea towel according to the general instructions above, fit tightly on the pan and place over high heat for 1 minute until sizzling. Reduce the heat to very ¹ ⏤nd *dam* for 45 minutes without lifting the lid. ⏤urn out onto a warmed serving plate.

Serve hot, with plain yoghurt.

PRODUCE OF THE CASPIAN

One year, my husband and I were invited to go with my sister, her husband and two children on a tour of the Caspian Sea. We drove the 400 miles from Tehran through groves where the oranges looked like gleaming light bulbs. The journey was all the more exciting knowing that we were so close to the borders of Russia.

One of the most fascinating things was seeing the sturgeon being caught and watching the extraction of the caviar, but for me a visit to see the rice cultivation, harvesting and preparation was a dream come true. It was very difficult to get a permit for this but my brother-in-law managed it by stressing how far we had travelled. I was thrilled to watch the planting of the seeds below inches of water, and actually to be in the mountains of rice and see how they thrashed it to remove the husks.

On the way back at the end of the holiday we stopped at various restaurants in the evenings and ate in the open air, enjoying the cool breezes from the mountains and the sea. The smell of the *jujeh kabab* (barbecued chicken) sprinkled liberally with lime juice came wafting temptingly as we sat beneath the trees with millions of stars shining through. In summer you could always guarantee brilliantly sunny days and clear skies in the evenings, and the mountains were incredibly beautiful. It always struck me what a contrast this was to the winter when often

those who trusted the mountains were killed by fatal avalanches.

Cherry Pilaf

Alubalu polov

Fresh cherries are always used when available, but as their season is so short most cooks rely on dried or frozen cherries at other times of year. If you are lucky enough to have fresh ones, you will need 1 lb/455 g for this recipe. Remove their stems and cut them in half, then simmer with the sugar for about 7 minutes until soft. Cool, then remove the stones. Use the cherries and cooking juice in exactly the same way as the frozen ones in this recipe.

Original Persian recipes for this pilaf used saffron to colour some of the rice. This was arranged like a border around the pilaf when served, as in the photograph on page 00. Saffron threads are very expensive, but powdered saffron is a cheaper alternative and may also be used. At the end of the cooking time, mix 3 tablespoons rice with ⅛ teaspoon powdered saffron dissolved in 1 tablespoon boiling water.

11 oz/315 g basmati rice
8 oz/230 g frozen black cherries
1 oz/30 g sugar
2 teaspoons lemon juice
1½ lb/685 g chicken breasts, skin removed, or very lean and tender boneless lamb (fillet or leg)
1 fl oz/25 ml oil
1 medium onion, peeled and coarsely chopped
¼ teaspoon turmeric
1¼ teaspoons ground cinnamon
salt and pepper
2 oz/60 g unsalted shelled pistachio nuts, cut into strips
2 oz/60 g blanched almonds, cut into strips
2½ oz/75 g butter or margarine

Clean, wash and soak the rice according to the general instructions on page 16. Put the frozen cherries in a bowl, sprinkling the sugar between the layers. Leave to defrost overnight.

The next day, place the cherries and their liquid in a small, heavy pan. Bring to the boil, then reduce the heat and simmer for 2 minutes. With a slotted spoon, transfer the cherries to a bowl. Add the lemon juice to the cherry juice in the pan and boil vigorously for 3 minutes until reduced to 1 fl oz/ 25 ml. Remove from the heat.

Wash the chicken or lamb and pat dry with kitchen paper. Heat the oil in a heavy saucepan, add the onion and fry gently until golden. Add the chicken or lamb and toss over gentle heat for 3 to 4 minutes. Add in the turmeric, cinnamon and peppers, stir for an additional minute. Pour in 4 fl oz/125 ml cold water and bring to the boil, then reduce the heat and simmer gently for 20 minutes or until the meat is tender. With a slotted spoon, transfer the meat to a plate. Increase the heat under the pan and boil the gravy vigorously until reduced to about 4 tablespoons. Remove from the heat.

Drain the rice, then parboil, drain and rinse according to the instructions on page 16. Melt half of the butter or margarine in the rinsed-out pan. Using both hands, sprinkle half of the parboiled rice into the pan. Cut the chicken or lamb into four or more pieces and place on the rice. Cover with half of the cherries and sprinkle on the remaining cinnamon. Put the pistachios in a corner of the pan and cover with a little rice to protect them from losing colour. Sprinkle the almonds all over the cherries and cover with the rest of the rice.

Melt the remaining butter or margarine and pour over the rice, then pour over the gravy. Wrap the lid of the pan in a tea towel according to the instructions above, fit tightly on the pan and place over high heat for 1 minute until sizzling. Reduce the heat to the lowest possible and *dam* for 1 hour without lifting the lid. Remove the pistachios carefully with a spoon. Turn the pilaf out onto a warmed plate, reserving the crispy base (*tahdig*). Reheat the cherry juice and pour over the dish. Place the crispy *tahdig* on top and sprinkle on the remaining cherries and the pistachios.

Note: this dish can also be prepared in the oven, a convenient method when entertaining as you will not have to worry about the rice catching on top of the stove and there is less chance of the cherries burning. Follow the recipe above, layering the ingredients in a deep 8 inch/20 cm square baking dish rather than the saucepan. Do not pour the gravy over the top. Cover the dish with foil instead of the insulated lid and cook in the coolest part of a preheated 300°F/150°C/gas mark 2 oven for 2 hours or until the bottom of the dish is crispy. Turn out and serve as in the recipe above.

Serve hot, with a seasonal salad for a complete lunch or evening meal.

LESSONS WITH FISH

My sister-in-law, who is also called Shirin, first taught me how to choose fish when the fishmonger used to call with his big basket at the door of my brother's apartment in Tehran. She told me to look first at the eyes to see that they are not sunken and that the gills are fresh, bright and pink. Then don't be afraid to smell the fish. Even if you are buying from a shop you should not be shy about examining it thoroughly.

GREY MULLET WITH CHESTNUTS, GRAPES AND HERBS is a real picture, and everyone loved it so much in our family that there never seemed to be enough to go round. The sweet and sour, crunchy taste of the nuts was heaven to me.

Once, when I returned from England for a long holiday I stayed with my parents in Tehran. We had what is called *dovreh* – a circle of friends who met once a week for lunch, bringing their knitting and sewing, etc. with them; I think I did more knitting then than at any other time of my life. Everyone took it in turn to be hostess and it was at these lunches that I met Mrs George from England. She kept pleading for someone to write down the fish recipe for her and begging one of us to write a book in English on Persian cooking. I kept quiet, but that was when I decided that one day I would reveal the secrets of how to prepare this tasty fish for the dinner table.

Grey mullet with Chestnuts, Grapes and Herbs

Mahi-e-safid-ba balut va-sabsi

Dried chestnuts are used in this recipe, but 8 oz/ 230 g fresh chestnuts can be used when available. Make a slit in the shells of each fresh nut with a sharp knife, then drop them into a saucepan of boiling water. When the shells split open, drain the nuts and remove both the shell and inner skin while they are still hot. Cut each nut in half, place in a small, heavy saucepan and cover with fresh cold water. Bring to the boil, then lower the heat, cover and simmer for 2–3 minutes until soft. Drain well before using.

2 oz/60 g dried chestnuts
3 fl oz/85 ml oil
1 medium onion, peeled and finely chopped
3 garlic cloves, peeled and crushed
8 oz/230 g black or white grapes, halved and seeded
2 teaspoons crushed dried tarragon
1 teaspoon crushed dried parsley
½ teaspoon crushed dried mint
salt and pepper
1 grey mullet, weighing about 2½ lb/1.25 kg, scaled and gutted with head left on
a little plain flour for cleaning fish
juice of 1 small or ½ large lemon

GARNISH
almond flakes, toasted
1 slice of lemon (optional)

Wash the dried chestnuts, place in a bowl and cover with lukewarm water. Leave to soak overnight.

The next day, drain the chestnuts, place in a small saucepan and cover with about 6 fl oz/175 ml cold water. Bring to the boil, reduce the heat and cover tightly. Simmer for 45 minutes until soft, then drain.

Make the stuffing. Heat 2 fl oz/50 ml of the oil in a heavy frying pan, add the onion and fry gently until golden. Add the garlic, stir for 1 minute, then add the chestnuts, half of the grapes, the herbs and salt and pepper to taste. Remove the pan from the heat and set aside to cool.

Preheat the oven to 350°F/180°C/gas mark 4. Rinse the fish under cold running water. Put a little flour inside the cavity of the fish and rub to remove any black bits. Rinse well and pat dry with kitchen paper. Squeeze the lemon juice inside the fish and rub over the flesh. Repeat with any remaining juice on the outside of the fish.

Place the fish in an ovenproof dish just large enough to hold it comfortably. Stuff the cavity with the cooled filling then arrange the fish in a swimming position, if necessary curling the tail inwards. Pour the remaining oil over the fish and cover loosely with foil. Cook in the oven for 1–1¼ hours until the liquid runs clear when the centre of the fish is pierced with a fine metal skewer. Remove the foil and drain off the cooking liquid into a sauceboat. Garnish the fish with the remaining grapes and the flaked almonds. Place the lemon slice in the mouth, if liked.

Serve hot, with plain rice. Hand the cooking liquid separately at the table.

A PERSIAN TASTE

The following dish, APPLE KHORESH WITH CHESTNUTS AND MINT, always reminds me of a very good German friend of my father's called Herr Mitr, who worked as a construction engineer. He came to dinner with his wife and small son and I think it was the first time they had tried Persian cooking. He explained to my mother that his son Peter was not used to anything but very simple food and so could he have a plain omelette for lunch. When we sat down to the meal Peter was served his omelette – but it was left untouched, as he enjoyed the *khoresh* with the rest of us.

From then on, whenever the Mitr family were expected a little extra was made, as Peter could hardly wait to try some new dish. His plate was always cleared first, but his favourite always remained KHORESH-E-SIB BA BALUT VA NAANA, his very first experience of Persian food.

Apple Khoresh with Chestnuts and Mint

Khoresh-e-sib ba balut va nanna

Fresh chestnuts may be used when in season and for this recipe you will need 12 oz/345 g. Prepare and cook them as in the introduction for GREY MULLET WITH CHESTNUTS, GRAPES AND HERBS

5 oz/140 g dried chestnuts
3 fl oz/85 ml oil
1 medium onion, peeled and finely chopped
½ teaspoon turmeric
salt and pepper
10 oz/285 g boneless lean lamb or beef (eg lamb fillet or frying steak), washed and cut into ½ inch/1 cm cubes
2 medium uncooked beetroots, peeled and cut into ¼ inch/5 mm cubes
3 medium sharp eating apples
2 teaspoons crushed dried mint
about 1 teaspoon sugar
about 2 teaspoons lemon juice

Wash the dried chestnuts, place in a bowl and cover with lukewarm water. Leave to soak overnight.

The next day, drain the chestnuts, place in a small saucepan and cover with about 11 fl oz/ 325 ml cold water. Bring to the boil, reduce the heat and cover tightly. Simmer for 45 minutes until soft, then drain.

Heat the oil in a large heavy saucepan, add the onion and fry gently until golden. Add the meat. Stir over moderate heat for about 5 minutes until the pieces of meat are browned on all sides, stir in the spices and stir for one minutes. Add the beetroot and chestnuts, cover with about 1¼ pints/ 750 ml cold water and bring to the boil. Reduce the heat cover tightly and simmer for 1–1¼ hours until the meat and beetroot are tender. Stir frequently during this time to prevent sticking and add up to 3–4 fl oz/85–120 ml water if the *khoresh* seems dry.

Peel, core and slice the apples. Add to the pan with the mint and sugar and lemon juice to taste.

Bring back to the boil, then reduce the heat, cover the pan again and simmer for a further 5–10 minutes. Do not stir during this time or the apples will disintegrate. Uncover the pan and check the liquid level – if the *khoresh* is too runny, boil it vigorously for a few minutes until reduced to a thick mixture.

Serve hot, with plain rice, NAN (page 138) or wholemeal bread.

SNOWY DAYS BUT WARM WITHIN

All the family looked forward to winter, and one of my most vivid childhood memories is of us all sitting round the *corsi*: a coal fire (*manghal*) was placed in the middle of the room with a large wooden stool on top, over which was draped a beautifully patterned hand-made eiderdown. As many as a dozen of us would sit round the *corsi* on hand-made mattresses, our legs stretched out beneath the warm eiderdown, and my father would take the opportunity to teach us children all about the world and broaden our education, and it was on one of those occasions that I learned that the word 'cheque' derives from Persia. Some of the grown-ups would be playing chess, while others played cards and some read or even dozed.

The trees were covered in snow like white bridal gowns and snow flakes danced down from the sky like confetti. Two of my brothers played the citar well and one of our cousins would accompany them on the violin. As we were lulled by the relaxing music we would hear in the background the voice of the snow-sweeper – *barf parookon*. On these cold days my mother would serve the most enjoyable, steaming hot *khoresh* with homemade NAN, and even the snow-sweeper would somehow manage to arrive at just the right moment to get his share.

French Bean Khoresh

Khoresh-e-lubia sabz

2 fl oz/50 ml oil
1 medium onion, peeled and finely chopped

½ teaspoon turmeric

salt and pepper

8 oz/230 g lean tender lamb or beef (lamb fillet or frying steak), washed and cut into ½ inch/1 cm cubes

8 oz/230 g French beans, trimmed and halved

2 medium or 1 large potato, peeled and cut into quarters

1 fl oz/25 ml tomato purée

Heat 2 fl oz/50 ml of the oil in a large heavy saucepan, add the onion and fry gently until golden. Add the meat. Stir over moderate heat for about 5 minutes until the pieces of meat are browned on all sides, then add the turmeric and stir for one minute. Cover with about 1 pint/600 ml cold water and bring to the boil, then reduce the heat and cover the pan tightly. Simmer for 20 minutes.

Add the beans and potatoes. Ladle about 3 fl oz/ 85 ml cooking liquid out of the pan and blend this with the tomato purée in a bowl. Stir back into the pan, bring back to the boil and cover tightly again. Reduce the heat and simmer for a further 15 minutes or until all the ingredients are well cooked. Uncover the pan and check the liquid level – if the *khoresh* is too runny, boil it vigorously for a few minutes until reduced to a thick mixture.

Serve hot, with plain rice, NAN (page 138) or other bread.

CHICKEN AND EGG

My brother Khodabakhsh always used a whistle to call the chickens in for their feed. Not far from the house there was a run with fifty chickens, and it was his responsibility to make sure that they were fed with fresh wheat. One blast of that whistle and they would all be at his feet, finishing the grain in two minutes flat.

He used to take one to two eggs a week, pierce them at either end with a needle, then suck out the raw yolk. Later, he would decorate the shells.

Sweet and Sour Chicken

*Khoresh-e-morghe
shirin torsh*

4 pieces of chicken breast, total weight about 1½ lb/685 g, skin removed

1 fl oz/25 ml oil

1 medium onion, peeled and finely chopped

3 garlic cloves, peeled and crushed

½ teaspoon turmeric

salt and pepper

3 oz/90 g shelled walnuts, ground

2 teaspoons crushed dried mint

1 oz/30 g sugar, preferably brown

6 fl oz/175 ml TAMARIND LIQUID

Wash the chicken and pat dry with kitchen paper. Heat the oil in a large, heavy saucepan, add the onion and fry gently until golden. Add the chicken pieces and stir for 4 minutes to brown, then turn over and stir in the spices and garlic.

Sprinkle over the walnuts, mint and sugar, then stir in the tamarind liquid. Bring to the boil, cover the pan tightly and then reduce the heat. Simmer for 30–40 minutes until the chicken is tender, adding a little water from time to time if the consistency is too dry.

Serve hot, with plain rice, NAN (page 138) or other bread.

Aubergine Gholyeh

Gholyeh-e-badimjan

2 oz/60 g split yellow lentils

2 aubergines, weighing about 8 oz/230 g each, sliced lengthways ¼ inch/5 mm thick

salt and pepper

oil for shallow frying

1 medium onion, peeled and finely chopped

¼ teaspoon turmeric
1 lb/455 g boneless lean lamb or beef (lamb fillet or frying steak), washed and cut into ½ inch/1 cm cubes
TO SERVE
1 pint/600 ml plain yoghurt
3 oz/90 g shelled walnuts, ground
HOT MINT (page 00)

Prepare and soak the lentils as in the recipe for PLUM AND MINT SOUP (page 11).

Put the aubergine slices on a tray or large plate. Sprinkle both sides with salt (about 2 teaspoons) and leave for 1 hour to extract the dark and bitter juices. Rinse under cold running water and pat dry with a clean tea towel. Heat shallow oil gently in a heavy frying pan, add the aubergine slices in batches and fry over gentle heat for 2 minutes on each side. Transfer to kitchen paper to drain while frying the remainder, then set aside for the garnish.

Heat 1 fl oz/25 ml oil in a large, heavy saucepan, add the onion and fry gently until golden. Add the meat. Stir over moderate heat for about 5 minutes until the pieces of meat are browned on all sides.

Drain the lentils and mix into the ingredients in the pan. Stir in turmeric. Slowly add 8 fl oz/225 ml cold water and bring to the boil. Reduce the heat, cover the pan tightly and simmer for 45 minutes until the meat and lentils are well cooked, adding a little water from time to time if the consistency is too dry. At the end of the cooking time the *gholyeh* should be thick. If it is too runny, uncover the pan and boil it vigorously for a few minutes until reduced.

To serve, spoon the *gholyeh* on to a warm serving dish, pour over the yoghurt and sprinkle with the nuts. Dot all over with the hot mint and garnish the edges with the fried aubergines.

Serve hot, with NAN (page 138) or other bread.

DOLMEH

Dolmeh, stuffed vegetables, are famous throughout the entire Middle East, but the original recipes came from ancient Persia. Generally served as a side dish to the main course, *dolmeh* can be made with or without meat. They freeze exceptionally well, and are therefore worth making up in large batches.

Important points to remember when making *dolmeh* are that the vegetables must not open or fall apart during cooking, and the water must be added very gradually to prevent burning without the *dolmeh* becoming soggy. When cooked, all the water should have been absorbed into the stuffed vegetables so that they are moist and juicy to eat.

STUFFED CABBAGE

Most of the countryside around Yazd was arid with little or no rain, so the water for irrigation had to be bought and hard work exerted on growing vegetables. This meant that all vegetables were appreciated to the last bit, and stuffed homegrown cabbages were particularly popular as they were so tasty and filling. When I was a young girl I used to pass the cabbage patch in the morning and twist off the middle part of the plant to crunch on my way to school.

My mother used to make DOLMEH-E-BARGE KALAM for large parties on summer evenings. We would eat out on the flat roof on a very large tablecloth spread over the Persian carpet, with tambourine music for entertainment. My friend Hoola was a very good tambourine player and the neighbours on their rooftops would watch, listen and encourage all the local children to do the traditional handkerchief dance. These impromptu parties would sometimes last until the early hours of the morning.

ᒷᢩᒷᡅᒷᡅᒷᢓ

Stuffed Cabbage

Dolmeh-e-barge kalam

These stuffed cabbage rolls are cooked on top of the stove by the *dam* method, which is exactly the same as for cooking rice the Persian way (page 16). If you prefer to cook them in the oven, simply place the stuffed leaves directly in a casserole dish (it is unnecessary to line the dish with broken leaves), cover with the lid (without the tea towel) and cook at 350°F/180°C/gas mark 4 for 1½ hours.

3 oz/90 g long grain rice, perferably basmati
1 large hard white cabbage, weighing about 3 lb/1.4 kg, washed
4 fl oz/20 ml oil
1 medium onion, peeled and finely chopped
1 teaspoon turmeric
½ teaspoon ground cinnamon
salt and pepper
8 oz/230 g lean minced lamb or beef
3 oz/90 g sultanas

Clean, wash and soak the rice according to the general instructions on page 16.

Bring 1½ pints/900 ml water to the boil in a large saucepan. Meanwhile, remove any broken leaves from the outside of the cabbage and reserve. Remove the saucepan from the heat and lower the cabbage, stalk end down, into the water. Return to the heat and bring back to the boil. Immediately reduce the heat and simmer, uncovered, for 8 minutes. Remove from the heat and leave for 10 minutes, then gently pour off the water, holding the cabbage with an oven glove.

Place the cabbage on a board or work surface with the stalk end uppermost. Using a sharp knife, separate the leaves from the stalk. Roll back from the crown to gently loosen each leaf and then lift off. Repeat until there are 12 good leaves altogether. If they are too brittle and stiff drop them one or two at a time into boiling water and simmer for another 2 minutes to soften a little. Leave to cool. Reserve the broken cabbage leaves.

Prepare the stuffing. Heat 2 fl oz/250 ml of the oil in a heavy frying pan, add the onion and fry gently until golden. Add the meat. Stir over moderate heat for about 5 minutes, stir in the spices and stir for one minutes, then stir in the sultanas and remove the pan from the heat. Leave to cool. Bring 1 pint/600 ml water to the boil in a separate pan. Add 2 teaspoons salt. Drain the rice, add to the water and bring back to the boil. Immediately reduce the heat and simmer gently for 4 minutes. Pour into a sieve and rinse under cold running water to remove the froth, then put into a large bowl, add the cooled meat mixture and toss well to mix.

Line a large non-stick or heavy saucepan with the reserved broken cabbage leaves. Place the good cabbage leaves on a board or work surface and pare away the hard stalk with a sharp knife. Place 2 teaspoonfuls of the stuffing on the stem end of one leaf. Fold the two sides inwards and roll up. Repeat with the remaining leaves, placing them tightly side by side in the pan. If there is any stuffing left, place it in the corners of the pan and cover it with broken cabbage leaves. Pour the remaining oil over the *dolmeh*, then pour in 6 fl oz/175 ml cold water. Wrap the pan lid in a tea towel, bringing all the ends to the centre over the handle and securing with a safety pin. Fit tightly on the pan and place over high heat for 1 mintue until sizzling. Reduce the heat to very low and cook for 1½ hours. Lift the *dolmeh* gently on to a warm serving dish and discard the broken leaves from the bottom of the pan.

Serve hot, with sweet chutney such as DATE AND TAMARIND CHUTNEY (page 143).

Orange and Yellow Heart Salad

Salade-e-zard ba porteghal

This exceptionally pretty salad goes well with cold fish. For a dramatic effect, use both red and green skinned apples .

a few lettuce leaves, washed and dried
6 oz/175 g celery hearts, finely diced
2 canned artichoke hearts, drained
8 oz/230 g eating apples, cored and sliced into rings
squeeze of lemon juice
8 oz/230 g orange segments
6 oz/175 g cooked baby corn-on-the-cob
DRESSING
juice of 1 large or 2 small lemons
3 fl oz/85 ml mayonnaise
2 fl oz/50 ml orange liqueur

2 teaspoons chopped fresh coriander

salt and pepper

Make the dressing: beat the lemon juice, mayonnaise and liqueur together, add the coriander and salt and pepper to taste, then pour into a sauce boat.

Arrange the lettuce leaves on a serving dish and sprinkle the celery on top. Dice one of the artichokes and add to the celery. Arrange the apple rings over the salad and sprinkle with a little lemon juice to prevent discoloration. Arrange the orange segments in a circle on top of the apple slices, then place the remaining whole artichoke heart in the centre. Tuck the baby corn-on-the-cob around the edge of the salad, then spoon over a little of the dressing.

Serve immediately, with the remaining dressing handed separately in the sauce boat.

ൟൟൟ

Spiced Meat Cakes

Shami ba sib zamini

8 oz/230 g old potato

salt and pepper

12 oz/345 g lean minced lamb or beef

1 medium onion, peeled

1 large egg, beaten

1 teaspoon ground cinnamon

garlic salt

6 fl oz/175 ml oil

Cook the potato in its skin in a saucepan of boiling salted water for 20 minutes or until tender. Drain, leave until cool enough to handle, then peel off the skin. Mash the flesh and leave to cool.

Put the meat and the mashed potato in a bowl. Grate the onion to a juice over the meat, then add the egg and cinnamon with garlic salt and pepper to taste. Knead with your hands for about 5 minutes until the meat binds together. Cover and leave to stand for 15 minutes.

Dampen the hands with a little water. Take a little of the dough and form it into a smooth ball a little larger than a walnut. Make a hole in the middle of the ball with your index finger, smooth the surface and press lightly between your palms until about ½ inch/1 cm thick. Repeat with the remaining mixture to make 12 *shami* altogether.

Heat the oil in a heavy frying pan until it is hot enough to turn a cube of bread golden brown in 10–15 seconds. Lower a few *shami* gently into the hot oil and fry over moderate heat for about 3 minutes on each side until golden brown. Transfer to a small saucepan with a slotted spoon. Repeat with the remaining *shami*.

Pour 1 fl oz/25 ml oil from the frying pan over the *shami* and add 2 tablespoons water. Wrap the lid of the pan in a tea towel according to the instructions on page 00, fit tightly on the pan and place over high heat for 1 minute until sizzling. Reduce the heat to very low and *dam* (page 16) for 15–20 minutes, without lifting the lid.

Serve hot or cold.

Makes 12 *shami*.

KUKU

Our holidays were often taken in the beautiful mountain region of Manshad. In the spring the water gushing down from the mountains sparkled with semi-precious stones. Brilliant gold pieces of mineral and brightly coloured stones were, for my father, overshadowed by the rarer small pieces of mountain quartz which could be found in almost inaccessible places. But nothing was 'impossible' for him, and he responded to the challenge.

On one occasion he hired a pair of asses to go in search of stones and my sister and I insisted on accompanying him. As we would have to be on foot for part of the way we deliberately avoided the hottest part of the day and set off in the late afternoon. It was all very exhilarating, especially when we reached our destination. I felt I was riding the wings of imagination. I stroked the precious quartz with my little hands, imagining that I could pick out a piece of the sparkling treasure, but sadly, we made our return journey empty-handed.

I sat on the front of one of the asses with my sister, who was tightly hugging the snack-box of *kuku* which my mother had packed in anticipation of our feeling peckish. It was getting dark – darker than we had reckoned. There was no light, save from millions of stars shining overhead, as we trotted down the mountain path far away from any sign of civilisation. With the hypnotic movement of the asses my sister and I began to doze off. I gently slid over the ass's head onto the rocky mountainside and only woke when my sister shouted to alert my father. I was soon back on the animal and holding on tightly. My sister put her arms round my waist, letting me know that I was even more precious to her than her box of *kuku*. To this day I treasure the memory of that family.

Cauliflower Savoury Cake

Kuku-ye-gole kalam

8 oz/230 g head of cauliflower
salt and pepper
3 fl oz/85 ml oil
1 medium onion, peeled and finely chopped
5 garlic cloves, peeled and crushed
1 teaspoon ground cinnamon
½ teaspoon turmeric
4 large eggs
¾ oz/25 g self-raising flour

Cook the cauliflower in a large saucepan of boiling salted water for 7 minutes until semi-soft. Drain well, mash coarsely with a fork, then leave to cool.

Heat 1 fl oz/25 ml of the oil in a small heavy frying pan, add the onion and fry gently until golden. Add the garlic, stir for 1 minute, then add the cinnamon, turmeric and salt and pepper to taste. Stir for a further minute, then remove from the heat and set aside to cool.

Preheat the oven to 350°F/180°C/gas mark 4. Pour the remaining oil into a 2 inch/5 cm deep, 8 inch/20 cm square baking dish. Place in the oven, shelf above centre, for 5–7 minutes until hot.

Beat the eggs with the flour (preferably using an electric mixer), then beat in the cooled onion mixture and the cauliflower. Remove the baking dish from the oven and pour in the *kuku*. Return to the

oven and bake for 15 minutes or until risen and golden. Cut into squares while still in the dish.

Serve hot, with sauté potatoes, or cold with a salad.

COOL DESSERT

In the hot summer, water was sprayed all over the garden, trees and terraces to give extra freshness to the air in the late afternoon and early evening. The warm air accentuated the perfume of the flowers and vegetables.

We found it pleasant to escape to Shemiran in the mountains near Tehran, where we would walk up the steep sides of Pole Tajrish (Tajrish Bridge) to enjoy the cooling stream from the melted snow. As we walked by the cafés packed with families and friends you could hear everyone cracking pumpkin and water melon seeds, and the empty shells would lie in a path along the street.

In the evenings the crowds would thin and we would eventually find room to be served in one of the little cafés. When we returned home, the delicious taste of ICE IN HEAVEN would still linger in my mouth.

Ice in Heaven

Yakh dar-behesht

An exquisite dessert. Please note that rose water can be obtained in oriental food shops: Do not mistake it for the essence that one buys at chemists' shops.

1 oz/30 g cornflour
1 oz/30 g rice flour
½ pint/300 ml milk
2½ oz/75 g sugar
3 fl oz/75 ml best-quality rosewater
1 oz/30 g ground almonds
¼ teaspoon freshly ground cardamom
chopped pistachio nuts and almonds, to decorate

Pour 6 fl oz/175 ml cold water into a bowl. With a fork, gradually whisk in the cornflour and rice flour. Bring the milk to just below boiling point in a heavy saucepan. Slowly stir in the water and flour mixture with a wooden spoon and stir continuously until the mixture comes to the boil. Reduce the heat, add the sugar and continue stirring over gentle heat for a further 4–5 minutes until the mixture thickens but does not become dry. Add the rosewater, ground almonds and cardamom, stir for a further 2 minutes, then remove from the heat. Spoon into individual dishes, leave to cool, then chill in the refrigerator. Sprinkle with nuts just before serving.

Serve well chilled.

LOUNGE WITH THE RUNNING STREAM

It was always a pleasure to be invited out to relatives and friends, and as a little girl I really looked forward to receiving their hospitality. Even though the houses were of simple construction, some had the most unusual architecture. My favourite trip was going to see our friend Banoo, whose house was built on a green and fertile piece of land just on the outskirts of Yazd, with fruit trees overlapping the high walls. Banoo and her family always welcomed us warmly. We passed through the garden and were led into the lounge where you could see a stream running through the middle! On either side of the stream was a decorative tiled floor with full-size Persian carpets laid on top, and the room was decorated all round with hand-made Persian ornaments. Lunch was *sofreh*-style: the cloth was laid on the floor over the Persian carpet. The running stream gushed underneath and gave the room a cool, relaxing atmosphere. The water was pure enough to drink and on some occasions Banoo would wash the mixed salad of mint and tarragon (*sabsi khordan*) in the stream.

REAL JUICE FROM A TREE

One day in late September when my youngest brother Firoz and I were both living in Tehran, he took me on a surprise trip away from the capital city towards Saveh, an agricultural town well known for its pomegranate cultivation. The pomegranate trees were planted row upon row, their branches laden with fruit almost touching the ground. You could see many, many baskets ready to be piled high with the shiny red fruit, but we were allowed to help ourselves from the trees. We chose the largest of the pomegranates and, holding the fruit in both hands, squeezed with our thumbs and made a small hole in the skin to suck out the juice. It was the most perfect surprise for me, as it took me back to my childhood days in Yazd when I used to squeeze the pomegranates from the trees in my grandfather's orchard.

MARRIAGE AND THE PERSIMMON TREE

Perhaps one of my most beautiful recollections is of the occasion when a Jewish lady called at our house in Tehran asking a favour. She wanted to place her unmarried daughter's dress overnight on our persimmon tree, which was laden with fruit, explaining that this was an old Jewish custom believed to bring good luck.

A few months later we were told that the lady's daughter had found a fiancé and would be married by the end of the year.

2

Persian Feasts

Jewish Festivals

PASSOVER

The festival of Passover commemorates the deliverance of the children of Israel from Egyptian bondage, and with it the birth of the Hebrew nation. The main meal on the eve of the first day of Passover is called Seder and consists of unleavened bread (*matzoh*), bitter herbs (to symbolise the bitterness of Egyptian bondage) and *xoreset*, a mixture of nuts, figs, dates, apples, sultanas, cinnamon and wine. At our Jewish friends' house the Passover meal was always very traditional, beginning with prayers over the wine and *matzoh*, after which passages were read from the *Haggada*, the Jewish prayer book which is only used at Passover. The glasses for wine were placed in a large bowl of water in the centre of the table and each time they were refilled the water was changed. Three *matzoh* covered with a cloth were placed in front of the eldest member of the family, then one *matzoh* was broken and sandwiched between the other two with *xoroset*, as is the Jewish custom. Unleavened bread is eaten throughout Passover until the eighth day, when it is the tradition for married men to visit their in-laws, taking with them flowers and boxes of sweets. On this occasion ordinary bread is eaten, and traditional dishes such as Herb Kuku, Yoghurt Ash and yoghurt.

Crispy Fish and Dill Rice

Berenj ba mahi va shevid

8 oz/230 g long grain rice
4 white-skinned plaice or other white fish fillets, each weighing 3–4 oz/90–115 g
3 tablespoons oil
salt
1 heaped tablespoon chopped fresh dill
2 oz/60 g margarine or butter

Clean, wash and soak the rice according to the general instructions on page 16. Wash the fish and pat dry with kitchen paper.

Heat 2 tablespoons of the oil in a heavy frying pan, add the fish and fry for 2–3 minutes on each side. Remove from the oil with a fish slice, drain and leave to cool.

Meanwhile, bring 1½ pints/900 ml water to the boil with 2 teaspoons salt in a 4 pint/2.25 litre heavy saucepan. Drain the rice, add it to the boiling water and bring back to the boil. Immediately lower the heat to simmer and parboil for 4 minutes. Drain into a sieve and rinse under cold running water. Thoroughly wash the pan to remove all scum.

Mix 1 ladleful of the rice with the chopped dill. Heat the remaining oil in the rinsed-out pan, then put in the cooled fish, skin side down, and cover with one-quarter of the remaining plain rice.

Sprinkle a little of the dill rice on top, then continue with alternate layers of plain and dill rice until both are used up.

Cut the margarine or butter into small pieces and dot all over the rice. Wrap the lid of the pan in a tea towel according to the instructions on page 16, fit tightly on the pan and place over high heat for 1 minute until sizzling. Reduce the heat to the lowest possible and *dam* for about 45 minutes without lifting the lid. Carefully turn the rice out on to a warm serving platter so that the fish is on top.

Serve hot, with plain yoghurt.

THE SABBATH

The various customs of the Jewish religion fascinated me and I used to spend many days with my Jewish friends during their 'high holidays' and festivals. My close girlfriend, Dalia, often invited me for the Sabbath (*Shabat*); she explained to me the significance of this important day, which lasts from Friday evening to Saturday evening.

Not only is the Sabbath a day of rest it is also a time of contemplation and prayers, a day of holiness when man can put aside the cares and material pursuits of life and devote himself to the refreshment of the spirit.

Four different meals were prepared in advance by Dalia's mother for the Saturday, as it was forbidden to work on the Sabbath. Prayers would be said over wine and bread, candles would be lit,

AUBERGINE AND YOGHURT STARTER

GREY MULLET WITH CHESTNUTS, GRAPES AND HERBS, AND ORANGE AND YELLOW HEART SALAD

CHERRY PILAFF

SWEET GOLDEN SOUP WITH ZOROASTRIAN NAN

STUFFED POTATO AND STUFFED ONION

BAKLAVA AND PISTACHIO BAKLAVA (left); CARDAMOM, ROSEWATER AND NUT
PASTIES (top right); RICE CRUMBLES AND ROSEWATER FONDANTS (bottom right)

ELEPHANT EARS (top); STUFFED FRIED FINGERS (top left); SOFT SYRUP FINGERS (top right); SWEET SYRUP CIRCLES (bottom left); HALVA (bottom right)

GOODBYE MEAL-IN-A-BOWL (top left); SWEET AND SOUR FISH (top right); MELON
SURPRISE (bottom left); FISH IN DILL SAUCE (bottom right)

followed by *Gondya Shahaty*, the traditional Sabbath meal eaten even to this day in Persia.

SHABAT

ℒℬℳℬℒ

Stuffed Chicken

Morgh-e-Porshodeh

Traditionally this dish should be made with a boiling fowl, but as these are not always easy to obtain nowadays this recipe uses a roasting chicken. If you can get a boiling fowl, simmer it in a large saucepan of water with 2 oz/60 g split yellow lentils (which have been soaked overnight and drained) for 1–1½ hours. Ten minutes before the end of cooking, add 4–5 dried limes or the juice of 3 fresh limes or lemons to the cooking liquid. This can then be served as a soup to start the meal; the stuffed chicken then follows as the main course.

3 oz/90 g long grain rice
about 2 oz/60 g chicken fat, diced, or 2 tablespoons oil
¼ teaspoon cumin seeds
¼ teaspoon turmeric
salt and pepper
3 lb/1.5 kg roasting chicken, washed

Clean, wash and soak the rice according to the general instructions on page 16.

Preheat the oven to 350°F/180°C/gas mark 4. Part-boil for 4 minutes, rinse and drain well. Place the rice in a bowl, add the chicken fat or oil, the spices and salt and pepper to taste. Toss well to mix. Stuff the neck end of the chicken with the mixture and sew it up with trussing string or thick thread. Place in a covered casserole or wrap well in foil and place in a roasting tin. Roast in the oven for 2–2½ hours or until the chicken is cooked and the meat is literally falling from the bones.

Serve hot, with plain rice.

ℒℬℳℬℒ

Chicken and Chick Pea Balls in Lime Soup

Gondy shabaty

Dried limes can be obtained in Persian supermarkets. Cut them in half and remove the seeds before using.

3 oz/90 g split yellow lentils
about 3 oz/90 g chicken fat, diced, or 2 tablespoons oil
1 medium onion, peeled and chopped
1 lb/455 g chicken, skin removed, washed and cut into quarters
8 oz/230 g minced chicken
3 oz/90 g lean minced beef
4 oz/115 g chick pea flour
½ teaspoon ground cardamom
¼ teaspoon turmeric
salt and pepper
4–5 dried limes or juice of 3 fresh limes or lemons

Prepare and soak the lentils as in the recipe for PLUM AND MINT SOUP (page 11).

Melt the chicken fat very slowly or heat the oil in a heavy saucepan. Add the onion and fry gently until golden. Drain the lentils, add to the pan and fry for a few minutes to seal, then add the pieces of chicken. Cover with about 2 pints/1.2 litres cold water and bring to the boil. Reduce the heat to the lowest possible simmer, cover and cook for 20–25 minutes.

Meanwhile, put the minced chicken and beef in a bowl and add the chick pea flour, spices and salt and pepper to taste. Knead with your hands for about 5 minutes until the meat binds together. Form into smooth balls the size of tangerines.

Drop the meatballs into the pan, cover again and simmer for 30–35 minutes. Ten minutes before the end of cooking, add the dried limes, lime or lemon juice.

Gondy Shabaty is served in three parts. The liquid is served as a soup, the pieces of chicken are served separately with plain rice, then the meatballs are served at the end of the meal with a seasonal salad.

A NIGHT IN SHUSH,
THE CITY OF PURIM

About 700 miles south of Tehran is Shush/Susa, the ancient capital of King Dariosh. We visited the archaeological site there, with its beautifully coloured and decorative enamelled bricks depicting soldiers, which can now be seen in the Louvre Museum in Paris and in the Tehran Museum. We also visited the legendary burial site of the prophet Daniel from the Old Testament. It was a sign of respect for ladies to wear *chador* (long cloths covering their clothes) and for the men to wear long-sleeved shirts before descending the narrow steps to the tomb.

The Jewish festival of Purim has its roots in the city of Shush, and in the book of Esther in the Old Testament you can read the story of the deliverance of the Jewish people in Persia from the hand of Haman, the King's officer who plotted their death.

Purim is a joyful festival, an occasion for parties and celebrations. Our Jewish friends Jacob and his wife Parvin met us after our tour of the city and welcomed us to their typical Shush home. Parvin's cooking was different from ours, and gave us a taste of the Khozestan cuisine. After dinner we were shown to our bedroom where three colourful *doshaks* (thick mattresses) were laid on the floor. There were pink satin hand-made eiderdowns and large heavy bolsters as pillows. We were suitably awed at spending the night in a 4000-year old city!

PURIM

Hamantaschen

Goosh-e-hayman

2 oz/60 g shelled walnuts, finely chopped
1 oz/30 g sultanas
1 oz/30 g stoned dates, finely chopped
3 tablespoons red kosher wine
1 teaspoon ground cinnamon

1 tablespoon clear honey
PASTRY
4 oz/115 g plain flour
4 oz/115 g self-raising flour
1 teaspoon ground cinnamon
pinch of salt
1 oz/30 g icing sugar
4 oz/115 g margarine
1 egg yolk
a little beaten egg white, to seal and glaze

Put the nuts and fruit together in a bowl with the wine and cinnamon. Warm the honey, add to the bowl and stir well to mix. Cover and leave to macerate for several hours, preferably overnight.

Make the pastry. Sift the flours, cinnamon and salt into a bowl and stir in the sugar. Add the margarine in small pieces and rub in with the fingertips. Make a well in the centre, add the egg yolk and 3 tablespoons chilled water and mix to a soft dough. Leave to rest for about 15 minutes.

Preheat the oven to 350°F/180°C/gas mark 4. Grease a heavy, flat baking tray and dust well with flour. Roll out the pastry on a lightly floured surface until ¼ inch/5 mm thick and cut into 20–25 3 inch/7.5 cm circles with a plain pastry cutter. Put 1 teaspoon of the nut and fruit mixture in the centre of each circle, then brush all the way round the edge of each circle with beaten egg white. Fold the circles over and press to seal. Twist or crimp the edges. Brush the pasties all over with egg white to glaze. Place the *hamantaschen* on the greased and floured tray and bake in the oven for 20 minutes or until golden. Transfer to a wire rack and leave to cool.

Makes 20–25

Zoroastrian Festivals

FAREWELL TO YAZD

It was an exciting experience as a teenager, travelling the 500 miles from Yazd to Tehran. I was one of the first to arrive at the bus depot, accompanied by my friends and relations. After saying goodbye, I climbed aboard the blue and white coach. Being the first passenger I took the seat by the window, with my packed lunch prepared by *memeh*.

It was an early Friday afternoon in September when the coach left the city of Yazd, a city of many happy childhood memories. It was a long journey, driving through the darkness of the night, with passengers falling asleep in their seats, then trying to wake up when we passed through various small towns such as Ardakan, Nain and Natanz. In each one there was a small café where black tea was served in small *estekan* glasses on floral patterned saucers with a sugar lump at the side. Everyone chose their own corner to eat their packed food. I remember how carefully my mother had packed my *sofreh* (white cloth) so that I could have a different snack at every stop.

Kashan was our major stop before passing through the Muslim holy city of Qum on the way to Tehran. I drank black tea and saved the rest of the packed food for Kayumars, my eldest brother who was waiting to meet me and had not tasted *memeh's* cooking for a few years.

ᏓᏋᏋᏗ

Goodbye Meal-in-a-Bowl

Ash-e-posht-e-pa

4 oz/115 g red kidney beans
3 oz/90 g chick peas
2 oz/60 g brown lentils
3 fl oz/85 ml oil
3 large onions, peeled and chopped
1 teaspoon turmeric
4 oz/115 g fresh spinach, washed and finely chopped
3 oz/90 g fresh coriander, finely chopped
3 oz/90 g fresh dill, finely chopped
1 small leek, finely chopped
1 teaspoon plain flour
½ pint/300 ml plain yoghurt, at room temperature

GARNISH

1 teaspoon sugar
½ teaspoon ground cardamom
2 teaspoons ground pistachios or other nuts

Prepare and soak the pulses as for the lentils in PLUM AND MINT SOUP (page 11).

Heat the oil in a large heavy saucepan, add the onion and fry gently until golden. Add the turmeric and stir for 1 minute. Drain the pulses and add to the pan, then cover with about 2 pints/1.2 litres cold water. Bring to the boil and boil vigorously for 10 minutes. Reduce the heat, cover the pan and simmer for about 1 hour or until the pulses are tender stirring occasionally.

Add the herbs and leek. Mix the flour to a paste with a little cold water and stir into the pan. Cover and simmer again for 10 minutes or until all the ingredients are well cooked and the liquid is reduced to a thick mixture. Remove the pan from the heat and stir in the yoghurt. Pour the *ash* into individual bowls. Mix the sugar and cardamom together and sprinkle on top, then garnish with the ground nuts.

Serve hot, with ZOROASTRIAN HUSHVA NAN (page 135).

ESFANDIAR AND THE WILLOW TREE

Esfandiar and his wife Azar were very proud of their walled land (*bagh*) in Yazd, with its beautiful fruit trees. Esfandiar would go off regularly in the early morning to inspect his *bagh*, not returning until the late afternoon. On the way there and back he would chat with the locals, so everyone knew him. One day he didn't return home at his usual time and the news spread fast that he must have been taken ill or got lost somewhere. A search was organised for him – and it lasted two whole days! Eventually he was found fast asleep under a weeping willow trees, miles away from his *bagh*. He must have been asleep for over 48 hours, but when he was woken up he thought he had been there just 15 minutes! A celebration was obviously called for, so Azar and the children invited everyone round to eat ASH-E-KHAIRAT, to share in their good fortune and say thank you for helping to find Esfandiar.

CHARITY ASH

Just about all Zoroastrian customs are based on charity or the helping of others, and it was most unusual if an interval of four weeks went by without someone organising *Ash-e-Khirat*, or Charity Ash. The family responsible would build a fire in the corner of one of the cobbled streets in Yazd and set over it a very large copper saucepan. the ladies of the family prepared the ingredients for the *ash*, then in the late afternoon the men would begin cooking and the aroma would gradually waft its way round the streets. By early evening all the neighbours would have gathered round the fire with their bowls and spoons, and the *ash* would be ladled out for them. The gathering was a mixed one – men and women from all different classes, young and old, rich and poor. The very old and infirm were not forgotten: volunteers carried bowls of *ash* round the town on large copper trays; for those who were not able to join in the party. the evening would end with tambourine music, clapping, singing and dancing.

ᒷᲛᏚᏚᒷᲛ

Charity Meal-in-a-Bowl

Ash-e-khairat

2 oz/60 g each red kidney beans, chick peas, butter beans and mung beans
1 oz/30 g black-eyed beans
1 oz/30 g long grain rice
3 tablespoons oil
1 large onion, peeled and chopped
½ teaspoon turmeric
1½ lb/685 g boneless chicken, skin removed, or lean tender lamb or beef, washed and cut into ½ inch/1 cm pieces
2 oz/60 g fresh coriander, finely chopped
2 oz/60 g fresh dill, finely chopped
1 small leek, finely chopped
salt and pepper

Prepare and soak the pulses as for the lentils in PLUM AND MINT SOUP (page 11). Clean, wash and soak the rice according to the general instructions on page 16.

Heat the oil in a large heavy saucepan, add the onion and fry gently until golden. Add the meat and fry over gentle heat for 4–5 minutes until browned on all sides. Stir in the turmeric. Drain the pulses. Drain the rice into a sieve and rinse until the water runs clear. Add the pulses and rice to the pan, cover with about 2 pints/1.2 litres cold water and bring to the boil and boil vigorously for 10 minutes. Reduce the heat to the lowest possible simmer, cover the pan tightly and cook until the meat is tender – about one to one and a half hours. If the pan becomes too dry during this time, add a little extra water.

Add the herbs, leek and salt and pepper to taste, cover and simmer again for 10 minutes. If there is too much liquid, increase the heat and boil until reduced to a thick mixture.

Serve hot, with NAN (page 138).

SARRESHTEH

If someone's husband had got a new job, it was an excuse for the ladies to have a lunch or midweek 'hen' party, and it was *memeh's* favourite to make ASH-E-RESHTEH. The scent of joss-sticks filled the house, the large brass samovar was boiling with the teapot (*ghoori*) on top and the old-fashioned gramophone was wound up and played European classical music.

To make enough space for the ladies, the large white *sofreh* (cloth) was spread out over the Persian carpet and each lady had an inverted polished copper tray and a rolling pin placed in front of her. They wore typical Zoroastrian costume with colourful headscarves (*maghna*). After chatting together over cookies and black tea drunk out of *estekhan* glasses, they would sit on hand-embroidered cushions beside their copper trays. Starting with *memeh*, they would sprinkle a little flour on each other's forehead (to bring good luck and for their husbands to have good jobs), then they would all start rolling out the prepared dough, watching each other's hands to see who could make the finest *reshteh*. If the dough was too thick, Aunt Gohar would give a gentle tap on the back of the hand with the rolling pin – she was the eldest and best! As each lady put her *reshteh* into the boiling *ash* she would make a wish. In the early evening all the families would gather in the house to have their share of the *ash*, and some would take home a bowl for dinner the next day. Reshteh, such as the following were a great delight.

❧❦❧

Vermicelli Pilaf

Reshteh polov

12 oz/345 g basmati rice
1½ fl oz/25 ml oil
1 medium onion, peeled and chopped
1 lb/455 g chicken breasts, skin removed, or very lean and tender boneless lamb (fillet or leg) or beef (frying steak), washed and cubed
salt and pepper
2 oz/60 g vermicelli
¼ teaspoon ground cinnamon
4 oz/115 g stoned dates, chopped
2 oz/60 g sultanas, rinsed
3 oz/90 g margarine or butter
¼ teaspoon ground saffron

Clean, wash and soak the rice according to the general instructions on page 16.

Heat the oil in a large heavy saucepan, add the onion and fry gently until golden. Add the meat and fry over gentle heat for 4–5 minutes until browned on all sides. Pour in about 6 fl oz/175 ml cold water and bring to the boil, then reduce the heat, cover the pan and simmer gently for 20–30 minutes or until the meat is just tender. (The cooking time will vary according to the type of meat used.) The ingredients should be juicy at the end of cooking; if there is too much liquid, increase the heat and boil until reduced and thick. Remove from the heat, add salt and pepper to taste, and leave to cool.

Meanwhile, simmer the vermicelli in a saucepan of water for 6–10 minutes until tender, then drain. Parboil, drain and rinse the rice as in the recipe for CRISPY FISH AND DILL RICE.

Put half of the rice in the bottom of a 4 pint/2.25 litre heavy saucepan and cover with the meat mixture, then the vermicelli. Sprinkle over the cinnamon, dates and sultanas, then top with the remaining rice.

Cut the margarine or butter into small pieces and dot all over the rice. Wrap the lid of the pan in a tea towel and reduce the heat to the lowest possible, *dam* for about 45 minutes, as in the recipe for CRISPY FISH AND DILL RICE.

Transfer 1 ladleful of rice to a bowl. Dissolve the saffron in 1 tablespoon boiling water and mix with the ladleful of rice. Turn the pilaf out onto a warm serving platter so that the crispy base (*tahdig*) is on top. Sprinkle the top and edge with the saffron rice.

Serve hot, with plain yoghurt.

❧❦❧

Vermicelli Soup

Abgoosht-e-reshteh

If using noodles rather than RESHTEH, precook them in boiling water for 8–10 minutes and drain well before adding to the soup.

1 fl oz/25 ml oil
1 large onion, peeled and finely chopped
1½ lb/685 g chicken, skin removed, washed and cut into quarters
½ teaspoon turmeric
2 garlic cloves, peeled and crushed
1 teaspoon dried tarragon
½ teaspoon crushed dried mint
1 fl oz/25 ml tomato purée
1 large or 2 medium potatoes, peeled and cut into ¼ inch/5 mm dice
salt and pepper
8 oz/230 g runner beans, topped and tailed and cut into ¼ inch/5 mm pieces

3 to 4 oz/60 g shredded RESHTEH
or any kind of noodles such as
  vermicelli

Heat the oil in a large, heavy saucepan, add the onion and fry gently until golden. Pat the chicken dry with kitchen paper, then add to the pan and fry gently until browned on all sides. Add the turmeric and stir for 1 minute.

Add the garlic and herbs. Dissolve the tomato purée in 4 fl oz/120 ml cold water and stir into the pan, then cover the ingredients with 1½–2 pints/ 900 ml–1.2 litres cold water. Bring to the boil, then reduce the heat and cover the pan. Simmer for about 45 minutes or until the chicken is tender, adding the potatoes and salt and pepper to taste half way through cooking and the runner beans about 10 minutes before the end. Add more water from time to time if the pan gets too dry. About 5 minutes before the end of cooking, add the RESHTEH or noodles.

Serve hot, with NAN (page 138).

❦❦❦

Occupation Meal-in-a-Bowl

Ash-e-reshteh

4 oz/115 g red kidney beans
3 oz/90 g chick peas
3 oz/90 g brown lentils
1½ lb/685 g minced chicken, lean lamb or beef
2 medium onions, peeled
3 tablespoons oil
1 teaspoon turmeric
2 oz/60 g fresh coriander, finely chopped
3 oz/60 g fresh parsley, finely chopped
1 small leek, chopped
3 oz/90 g shredded RESHTEH or any kind of noodles such as vermicelli
2 teaspoons plain flour
½ pint/300 ml plain yoghurt
salt and pepper

Prepare and soak the pulses as for the lentils in PLUM AND MINT SOUP (page 11).

Put the meat in a bowl. Grate 1 oz/30 g of the onion to a juice over the meat. Knead with your hands for about 5 minutes until the meat binds together. Form into smooth small balls.

Finely chop the remaining onion. Heat the oil in a heavy saucepan, add the onion and fry gently until golden. Add the meatballs and toss in the onion and oil for a few minutes until lightly coloured on all sides, then add the turmeric and stir for a further minute. Remove from the heat.

Drain the pulses, place in a large saucepan and cover with about 2 pints/1.2 litres cold water. Bring to the boil and boil vigorously for 10 minutes to allow the steam to escape. Reduce the heat, cover the pan and simmer for about 1 hour or until tender.

Drop the meatballs into the pan and add the herbs, leek and *reshteh* or noodles. Cover and simmer again for 15 minutes. Mix the flour to a paste with a little cold water and stir into the pan. Continue cooking until the liquid is reduced to a thick mixture. Add the yoghurt and salt and pepper to taste before serving.

Serve hot, with HOT MINT (page 150) accompanied by SPICED MEAT CAKES

BAHMAN ROOZ (ANIMAL APPRECIATION)

Each day in the Zoroastrian calendar is named after a special angel, some of which are the guardians of animals, called Bahman, Mah, Goosh and Ram. 'Animal' days fall at the beginning of the Zoroastrian month, and on these a true Zoroastrian must neither kill animals nor eat meat of any sort.

I remember one occasion when I was at a cinema in Tehran with friends. During the interval I was eating a meat sandwich. Halfway through I suddenly realised it was Bahman Rooz! The others continued eating, but I went hungry until the next day.

❦❦❦

Mung Beans and Rice

Mash-va-berenj

4 oz/115 g mung beans
4 oz/115 g long grain rice
1 fl oz/25 ml oil
1 medium onion, peeled and finely chopped
½ teaspoon turmeric
1 tablespoon tomato purée
1 medium potato, peeled and cut into 'chip' (french fry) shapes
3 oz/90 g margarine or butter
salt
sprigs of fresh mint or parsley, to garnish

Prepare and soak the mung beans as for the lentils in PLUM AND MINT SOUP (page 11). Clean, wash and soak the rice according to the general instructions on page 16.

Heat the oil in a heavy frying pan, add the onion and fry gently until golden. Add the turmeric and stir for 1 minute, then dissolve the tomato purée in about 3 fl oz/85 ml cold water and mix into the onion. Remove from the heat and leave to cool.

Meanwhile, drain the mung beans and place in a large heavy saucepan, cover with 1 pint/600 ml cold water and bring to the boil. Reduce the heat, cover and simmer for about 45 minutes or until the beans are soft, adding more water from time to time if the pan becomes dry.

Wash the rice into a sieve and rinse until the water runs clear. Add the rice and potatoes to the pan, pour in 12 fl oz/375 ml cold water and bring to the boil. Add the onion and tomato purée mixture, stir once or twice, then add the margarine or butter and a little salt. Cover the pan and simmer again on the lowest heat for about 45 minutes. Garnish with mint or parsley before serving.

Serve hot, with a seasonal salad.

Okra and Tomato Soup

Eshkaneh-e-bamya

3 tablespoons oil
1 large onion, peeled and chopped
1 teaspoon turmeric
salt and pepper
1 teaspoon plain flour
8 oz/230 g okra, topped and tailed and cut in half if large
8 oz/230 g tomatoes, skinned and quartered

Heat the oil in a large heavy saucepan, add the onion and fry gently until golden. Add the turmeric, stir and add salt and pepper to taste, make a paste with the flour and 3 oz water, and add to the other indredients then about 1 pint/600 ml cold water. Bring to the boil.

Add the okra and tomatoes, cover and simmer for about 10 minutes until the vegetables are cooked to your liking. Add more water if necessary during cooking, but do not stir or the okra will break up.

Serve hot, with NAN (page 138).

GOHANBAR

Gohanbar was a traditional Zoroastrian custom to commemorate the good deeds of deceased members of the family who had bequeathed part of their estate to the benefit of the poorer members of the community. Five days before New Year (Nov Rooz), a large assortment of dishes was set out in the most spacious room in the house, which was beautifully decorated with freshly cut spring flowers. The dishes were spread out on a large tablecloth on the floor, together with a very large copper tray piled high with dried fruit, nuts and sweets (lork). The front door was left open as everyone was welcome, and the gathering would often reach a hundred or more.

Everyone sat in silence listening to the Zoroastrian priest (*moobed*), who was dressed in traditional white gown and cap. He recited passages from the holy

Avesta, chanting away in a low musical voice, his eyes half closed. This chanting had such a hypnotic effect that some of the smaller children dozed off, while others waited with barely concealed impatience to get at the tray of delicious nuts and sweets.

The ceremony lasted about an hour and ended with the *moobed* blessing members of the family and all those present. Then there was a sudden burst of activity, laughter would fill the air and the tray of nuts and sweets (lork) would be offered round to everyone. I remember changing places several times in order to fill my small cloth bag with my share and more!

A little later guests would start to leave till only very close relatives and friends were left in the house. Volunteers took trays of cooked food around the community, to both rich and poor, symbolising that all men are born equal. On returning to the house everyone would sit down to dinner, consisting of the traditional Kohlrabi and Quince Soup (BEH-VA-KALAM), Roast Leg of Lamb (BAREH-E-KABAB SHODEH) and many other dishes.

Turmeric Loaf

Nan-e-zardchoobeh

2 tablespoons oil
1 medium onion, peeled and finely chopped
1 teaspoon turmeric
¼ oz/10 g dried yeast or ½ oz/15 g fresh
1 teaspoon sugar
1½ lb/685 g wholemeal flour
1 teaspoon salt
¼ teaspoon cumin seeds
a little milk, to glaze

Heat the oil in a heavy frying pan, add the onion and fry gently until golden. Add the turmeric and stir for 1 minute, then remove from the heat and leave to cool.

Dissolve the yeast and sugar in 2 fl oz/50 ml warm water and leave in a warm place for 10–15 minutes until frothy. Mix the flour, salt and cumin

seeds together in a large bowl. Make a well in the centre, add the frothing yeast and the cooled onion and turmeric and knead in the bowl, gradually working in 16–18 fl oz/475–500 ml warm water to form a soft dough. Knead in the bowl for a further 10 minutes, then dust the dough lightly with flour and cover with a damp cloth. Leave in a warm place until doubled in bulk.

Turn the dough out onto a lightly floured surface and knead for 5 minutes. Place in a greased and floured 1½ lb/685 g loaf tin and brush with a little milk to glaze. Leave in a warm place until the loaf has reached the top of the tin. Meanwhile, preheat the oven to 400°F/200°C/gas mark 6.

Bake the loaf in the oven for 20 mintues, then reduce the temperature to 350°F/180°C/gas mark 4 and bake for a further 35–40 minutes or until the loaf sounds hollow when tapped on the bottom. Transfer to a wire rack and leave to cool before serving.

Roast Leg of Lamb

Bareh-e-kabab shodeh

1 leg of lamb weighing about 4 lb/1.75 kg
1 head of garlic or about 8 garlic cloves, peeled and quartered
1 teaspoon turmeric
salt and pepper
sprigs of fresh mint, to garnish

Preheat the oven to 425°F/220°C/gas mark 7. Wash the meat and pat dry with kitchen paper. Make deep incisions all over the joint with a sharp knife and insert the pieces of garlic into them. With your hands, rub the turmeric and a little salt and pepper all over the joint.

Wrap the meat in foil and place in a roasting tin. Roast in the oven for 15 minutes, then reduce the temperature to 325°F/170°C/gas mark 3 and roast for a further 2½–3 hours or until tender. Before serving, pour off the excess fat and garnish with mint.

Serve hot, with plain rice or SAFFRON RICE

WITH ORANGE AND ALMONDS (page 48) and
OKRA KORESH (page 82).

Kohlrabi and Quince Soup

Abgoosht-e-beh-va-kalam

3 oz/90 g chick peas
2 lb/900 g stewing lamb or beef, washed and cut into large serving pieces
1 large onion, peeled and quartered
1 teaspoon turmeric
8–10 oz/230–285 g kohlrabi, peeled and cut into 2 inch/5 cm squares
5–6 oz/140–175 g quinces, quartered and seeded
salt and pepper
fresh coriander leaves, to garnish

Prepare and soak the chick peas as for the lentils in
PLUM AND MINT SOUP (page 11).

Put the meat in a large, heavy saucepan. Cover
with about 2 pints/1.2 litres cold water and place
over moderate heat until the froth rises. Immediately remove the pan from the heat to prevent
boiling over, spoon off and discard the froth.
Return the pan to the heat and add the turmeric.
Drain the chick peas, add to the pan and bring to
the boil, then reduce the heat to simmer. Cover the
pan and cook for 1–2 hours until the meat is tender.
(The cooking time will vary according to the type,
cut and quality of the meat used.) Half an hour
before the end of cooking add in the prepared
vegetables, continue simmering until the ingredients are cooked, add in the salt and pepper.
Before serving, add salt and pepper to taste and
garnish with the coriander.

Serve hot in soup bowls with NAN (page 138) or
other bread.

Rue and Mint Sauce

Sir-va-sedab

Traditionally this sauce is made more runny and
served poured over bread in a bowl. This version is
thicker and is excellent with grilled or fried fish.

1 tablespoon oil
5 garlic cloves, peeled and chopped
1 teaspoon turmeric
leaves of 1 mint sprig finely chopped
2 teaspoons finely chopped fresh rue
1 teaspoon crushed dried mint
2 heaped teaspoons sugar, preferably brown
3 fl oz/85 ml vinegar
salt and pepper

Heat the oil in a heavy frying pan, add the garlic
and fry very gently for a few minutes. Add the
turmeric and herbs and toss a few times to mix with
the garlic. Remove from the heat. Dissolve the
sugar in the vinegar, stir into the pan, then return
to the heat and add salt and pepper to taste. Simmer
gently for 2–3 minutes until the mixture is fairly
thick. Remove from the heat and leave to cool.

Serve cold, with grilled or fried fish.

Sweet Paste

Halva

If the flour and butter mixture becomes lumpy,
simply pour it into a blender and work until smooth.

2 oz/60 g unsalted butter or 2 fl oz/50 ml oil
4 oz/115 g plain white flour
4 oz/115 g granulated sugar
1 heaped teaspoon ground cinnamon
3 fl oz/85 ml rosewater
a few pistachios, finely chopped, to decorate

Heat the butter or oil in a heavy frying pan, add the flour and stir over gentle heat for 3–4 minutes until golden. Remove from the heat and leave to cool, then sieve into a bowl. Set aside.

Put the sugar in a clean heavy pan, pour in 3 fl oz/85 ml cold water and heat gently until the sugar has dissolved. Bring to the boil, then reduce the heat to moderate and add the cinnamon. Cook for 2–3 minutes until bubbles appear, then remove from the heat and pour in the rosewater. Slowly stir in the sieved flour mixture until a thick paste is formed, then return to the heat and stir for 30–60 seconds. Pour the *halva* into a shallow dish (½ inch/ 1 cm deep), smooth the surface and leave to cool. Cut into diamond shapes and sprinkle with chopped pistachios before serving.

Serve with NAN (page 138).

PIR-E-SABZ
(THE GREEN SHRINE)

The astonishing Zoroastrian shrine, Pir-e-sabz, was like something out of a fairy tale. The scenery behind me was inhospitable desert as I stood almost at the top of the mountain peak in front of the shrine. The large room glittered with the burning candles and all around was vivid green, as it was fed by the water which trickled down from a giant rock. I was entranced by the peace and tranquillity as I stood by the pond. I was so completely absorbed by the magnificence of it all that I was taken completely by surprise when a pilgrim lady offered me a piece of fried nan (*soorog*) as a sign of charity.

Fried Nan
Soorog

¼ oz/10 g dried yeast or ½ oz/15 g fresh
1 teaspoon sugar
1 lb/455 g plain flour
¼ teaspoon salt
3 fl oz/85 ml plain yoghurt
2 tablespoons oil, plus extra oil for shallow frying

icing sugar and ground unsalted pistachios, to serve

Dissolve the yeast and sugar in 3 fl oz/ 85 ml warm water and leave in a warm place for 10–15 minutes until frothy. Mix the flour, and salt together in a large bowl. Make a well in the centre, add the foaming yeast, yoghurt and 2 tablespoons oil and knead in the bowl, gradually working 4–6 fl oz/ 120–175 ml warm water to form a firm dough. Knead in the bowl for a further 5 minutes, then dust lightly with flour and cover with a damp cloth. Leave in a warm place until doubled in bulk.

Turn the dough out onto a lightly floured surface and knead for 5 minutes. Leave in warm place until doubled in bulk again.

Heat ¼–½ inch/5–10 mm oil in a heavy frying pan until moderately hot. Meanwhile, take a ball of dough (about the size of an orange) and roll out on a lightly greased work surface to a circle about 7–8 inches/18–20 cm in diameter. Lift up the *soorog* and make 2 holes in the dough with your fingers. Place the *soorog* in the hot oil and fry over moderate heat for about 1 minute. Lift the *soorog* out of the pan by putting a fork in one of the holes, turn the *soorog* over and fry for a further minute on the other side. Drain on kitchen paper. Repeat with the remaining dough to make 7–8 *soorog*. Sprinkle with icing sugar and ground pistachios before serving. Serve warm or cold.

Makes 7–8.

NAMZADI (ENGAGEMENT)

Hazelnut Sweets
Shirini-e-fandogh

5½ oz/155 g plain white flour
3 oz/90 g shelled hazelnuts
2 large eggs
2½–3 fl oz/65–85 ml oil
2 teaspoons ground cardamom
6 oz/175 g icing sugar
2 oz/60 g ground almonds

Put the flour in a heavy frying pan and stir over gentle heat for a few minutes until light brown in colour. Remove from the heat and leave to cool.

Put the hazelnuts in the grill pan and toast under a preheated grill for about 6 minutes, shaking the pan frequently to ensure the nuts become evenly browned. Remove from the heat and rub in a clean tea towel while still hot, to remove the skins. Grind the nuts finely in a food processor or nut grinder.

Break the eggs into a large bowl, add 2–2½ fl oz/ 50–65 ml oil and the cardamom and stir well to mix. Slowly add the sugar, hazelnuts and ground almonds and mix with your hands to form a dough. Sift in the cooled flour and mix in a further ½ fl oz/ 12.5 ml oil if necessary to give a soft dough.

Preheat the oven to 350°F/180°C/gas mark 4 and grease a flat, heavy baking tray. Moisten your hands with water. Take hazelnut-sized balls of the dough and roll until smooth. Gently press to ¼ inch/5 mm thick in the palms of your hands. Place on the greased tray, spacing them about ½ inch/1 cm apart to allow for spreading. Bake in the oven on the shelf just above centre for about 12 minutes or until risen and light golden. Transfer to a wire rack and leave to cool.

Makes 90–95.

JASHN-E-TIREGAN-VA-TIRMAH

The longest and hottest day of the year was Tiregan in the month of Tir (Tirmah). Two or three days before Tiregan it was the custom to collect together various items such as a ring, a bracelet, chains in precious metal, or articles in wrought iron such as a key or lock. Each one was named after a member of the family and placed in a pottery pot (called a *chak-va-doreh*). The pot was filled with water, covered with a cloth and tied with string, then placed under a pomegranate tree in the garden. On the actual day of Tiregan, everyone filled bowls, jars and baskets with water and hid them behind their walls or on their balconies. The first Zoroastrian passer-by, whether it was a child, a woman or even a man in his best suit on his way to work, would be showered with the water. The sound of giggles and laughter filled every corner of the street! Some families even soaked each other inside their houses and got the

heavy Persian carpets saturated. We had many changes of clothes during the day and the fun went on until late afternoon when the sun was getting pale. A young girl who had not yet reached puberty was chosen to pull the items out of the pot one by one, each object symbolising the future or fate of each member of the family. The ceremony lasted for up to three hours or more, with the ladies reciting or singing poems, playing the tambourine and dancing. And for everyone there was a bowl of *Sholy* – Spinach and Beetroot Soup.

Spinach and Beetroot Soup

Shooly

3 oz/90 g brown lentils
2 oz/60 g long grain rice
1½ lb/685 g lean minced lamb or beef
1 large or 2 medium onions, peeled
3–4 tablespoons oil
½ teaspoon turmeric
8 oz/230 g uncooked beetroot, peeled and grated
2 teaspoons plain flour
8 oz/230 g fresh spinach, washed and coarsely chopped
3–4 fl oz/85–120 ml vinegar, or a little more according to taste
salt and pepper

Prepare and soak the lentils as in the recipe for Plum and Mint Soup (page 11). Clean, wash and soak the rice according to the general instructions on page 16.

Put the meat in a bowl. Grate 2 oz/60 g of the onion to a juice over the meat, then knead with your hands for about 5 minutes. Form into smooth balls the size of hazelnuts.

Finely chop the remaining onion. Heat the oil in a large, heavy saucepan. Add the chopped onion and fry gently until golden, then add the meatballs and fry for a few minutes until browned on all sides. Add the turmeric and stir for 1 minute. Drain the lentils. Drain the rice into a sieve and rinse until the water runs clear. Add the lentils and rice to the pan, then add the beetroot and about 2 pints/1.2 litres cold water. Bring to the boil, then reduce the heat, cover the pan and simmer gently for 30 minutes.

Mix the flour to a paste with ¼ pint/150 ml cold water and stir into the pan with the spinach. Continue simmering for about 5 minutes, stirring constantly, then remove from the heat, add vinegar and salt and pepper to taste.

Continue simmering, stirring constantly, add vinegar and salt and pepper to taste and them simmer for at least 15 to 20 minutes, to eliminate the vinegar's acidity.

Serve hot.

THE BIRTHPLACE OF ZOROASTER (ZARDOSHT)

One of the earliest lessons I had at school was about Lake Rezaiyeh, where the prophet and philosopher Zoroaster was born, 300 kilometres from Tabriz. The land is surprisingly fertile just a few kilometres away from this saltwater lake, but near the lake you can see many holes deep in the ground. These are filled with salt water by individual families so that they can produce their own salt.

It is said that the three wise men of biblical times passed through this area of western Persia on their way to Bethlehem.

JASHN-E-MEHREGAN

According to Zoroastrian teaching, the angel of Mehr is the angel of promise – 'your word is your bond'. The month of Mehr is the seventh month of the year in the Zoroastrian calendar, coinciding with September, which is harvest time. It was a time of celebrating and family gatherings, for remembering old people and the less well off. A few days before the celebration, crops were harvested and fruits and vegetables neatly displayed for all to see. On the morning of Mehregan, Bahman the old Zoroastrian baker would call at our house to make

bread (*nan*) in our traditional oven (*tanoor*) and would make at least a hundred loaves. A whole lamb was roasted and cut into portions to cool, then garnished with cold sliced potatoes, onion rings, coriander leaves and a sprinkling of cumin seeds. The lamb and garnish were sandwiched together between *nan* and distributed amongst the Zoroastrian community, rich and poor alike. In the evening it was the custom to make a bonfire in each street and the local people gathered round offering each other roasted nuts from their hand-made silk bags (*doolog*). When the fire died down the crowd would return home to finish celebrating Jashn-e-Mehregan with their families.

Mung Bean and Aubergine Meal-in-a-bowl

Ash-e-mash va badimjan

8 oz/230 g mung beans
1½ lb/685 g aubergines, peeled and sliced lengthways ¼ inch/5 mm thick
salt and pepper
3 tablespoons oil
1 large onion, peeled and chopped
1½ lb/685 g chicken, skin removed, or lean tender lamb or beef, washed and cut into serving pieces
1 teaspoon turmeric

Prepare and soak the mung beans as for the lentils in PLUM AND MINT SOUP (page 11).

Put the aubergine slices on a tray or large plate. Sprinkle both sides with salt (about 2 teaspoons) and leave for 1 hour to extract the dark bitter juices.

Meanwhile, heat the oil in a large heavy saucepan, add the onion and fry gently until golden. Add the meat, toss and stir to mix with the onion, then add the turmeric and stir for 1 minute. Drain the mung beans and add to the pan. Cover with about 2 pints/ 1.2 litres cold water and bring to the boil.

Rinse the aubergines under cold running water

to remove the salt, then add to the pan. Reduce the heat to the lowest possible simmer, cover the pan and cook until the meat is tender – about 45 minutes for chicken, up to one hour for lamb or beef. Before serving, add salt and pepper to taste and mash the ingredients with a wooden spoon or potato masher to make them as smooth as possible.

Serve hot, with plain yoghurt.

Lentil and Yoghurt Meal-in-a-bowl

Riseh-e-badimjan

8 oz/230 g brown lentils
12 oz/345 g aubergines
4–5 tablespoons oil
1 large or 2 medium onions, peeled and roughly chopped
5 garlic cloves, peeled and crushed
1 teaspoon turmeric
salt and pepper
1 lb/455 g lean stewing lamb or beef, washed and cut into small cubes
8 tablespoons plain yoghurt; to serve

Prepare and soak the lentils as in the recipe for PLUM AND MINT SOUP (page 11).

Put the aubergines under a preheated grill and turn until charred and soft on all sides. Leave until cool enough to handle, then peel off the skin and coarsely chop the flesh.

Heat the oil in a large, heavy saucepan, add the onion and fry gently until golden. Add the garlic, turmeric and salt and pepper to taste, stir to mix then remove half of this mixture from the pan and set aside.

Drain the lentils, add to the pan then add the aubergines and meat and cover with about 2 pints/1.2 litres cold water. Bring to the boil, then reduce the heat to the lowest possible simmer, cover the pan and cook for 1–2 hours until the meat is tender. (The cooking time will vary according to the type, cut and quality of the meat used.) If the pan becomes dry during this time, add a little extra water.

If there is too much liquid at the end of the cooking time increase the heat and boil until reduced to a thick mixture. Remove from the heat and mash the ingredients in the pan with a potato masher or meat tenderiser until almost smooth. Spoon into warm soup bowls, top with the yoghurt and garnish with the reserved onion mixture.

Serve hot, with NAN (page 138).

JASHN-E-SADEH

A story tells that Hooshang Shah, the legendary King of ancient Persia, was out riding with his soldiers one day when he came across a large boulder with a giant snake curled on top. He threw a stone at the snake, missed it, but hit the rock, causing sparks to fly and a fire to blaze which burnt the snake. This event (so the legend goes) marked the festival of Jashn-e-Sadeh – fifty days before the Zoroastrian New Year (Nov Rooz).

When I was a little girl in Yazd this festival was celebrated in the school hall. We re-enacted the Hooshang Shah legend with great enthusiasm; for me it was wonderful to be dressed in Zoroastrian costume and to act on stage. Once the show was over refreshments were provided by the local community and young boys and girls held hands and danced around the burning fire. Every street had its own bonfire and after the dancing and singing, as the fire was going out, everyone would jump over the edge and make a wish. In the late evening, chestnuts were roasted and lots of potatoes were buried to bake under the hot ash.

Tamarind Meal-in-a-bowl

Ash-e-tambr

3 oz/90 g brown lentils
1 oz/30 g chick peas
1 oz/30 g pin barley
2 oz/60 g short grain rice
2 fl oz/50 ml oil
1 large or 2 medium onions, peeled and chopped

1 lb/455 g lean tender lamb or beef, washed
and cut into ½ inch/1 cm cubes

2 medium uncooked beetroot, peeled and
finely chopped or grated

8 oz/230 g fresh spinach, washed and finely
chopped

2 oz/60 g leek (white part only), finely
chopped

2 oz/60 g fresh parsley, finely
chopped

2 teaspoons crushed dried mint

8 fl oz/225 ml TAMARIND LIQUID
(page 00)

4 teaspoons sugar

3 garlic cloves, peeled and crushed

1 teaspoon turmeric

Prepare and soak the pulses and barley as for the
lentils in PLUM AND MINT SOUP (page 11).

Heat half of the oil in a large, heavy saucepan,
add half of the onion and fry gently until golden.
Drain the pulses. Add the pulses to the pan, then
add the meat and cover with about 2 pints/1.2 litres
cold water. Bring to the boil, then reduce the heat to
the lowest possible simmer, partially cover the pan
(to allow steam to escape) and cook for 1–2 hours
until the meat is tender stirring occasionally. (The
cooking time will vary according to the type, cut and
quality of the meat used.) If the pan becomes dry
during this time, add a little extra water.

Add the beetroot, spinach, leek, parsley and half
of the mint. Cover the pan and simmer again for
10–15 minutes, pour in the tamarind liquid, add
the sugar.

Meanwhile, heat the remaining oil in a small,
heavy frying pan, add the remaining onion and fry
gently until golden. Stir in the garlic and turmeric,
fry for 1 minute, then stir in the remaining mint
and immediately remove from the heat to prevent
burning.

If there is too much liquid in the *ash* at the end of
the cooking time uncover the pan, increase the heat
and boil until reduced to a thick mixture. Spoon
into warm soup bowls and garnish with the onion,
garlic and mint mixture.

Serve hot. Hand extra sugar separately at the
table.

Stuffed Potatoes

Dolmeh-e-sibzamini

2 oz/60 g long grain rice

¼ pint/150 ml oil

1 medium onion, peeled and chopped

½ teaspoon turmeric

¼ teaspoon ground cinnamon

salt and pepper

4 oz/115 g minced chicken, lean lamb
or beef

2 teaspoons tomato purée

10 potatoes, each weighing 3–4 oz/90–115 g

Clean, wash and soak the rice according to the
general instructions on page 16.

Heat 2 fl oz/50 ml of the oil in a heavy saucepan,
add the onion and fry gently until golden. Add the
meat and fry, stirring, for 3–4 minutes until
browned, add the spices and stir. Dissolve the
tomato purée in 4 fl oz/120 ml cold water, stir into
the pan and cook over moderate heat until the
liquid has evaporated and the mixture is thick.
Remove from the heat and set aside.

Parboil, drain and rinse the rice as in the recipe
for CRISPY FISH AND DILL RICE, add to the
meat mixture and toss well to combine.

Preheat the oven to 400°F/200°C/gas mark 6.
Scrub the potatoes, then carefully cut a ¼ inch/5 mm
thick slice horizontally off each one. Reserve the
slices for lids. Using an apple corer or sharp-edged
teaspoon, hollow out the centres. Reserve the pulp.

Fill the potatoes with the meat and rice mixture,
replace the lids, then place the potatoes side by side
in a baking dish. Pour over 1 fl oz/25 ml of the
remaining oil and bake in the oven for about 1 hour
or until the potatoes are soft.

Serve hot, with plain yoghurt and a seasonal
salad.

HAFTEH ROOZ

White Sweet

Halva berenji

4 oz/115 g basmati rice
1 oz/30 g margarine or butter or 2 fl oz/50 ml oil
1 heaped teaspoon ground cardamom
2–3 fl oz/50–85 ml golden syrup
2 teaspoons ground unsalted pistachios

Clean, wash and soak the rice according to the general instructions on page 16.

Heat the margarine, butter or oil in a heavy frying pan and swirl it all over the inside of the pan (to prevent the rice burning during cooking).

Drain the rice into a sieve and rinse until the water runs clear. Place in the pan, cover with 1 pint/600/ml cold water and bring to the boil. Reduce the heat, add the cardamom and simmer for 45 minutes to 1 hour until the rice is soft, stirring occasionally to prevent burning and adding more water if the pan becomes dry.

Remove the pan from the heat, add golden syrup to taste and stir slowly with a wooden spoon to make the *halva* as smooth as possible. Divide equally between individual dishes, sprinkle ground pistachios on top and leave to cool. Chill in the refrigerator for at least 1–2 hours before serving.

SENNE BOLOOGH (Coming of age)

For a Zoroastrian girl, the onset of puberty is an important occasion. I recall arriving home from school, as a girl of only nine, to find the house packed with young ladies and their mothers. It was a surprise party from my mother for my sister Sarvar, with non-stop gramophone music and hot bowls of Sweet Golden Soup. Everyone showered my sister with presents as she sat there, in her frilly, girlish pink dress with white patent shoes, looking so shy. That moment I made a decision. When my time came, *memeh* should give me just one big present rather than announcing the news far and wide!

Sweet Golden Soup

Tafteh

White basil seeds can be obtained from specialist Oriental shops.

1 oz/30 g butter or margarine
1 teaspoon turmeric
1½ tablespoons ground rice or rice flour
1 teaspoon white basil seeds, washed and soaked in cold water for a few minutes
2 teaspoons sugar, or to taste

Melt the butter or margarine in a large heavy saucepan, add the turmeric and fry for 1–2 minutes. Dissolve the ground rice or rice flour in 1½ pints/900 ml cold water, stir into the pan and bring to the boil.

Reduce the heat, add the seeds and their soaking water and simmer for 5–7 minutes until the soup thickens. Add more water if you prefer a thinner consistency. Remove the pan from the heat and stir in sugar to taste.

Serve hot as a starter with warm ZOROASTRIAN NAN (page 138).

Split Yellow Lentil and Lime Khoresh

Khoresh-e-ghimeh

3 oz/90 g split yellow lentils
oil for shallow frying
1 large onion, peeled and chopped
1 lb/455 g boneless chicken, skin removed, or lean fillet/leg of lamb (beef) or frying steak washed and cut into ½ inch/1 cm pieces
1 teaspoon turmeric
¼ teaspoon ground cinnamon
salt and pepper
2 teaspoons tomato purée

juice of 3–4 limes, or lemon juice to taste
4 medium potatoes, peeled and cut into 'chip' (french fry) shapes
a few red plums or prunes, to garnish

Prepare and soak the lentils as in the recipe for PLUM AND MINT SOUP (page 11).

Heat 3 tablespoons oil in a large, heavy saucepan, add the onion and fry gently until golden. Add the meat and fry for 2–3 minutes until browned on all sides. Drain the lentils and add to the pan, stir for 2–3 minutes to seal, then add the spices and salt and pepper to taste. Cover the ingredients with 10–12 fl oz/300–350 ml cold water and bring to the boil.

Reduce the heat to simmer, cover the pan and cook until the meat is tender – about 45 minutes. If the pan becomes dry during this time, add a little extra water in the meantime, add in the lime or lemon juice.

Dissolve the tomato purée in a few tablespoons cold water and add to the pan. Fry the potato chips in shallow oil in a separate frying pan until golden and crisp. Drain on kitchen paper.

If the *khoresh* is too liquid at the end of cooking, increase the heat and boil until reduced to a thick mixture. Transfer to a warm serving platter, arrange the potatoes around the edge and garnish with plums or prunes.

Serve hot, with plain rice.

Plum and Potato Khoresh

Khoresh-e-sibzamini ba alu

3 oz/90g split yellow lentils
2–3 tablespoons oil
1 large onion, peeled and chopped
1½ lb/685 g boneless chicken, skin removed, or lean stewing lamb or beef, washed and cut into cubes
1 teaspoon turmeric
½ teaspoon ground cinnamon
salt and pepper
1 lb/455 g potatoes, peeled and quartered
1 lb/455 g red plums

juice of 1 large lemon, or to taste
1 teaspoon sugar, or to taste

Prepare and soak the lentils as in the recipe for PLUM AND MINT SOUP (page 11).

Heat the oil in a large heavy saucepan, add the onion and fry gently until golden. Add the meat and fry for 1–2 minutes until browned on all sides. Drain the lentils and add to the pan, stir for 2–3 minutes to seal, then add the spices and salt and pepper to taste. Cover the ingredients with 8–10 fl oz/225–300 ml cold water and bring to the boil.

Reduce the heat to the lowest possible simmer, cover the pan and cook until the meat is tender – about 30/45 minutes. If the pan becomes dry during this time, add a little extra water.

About 20 minutes before the end of cooking, add the potatoes, then add the plums about 10 minutes later, with the lemon juice and sugar to taste. Do not stir or the potatoes and plums will break up.

If the *khoresh* is too liquid at the end of cooking, increase the heat with the pan uncovered, and boil until reduced to a thick mixture.

Serve hot, with NAN (page 138) or plain rice.

A ZOROASTRIAN PROPOSAL IN YAZD

If a boy and girl liked each other, two members of the boy's family (usually ladies) would call on the girl's parents to acquaint them of the boy's serious intentions. I remember one summer when I was spending the day with my cousin Mahin, two ladies arrived, colourfully dressed, and carrying green silk handkerchieves containing white fondant sweets, sugar plums and marjoram leaves. They had called to ask my aunt Govhar for the hand of Mahin for Iraj.

The answer was 'yes', and they placed a piece of the sugar plum into Mahin's mouth to signify her acceptance of the proposal. They were then invited to sit down and were offered tea, home-made wine, sweets and fruit. My aunt's beautiful brass samovar was lit and soon the house was full of guests. The sound of tambourine music could be heard until gone midnight.

ZOROASTRIAN ENGAGEMENT IN YAZD

One day, as a girl of eight, dressed in a frilly pink dress and black patent shoes, I watched my aunt Pari prepare the traditional engagement trays for her eldest son Kaykhosrov. On one tray she placed a gold ring and a pomegranate with thirty-three (a Zoroastrian holy number) silver coins inserted in it all the way round, a piece of raw green silk and some jewels. On the other tray she arranged several sugar loaves, candies, cookies and various presents, then both trays were covered with green silk cloth. Iraj and Parviz, the two younger brothers, carried the trays, while Kaykhosrov and the rest of the family followed behind, walking slowly through the narrow cobbled streets of Yazd towards the bride's house.

The procession was greeted with loud cheering from the girl's family and the old aunt Abnahir showered Kaykhosrov and the trays with the marjoram leaves and sugar plums, while reciting a prayer over them. The two trays were then placed in the middle of the reception room next to another tray covered with raw green silk which had been prepared by the girl's family. We all sat round the trays. Abnahir removed the cloths and gave the raw silk material and the jewels to Mahin, the bride-to-be. She gave a present of a skull cap to the father, a sugar loaf to the mother and a present each to all the other members of the family. Then a complete suit was presented to Kaykhosrov, plus shoes! Kaykhosrov placed the ring on Mahin's finger and gave her the pomegranate with the thirty-three silver coins. Mahin responded by putting a ring on Kaykhosrov's finger, then the couple embraced and kissed, to cheers from everyone around. Finally the priest blessed the couple, the parents announced the wedding date – and the party began!

꧁꧂

Aubergine Khoresh

Khoresh-e-badimjan

2 aubergines, weighing about 8 oz/230 g
each, sliced lengthways ¼ inch/ 5 mm thick
salt and pepper
oil for shallow frying
1 large onion, peeled and chopped
1 teaspoon turmeric
1½ lb/685 g boneless chicken, skin removed, or lean stewing lamb or beef, washed and cut into cubes
2 teaspoons tomato purée
1 teaspoon crushed dried mint

Put the aubergine slices on a tray or large plate. Sprinkle both sides with salt (about 2 teaspoons) and leave for 1 hour to extract the dark and bitter juices. Rinse under cold running water and pat dry with a clean tea towel.

Heat shallow oil gently in a frying pan, add the aubergine slices in batches and fry over gentle heat for 2 minutes on each side. Transfer to kitchen paper to drain while frying the remainder, then set aside.

Heat 3 tablespoons oil in a large, heavy saucepan, add the onion and fry gently until golden. Add the meat. Stir over moderate heat for about 5 minutes until the pieces of meat are browned on all sides, stir in the spices.

Cover with 8–10 fl oz/225–300 ml cold water and bring to the boil. Reduce the heat to simmer, cover the pan and cook until the meat is tender – about 45 minutes for chicken, up to 2 hours for lamb or beef. If the pan becomes dry during this time, add a little extra water, in the meantime add the tomato puree, with a little water and the mint.

Place the fried aubergine slices on top of the meat. Baste with a little of the gravy, but *do not stir* or the aubergines will lose their shape. Cover and simmer again for 5–10 minutes. If the *khoresh* is too liquid at the end of cooking, increase the heat and boil until reduced to a thick mixture.

Serve hot, with plain rice or SAFFRON RICE WITH ORANGE AND ALMONDS.

ZOROASTRIAN WEDDING INVITATION IN YAZD

Wedding invitation cards were only sent to relations and friends living far away. For those living within walking distance, an old Zoroastrian custom was observed. Two ladies, a relation from either side of the boy and girl, would walk through the twisted narrow cobbled streets of Yazd with the wedding guest list and call unexpectedly at individual houses to offer invitations. As a little girl on the way home from school, I used to watch the direction of the ladies' footsteps to make sure they were heading for our street. I would run to let *memeh* know that the 'invitation ladies' were on their way, so that she had enough time to light the samovar and place some cookies on a plate. I would be so anxious waiting for the ladies, hoping it was not a false alarm – as they *might* be for the next-door neighbour and not for us.

A WEDDING IN A HOUSE

Arooskeshan is an old Zoroastrian custom for welcoming the bride. The colourful procession from the bride's to the groom's house usually started in the afternoon. The shy bride held on to her father's waist as he stopped along the street demanding the bride's 'welcoming fee' from the groom's family. It took several hours to cover the short distance. On the way the bride was showered with marjoram leaves and sugar lums and women would light small fires of soft wood and sing poems of 'good luck'.

The wooden door to the groom's house was left open and the scent of burning sandlewood and joss-sticks filled the cobbled entrance. Around the shallow octagonal pond in the open-style house, families and friends handed round fern and marjoram leaves to congratulate each other on such a happy occasion, some helping themselves to tea (*chay*) from the brass samovar. Large plates were piled high with various sweets, tambourine music filled the air and many of the guests would take part in the handkerchief dance.

The bride was greeted with cheers as she entered her husband's house, where he announced he was to give her property and jewellery. The priest led the young couple round a small fire in the garden, which was lit to signify warmth and sincerity. Everyone showered the couple with marjoram leaves, white sweets, sugar plums and silver coins in celebration of the happy event, then they were led

through to the lounge where the wedding ceremony was to take place.

Potato Khoresh

Khoresh-e-sibzamini

2–3 tablespoon oil
1 large onion, peeled and chopped
1 teaspoon turmeric
salt and pepper
1½ lb/685 g boneless chicken, skin removed, or lean stewing lamb or beef, washed and cut into cubes
1½ lb/685 g potatoes, peeled and quartered
1 lb/455 g tomatoes, skinned and quartered

Heat the oil in a large, heavy saucepan, add the onion and fry gently until golden. Add the meat. Stir over moderate heat for about 5 minutes until the pieces of meat are browned on all sides, add the spices and stir.

Cover with 8–10 fl oz/225–300 ml cold water and bring to the boil. Reduce the heat to the lowest possible simmer, cover the pan and cook until the meat is tender – about 45 minutes for chicken, up to 2 hours for lamb or beef. If the pan becomes dry during this time, add a little extra water.

About 20 minutes before the end of cooking, add the potatoes and tomatoes. If the *khoresh* is too liquid at the end of cooking, increase the heat and boil until reduced to a thick mixture.

Serve hot, with NAN (page 138) or plain rice.

Spinach and Plum Khoresh

Khoresh-e-esfenaj-va-alu

If fresh plums are not in season, use 4 oz/115 g prunes and soak them overnight. Cook them for the same length of time as the plums in the recipe.

2–3 tablespoons oil

1 large onion, peeled and finely chopped
1 lb/455 g lean stewing lamb or beef, washed and cut into ½ inch/1 cm pieces
1 teaspoon turmeric
¼ teaspoon ground cinnamon
1 lb/455 g red plums
8 oz/230 g fresh spinach, washed and coarsely chopped
salt and pepper

Heat the oil in a large, heavy saucepan, add the onion and fry gently until golden. Add the meat and stir for 3–4 minutes until browned on all sides, then add the turmeric and cinnamon and toss to coat the meat evenly. Add 1–1½ pints/600–900 ml cold water and bring to the boil.

Reduce the heat to the lowest possible simmer, cover the pan and cook for up to 2 hours until the meat is tender.

Add the plums, spinach and salt and pepper to taste, with a little more water if necessary. Cover and simmer again for 10–15 minutes until the plums are soft. If there is too much liquid at the end of cooking, uncover the pan, increase the heat and boil until reduced to a thick mixture.

Serve hot, with CRISPY POTATO RICE (page 86).

WEDDING CEREMONY IN TEHRAN

My sister Sarvar was dressed in a long white gown with lace covering her hair and forehead. She was beside Khosrov, her husband-to-be, in the hall of the fire temple in Tehran, smiling at the relations and friends around her. A candle was lit and placed beside the display of flowers on the table next to a large copper tray containing various nuts, sweets and sugar plums. Rostam, the young son of a close family friend, held a green silk cloth over the groom's head. In the cloth was a pomegranate (a sign of fertility), a boiled egg (meaning past sin), a needle and cotton (for future occupation), scissors (symbolising compatibility) and some marjoram leaves and sugar plums.

Mobed Ardeshir the priest began the ceremony, reciting from the Avesta (holy book) in a musical voice. The marriage bond was said and the bene-diction announced asking Sarvar to devote one day in the Zoroastrian calendar for charity, to help the poor and disabled. At the end of the service the couple placed a sweet in each other's mouths to a loud cheer from the congregation.

My mother got hold of the egg and wrapped it up to throw away past sin as soon as possible. Everyone waited behind while the priest accompanied the couple to the fire temple. According to Zoroastrian history, a fire has burnt continuously in a brazen vessel in this temple for the past 3000 years. The priest blessed the couple and recited again from the holy Avesta, while walking three times in a circle around the vessel. *Lork,* a nut and sweet mixture, was distributed amongst the congregation, and then everyone took their seats in a large hall in the temple grounds for a dinner to celebrate the big occasion.

Rice in Meat and Tomato Sauce

Eslamboli polov

2 tablespoons oil
2 medium onions, peeled and chopped
1 lb/455 g very lean and tender boneless lamb (fillet or leg) or beef (frying steak), washed and cut into 1 cm/½ inch cubes
salt and pepper
1 fl oz/25 ml tomato purée
1½ lb/685 g tomatoes, roughly chopped
8 oz/230 g basmati rice
3 oz/90 g margarine or butter
¼ teaspoon turmeric

Heat the oil in a heavy saucepan, add half of the chopped onions and fry gently until golden. Add the meat and stir over moderate heat for about 5 minutes until the pieces of meat are browned on all sides. Stir in the salt and pepper. Dissolve the tomato purée in 3 fl oz/85 ml cold water, stir into the pan, remove from the heat and set aside.

Put the tomatoes in a saucepan, pour in 12 fl oz/350 ml cold water and bring to the boil. Simmer for

5 minutes, then work in a blender or food processor and sieve. There should be about 1½ pints/900 ml tomato juice; if there is not enough, make up to this amount with water.

Put the rice in a sieve and rinse until the water runs clear. Melt a little of the margarine or butter in a 4 pint/2.25 litre heavy saucepan, add the remaining chopped onion and fry gently until golden. Stir in the turmeric, then remove the pan from the heat and add the rice and remaining margarine or butter. Stir once or twice to mix. Return the pan to the heat, add 1 pint/600 ml of the tomato juice and bring to the boil. Reduce the heat, add salt and pepper to taste, then cover the pan and simmer gently for about 15 minutes. Add more tomato juice from time to time as the pan becomes dry.

Remove the pan from the heat and make a well in the centre of the rice. Fill with the meat mixture, then cover it over with rice. Wrap the lid of the pan in a tea towel and *dam* for about 30 minutes, as in the recipe for CRISPY FISH AND DILL RICE (page 28). Turn the rice out onto a warm serving platter so that the crispy base (*tahdig*) is on top.

Serve hot, with a seasonal salad.

Saffron Rice with Orange and Almonds

Shirin polov

11 oz/315 g basmati rice
salt
2 large or 4 small oranges
2 teaspoons sugar
3 oz/90 g blanched almonds, shredded
1 tablespoon oil
¼ teaspoon ground saffron
3 oz 90 g margarine or butter

Clean, wash and soak the rice according to the general instructions on page 16, then parboil, drain and rinse as in the recipe for CRISPY FISH AND DILL RICE.

Remove the rind from the oranges with a canelle knife or zester. Place in a small heavy saucepan with the sugar, almonds and 2 fl oz/50 ml cold water. Bring to the boil, then reduce the heat to moderate and cook for 10 minutes or until the ingredients become fairly dry.

Swirl the oil over the inside of a 4 pint/2.25 litre heavy saucepan. Put half of the rice in the bottom and cover with the orange and almond mixture. Sprinkle over the saffron, then top with the remaining rice.

Cut the margarine or butter into small pieces and dot all over the rice. Wrap the lid of the pan in a tea towel and *dam* for 30–45 minutes, as in the recipe for CRISPY FISH AND DILL RICE (page 28).

Turn the rice out on to a warm serving platter. Remove the crispy base (*tahdig*) and drain off any excess oil. Spoon the orange and almond mixture on top of the rice, break the *tahdig* into pieces and use as a garnish.

Serve hot, with CHICKEN AND HERBS IN LIME SAUCE (page 52).

Herb and Lime Pilaf

Polov-e-ghormeh sabsi

11 oz/315 g basmati rice
3 tablespoons oil
1 medium onion, peeled and chopped
1½ lb/685 g boneless chicken, skin removed, or very lean and tender lamb (fillet or leg) or beef (frying steak), washed and diced
juice of 1 large lemon, or to taste
1 heaped tablespoon finely chopped fresh parsley
1 heaped tablespoon finely chopped spring onion or leek
1 teaspoon finely chopped fresh fenugreek
½ teaspoon each ground cinnamon, cardamom, ginger, turmeric and paprika
salt
3 oz/90 g margarine or butter
¼ teaspoon ground saffron

Clean, wash and soak the rice according to the general instructions.

Heat the oil in a large, heavy saucepan, add the onion and fry gently until golden. Add the meat and fry over gentle heat for 4–5 minutes until browned on all sides. Add the chopped herbs and stir for one or two minutes. Combine in the spices, stir for a further minute. Pour in 8 fl oz/225 ml cold water and bring to the boil. Reduce the heat, cover the pan and simmer gently for 20–45 minutes until the meat is tender (the cooking time will vary according to the type of meat used.) In the meantime, when the meat is cooked add the lemon juice, continue simmering for a further 5–10 minutes. The ingredients should be juicy at the end of cooking; if there is too much liquid, increase the heat and boil until reduced and thick. Remove from the heat and leave to cool.

Meanwhile, parboil, drain and rinse the rice as in the recipe for CRISPY FISH AND DILL RICE (page 28). Melt 1 oz/30 g of the margarine or butter in a 4 pint/2.25 litre heavy saucepan. Remove from the heat. Put one-quarter of the rice in the bottom of the pan, add half of the meat mixture, then another quarter of the rice. Repeat with the remaining meat mixture and rice.

Cut the remaining margarine or butter into small pieces and dot all over the rice. Wrap the lid of the pan in a tea towel and *dam* for about 45 minutes, as in the recipe for CRISPY FISH AND DILL RICE (page 28).

Transfer 4 tablespoons rice to a bowl. Dissolve the saffron in 1 tablespoon boiling water and mix with the rice. Turn the pilaf out onto a warm serving platter so that the crispy base (*tahdig*) is on top. Sprinkle the saffron rice around the edge.

Serve hot, with a seasonal salad.

A TRAY OF WEDDING FOOD

There was always someone who was unable to attend a wedding, and on such happy occasions the less well off were always remembered too. Large numbers of dishes filled with wedding food were placed on highly polished copper trays and carried to various local houses by volunteers. According to Zoroastrian tradition, the recipient would wash and dry the empty dishes after eating, then place a handful of marjoram leaves, sweets and cookies in them to return to the sender. After a wedding I used to love sorting out the sweets, which lasted me several days.

THE EVERLASTING MARRIAGE

I remember, as a little girl of seven, pushing myself in front of family and friends as they gathered to watch the colourful and traditional Zoroastrian ceremony which took place on the second day of a wedding. The atmosphere was filled with happiness and joy and shouts of 'hurrah' as Tahmoores, the groom, gently removed the stocking from one of his wife Banoo's feet. She reciprocated by removing one of his socks, then the two bare feet were put on top of one another on a tray on which was placed a type of grass (called *movr*) to symbolise everlasting vegetation. The cheering continued as the groom poured cold milk on his bride's foot and, stroking gently with his other hand, began to wash it. The bride repeated the ritual, which symbolises strength. The groom then offered a rosewater drink to his bride to sip and the bride repeated this for her husband. Finally the tray was moved away and the spilt milk was poured into the nearest running stream. At this moment the priest and bridegroom recited prayers from the Avesta (holy book) wishing the couple a healthy and happy life.

DOWRY DAY IN YAZD

On the second day of a wedding the groom's house was pleasantly untidy, with marjoram leaves, pieces of fern and silver coins sprinkled on the highly patterned Persian carpet from the day before. *Estekan* glasses with their silver holders were placed beside the bubbling samovar and sweets were piled high on large plates. The kitchen was busy with cooks in their traditional clothes preparing food for relations and close friends.

In early afternoon a cheer went up as the bride's family procession approached the house with trays of presents. On entering the front door they were showered with marjoram leaves, white sweets and silver coins. Their presents were carried into the reception room to be placed with the others next to where the bride sat with her new husband welcoming her family into her new home. The joyful atmosphere was filled with the scent of joss-sticks. Tea (*chay*) and Rosewater Drink (Sharbat-e-Golab) were offered as everyone gathered round to see the presents. As a Zoroastrian custom, the eldest lady in the family would remove the bright cover from the trays to reveal the gifts, lifting each item and announcing the name of the person who had given it. At the end of the ceremony, there was another loud cheer as the bride and groom were the first to help themselves from the dinner table.

AN OFFICIAL INVITATION FOR THE BRIDE TO HER OLD HOME

Following the old Zoroastrian custom, my sister Sarvar had to wait for an 'official' invitation from our parents to visit them at the home she had left before getting married. Without this invitation she would not be able to visit them freely in the future!

On the arranged date some soft wood was lit in the barbecue (*manghal*) and sprinkled with sandlewood and wild rue. Sarvar and her husband Khosrov stretched their arms over the low flamed and stroked their faces to signify warmth and sincerity. Then *memeh* presented them with a gold sovereign placed on a piece of green silk with some marjoram leaves, sweets and a piece of fern, together with a sugar loaf wrapped in shiny green paper for Sarvar. Rosewater Drink was offered to the couple on entering the house, which was packed with close relatives. Over a buffet-style lunch, everyone issued lunch or dinner invitations to the newly married couple.

Wedding Cake

Cake

4 eggs, separated
6 oz/175 g caster sugar
6 oz/175 g self-raising flour, sifted
2 tablespoons granulated sugar
2 tablespoons dark navy rum
4–6 tablespoons jam

12 fl oz/350 ml double cream
2 teaspoons cocoa powder
2 teaspoons instant coffee powder
1 tablespoon caster sugar
1 teaspoon vanilla essence

TO DECORATE
grated chocolate
fresh strawberries

Preheat the oven to 400°F/200°F/gas mark 6. Grease an 8 inch/20 cm round cake tin with a removable base and dust lightly with flour.

Beat the egg yolks with the caster sugar until creamy and white, then fold in the flour. Whisk the egg whites in a separate bowl until stiff, then fold into the flour mixture with a large metal spoon until thoroughly blended. Pour into the prepared tin and bake in the oven for 30–40 minutes until risen and golden. Remove the tin from the oven, turn the cake out on to a wire rack and leave to cool.

Put the granulated sugar in a small, heavy saucepan, add 6 fl oz/175 ml cold water and heat gently until the sugar has dissolved. Stir in the rum and remove from the heat. Set aside to cool.

Cut the cold cake horizontally into 3 layers.

Whip the cream until it will hold its shape and carefully add caster sugar and vanilla essence. Set 3 heaped tablespoons aside. Divide the remaining cream into 3 equal parts. Then mix the cocoa and coffee powders into the other portions.

Place the base layer on a plate, sprinkle with two tablespoonsful of the rum syrup and spread with the jam. Place another layer on top, sprinkle again with two tablespoonsful of the rum mixture. Top up with some of the flavoured cream. Repeat with the other layers. Finally spread the plain cream over the top and sides of the cake and decorate with grated chocolate and strawberries. Chill in the refrigerator until serving time.

NOV ROOZ (NEW YEAR)

The end of the snow and the beginning of the roses and nightingales would lead to Nov Rooz, 1st of Farvadin or March 21st. It has been said that on this day the legendary King Jamshid Shah was crowned, when the first blossom appeared through the snow, signifying the birth of spring.

Preparation and excitement for Nov Rooz started weeks in advance. Wheat and lentils were germinated in traditional earthenware pots (*koozeh*) and each day the growing shoots would proclaim the coming of Nov Rooz. *Khaneh takani*, or spring cleaning, would be undertaken by all members of the house, and gifts of nuts and sweets were distributed amongst relations and friends. The grey, sad garden which winter had left behind bloomed with high-scented narcissi (*nargess*), mauve-coloured pansies (*banafsheh*) and numerous different Persian roses. The blossom on the fruit and almond trees attracted butterflies and bees, and in the cobblestoned streets of Yazd, the housewives could be seen sweeping in the early morning sun. It was obvious which houses were Zoroastrian as, a few days before the equinox, Nov Rooz was welcomed with a piece of conifer, a handful of marjoram leaves, a few fondant sweets (*noghl*) and sorb placed in the corner of the front door.

Fish in Dill Sauce

Mahi ba shevid

3–4 tablespoons oil
1 medium onion, peeled and chopped
1 medium courgette, sliced into rings
½ teaspoon turmeric
4 small or 2 medium potatoes (total weight about 10 oz/285 g), peeled and coarsely diced
1 small bunch of fresh dill, finely chopped
salt and pepper
1 oz/30 g butter or margarine
1½ lb/685 g cod or other white fish fillets

GARNISH

1–2 carrots, peeled and coarsely grated
4 tomatoes, skinned and halved
fresh coriander

Heat the oil in a large, heavy frying pan, add the onion and fry gently until golden. Add the courgettes and fry for a few minutes on each side until lightly coloured and just tender. Remove with a slotted spoon and keep warm. Stir in the turmeric.

Add the potatoes with the dill and salt and pepper to taste. Stir for 1–2 minutes, then add 3–4 fl oz/85–120 ml cold water, cover and simmer gently for about 10 minutes or until the potatoes are tender.

Meanwhile, preheat the grill to hot. Melt the butter or margarine in a small pan and brush over the flesh side of the fish. Place under the grill for 7–10 minutes until cooked.

Arrange the fish in the centre of a warm serving platter and surround with the potato and dill mixture and the courgettes. Add the carrots to the pan in which the potato mixture was cooked and stir to mix with the oil, then use to garnish the fish with the tomatoes and coriander.

Serve hot, with plain rice and yoghurt.

HERBS FOR SNOWY DAYS

In midsummer, when the sun shone on the cobbled narrow streets in the residential area of Yazd, tranquillity filled the air. Only the odd sound of a bicycle bell would break the silence, a warning for the occasional pedestrian out at that time of day to pull to one side. The wooden doors were left open in rows against the high walls of the terraced houses and the ladies sat in their colourful dresses on hand-made mattresses (*doshak*) and embroidered cushions. Some would be quietly spinning wool, knitting or crocheting garments for winter, but the sight I love to remember is of the women crouching over highly polished copper trays sorting out the herbs which had to be washed, dried, crushed and put away for winter use. I remember the rows of brightly coloured batique cloths covered with crushed herbs and the bags for storing them in. The aroma filled the whole house, and when we used the herbs in winter they would always evoke memories of those days in midsummer.

Savoury Herb Cake

Kuku-ye-sabsi

5–6 tablespoons oil
1 medium onion, peeled and finely chopped

| 5 oz/140 g fresh spinach, washed and finely chopped |
| 1 small leek, weighing about 3 oz/90 g, finely chopped |
| 1 oz/30 g each fresh parsley, dill and coriander, finely chopped |
| 2–3 lettuce leaves, finely chopped |
| ¼ teaspoon turmeric |
| ¼ teaspoon cinnamon |
| 4 large eggs |
| 1 teaspoon self-raising flour |
| 2 oz/60 g shelled walnuts or other nuts, chopped |
| salt and pepper |

Heat 3–4 tablespoons of the oil in a small, heavy frying pan, add the onion and fry gently until golden. Add the spinach, leek, herbs and lettuce leaves and stir over low heat for 3–4 minutes, stir in turmeric and cinnamon, then remove from the heat and set aside to cool.

Preheat the oven to 350°F/180°C/gas mark 4. Pour the remaining oil into a 2 inch/5 cm deep, 8 inch/20 cm square baking dish. Place in the oven, on the shelf above centre, for 5–7 minutes until hot.

Beat the eggs with the flour, nuts and salt and pepper to taste (preferably using an electric mixer), then beat in the cooled onion and herb mixture. Remove the baking dish from the oven and pour in the *kuku*. Return to the oven and bake for 15 minutes or until risen. Cut into squares while still in the dish.

Serve hot or cold, with plain rice and fried fish.

ON THE DAY OF NOV ROOZ (NEW YEAR)

On this special day, fresh flowers would be displayed in each room. Narcissi and roses were the favourites, their fragrance permeating throughout the house. It is still the custom for a traditional Zoroastrian home to have a table set with *Haft Sheen*, seven items starting with the letters 'sh' symbolising prosperity and plenty in the New Year. A small walnut table is covered with a hand-embroidered white tablecloth placed on a royal blue Persian carpet and reflected in a full-sized mirror. Fully grown cress in an earthenware pot (*koozeh*) is placed in the centre of the table and surrounded with wine (*sharab*), milk (*shir*), jujube (*shilooneh*), sweets (*shirini*), a drink made from rosewater, sugar and basil seeds (*sharbat*) and three candles (*shaam*). These seven things symbolise the making of a wish to our lord asking for food and nourishment in the coming year. The three candles placed in front of the display symbolise good thought, good word and good deed, the words Zoroaster taught his people. Other items also placed on the table include a hand mirror, a rosewater pourer containing rosewater, an apple studded with silver coins in a bowl of water and thyme (the sign of wealth), the holy Zoroastrian book (Avesta), a picture of Zoroaster, a bowl of fruit, some bread (*nan*) and cheese (*panir*).

In a Muslim home a table is also set with seven things, but these are different from the Zoroastrian and all begin with the letter 's'. On a Muslim New Year table there is greenery (*sabsi*), an apple (*sibsan*), vinegar (*serkeh*), garlic (*seer*), sumac (*sumach*), hyacinth (*soubol*) and a sweet drink (*sharbat*).

Chicken and Herbs in Lime Sauce

Khoresh-e-ghormeh sabsi

| 4 oz/115 g red kidney beans |
| 3 tablespoons oil |
| 1 medium onion, peeled and chopped |
| 1 lb/455 g boneless chicken, skin removed, or lean lamb (fillet or leg) or beef (frying steak), washed and cut into ½ inch/1 cm cubes |
| 1 teaspoon ground mixed spices (cinnamon, cardamom, ginger, turmeric and paprika), mixed together |
| 8 oz/230 g fresh spinach, washed and finely chopped |
| 1 medium leek, weighing about 5 oz/140 g, finely chopped |
| 3 oz/90 g fresh parsley, finely chopped |
| 1 teaspoon finely chopped fresh fenugreek |
| 4–5 dried limes, halved and seeded, or juice of 5–6 fresh limes or lemons |

salt and pepper

a little extra chopped fresh parsley, to garnish

Prepare and soak the kidney beans as for lentils in PLUM AND MINT SOUP (page 11).

Heat the oil in a 4 pint/2.25 litre heavy saucepan, add the onion and fry gently until golden. Add the meat and stir over moderate heat for about 5 minutes until the pieces are browned on all sides. Add the spices and stir for a further minute, then add the spinach, leek, parsley and fenugreek. Cover with about 8 fl oz/225 ml cold water and bring to the boil, then reduce the heat and cover the pan tightly. Simmer for 45 minutes to 1 hour or until the meat is tender.

Meanwhile, transfer the beans and their soaking water to a separate saucepan. Bring to the boil and boil rapidly for 10 minutes. Reduce the heat, half cover the pan and simmer for about 50 minutes or until the beans are tender.

Add the beans to the *khoresh* with the limes, lime or lemon juice and salt and pepper to taste. Stir to combine, then cover and simmer for 15–20 minutes. Sprinkle with parsley before serving.

Serve hot, with plain rice.

Chicken with Chick Peas and Cinnamon

Morgh ba nokhod va darchin

2 oz/60 g chick peas

2 tablespoons oil

1 medium onion, peeled and chopped

2 lb/900 g roasting chicken, washed, skin removed and cut into serving pieces

½ teaspoon ground cinnamon

¼ teaspoon turmeric

1 medium potato, peeled and quartered

salt and pepper

Prepare and soak the chick peas as for the lentils in PLUM AND MINT SOUP (page 11).

Heat the oil in a 4 pint/2.25 litre heavy saucepan, add the onion and fry gently until golden. Add the chicken and stir over moderate heat for about 5 minutes until the pieces are browned on all sides, then add the spices and stir for a further minute.

Drain the chick peas and add to the pan. Cover with about 8 fl oz/225 ml cold water and bring to the boil. Reduce the heat, cover the pan tightly and simmer for about 45 minutes until the chicken and chick peas are tender, 15–20 minutes before the end of cooking add in the potato, adding a little water from time to time if the pan becomes dry. If there is too much liquid at the end of cooking, increase the heat and boil vigorously until reduced to a thick mixture. Add salt and pepper to taste before serving.

Serve hot, with plain rice.

FAMILY GREETINGS ON NOV ROOZ DAY

Everyone got very excited and emotional as the time of the equinox approached. Dressed in new clothes, we all gathered together in the lounge. Candles were lit and the incense dish (*obregooni*) was prepared with a little hot coal or wood, some incense and wild rue. A green raw silk cloth was spread on the table containing strands of fern from the garden, thyme, sorb and a few white fondant sweets (*noghl*). At the exact time of the equinox (*salgardesh*), my parents would greet each other, then make a present of a silver coin to each member of the family and bless and embrace us. We would exchange gifts and my mother would pour a little rosewater (*golab*) into our cupped hands. Some of the liquid would pour on to the Persian carpet as we stroked our hair with the perfumed water, which spread a very special fragrance throughout the room. We then looked into the mirror for bright days ahead, handed each other a strand of fern, a small sprig of thyme and a white sweet, which in turn would be placed back on the green silk cloth. Finally we would eat a fondant sweet and make a New Year wish.

Herb Pilaf

Sabsi Polov

11 oz/315 g basmati rice
2 tablespoons finely chopped fresh dill
1 tablespoon each finely chopped fresh coriander, chives or young leek and parsley
4 oz/115 g margarine or butter

Clean, wash and soak the rice according to the general instructions on page 16, then parboil, drain and rinse as in the recipe for CRISPY FISH AND DILL RICE (page 28).

Put 1 ladleful of the rice in a bowl and stir in the herbs. Put one-quarter of the remaining rice in the bottom of a heavy saucepan. Sprinkle in a little of the herb rice, then alternate layers of plain and herb rice until both are used up.

Cut the margarine or butter into small pieces and dot all over the rice. Wrap the lid of the pan in a tea towel and *dam* for about 45 minutes, as in the recipe for CRISPY FISH AND DILL RICE.

Serve hot, with plain yoghurt.

Sweet and Sour Fish

Mahi-e-shirin torsh

1 grey mullet (weighing about 2 lb/900 g), scaled and gutted, with head and tail removed
a little plain flour for cleaning fish
¼ teaspoon turmeric
4 fl oz/120 ml oil
1 oz/30 g sugar, preferably brown
4 fl oz/120 ml vinegar
a few flaked almonds, toasted, to garnish

Rinse the fish under cold running water. Put a little flour inside the cavity of the fish and rub to remove any black bits. Cut the fish widthways into 3 inch/7.5 cm slices, then open up each piece and gently remove the bone. Pat dry with kitchen paper.

Rub a little turmeric on each piece of fish. Heat the oil in a heavy frying pan, add 1–2 pieces of fish and fry for about 3 minutes on each side until golden. Repeat with the remaining pieces of fish.

Put the sugar and vinegar in a heavy saucepan and heat gently until the sugar has dissolved. Place the fish in the pan and spoon over the vinegar, then pour in the oil left over from frying the fish. Bring to the boil, then reduce the heat, cover and simmer for 20 minutes or until the vinegar has evaporated.

Remove the fish from the pan with a fish slice and drain off any excess oil. Arrange on a serving plate and garnish with almonds.

Serve hot or cold, with CRISPY POTATO RICE (page 86) and any *khoresh*.

Grey Mullet with Vinegar Sauce

Mahi-e-safid ba serkeh

1 grey mullet (weighing about 2 lb/900 g), scaled and gutted, with head and tail removed
a little plain flour for cleaning fish
¼ teaspoon turmeric
2 fl oz/50 ml oil
3 fl oz/85 ml vinegar
sprigs of fresh mint or parsley, to garnish

Rinse the fish under cold running water. Put a little flour inside the cavity of the fish and rub to remove any black bits. Cut the fish widthways into 3 inch/7.5 cm slices, then open up each piece and gently remove the bone. Pat dry with kitchen paper.

Rub a little turmeric on each piece of fish. Heat the oil in a heavy frying pan, add 1–2 pieces of fish and fry for about 3 minutes on each side until golden. Transfer to a heavy saucepan. Repeat with the remaining pieces of fish.

Pour the vinegar over the fish, then 2 tablespoons of oil from the frying pan. Bring to the boil, then reduce the heat, cover and simmer for 20 minutes or until the vinegar has evaporated. Garnish with sprigs of herbs before serving.

Serve hot or cold, with plain rice and yoghurt.

Saffron Toffee

Sohan-e-asali

¼ teaspoon ground saffron
3½ oz/100 g thick honey
3½ oz/100 g caster sugar
2½ oz/65 g unsalted butter or 2½ fl oz/ 65 ml oil
3½ oz/100 g blanched almonds, shredded

Grease a heavy flat baking tray. Dissolve the saffron in 2 teaspoons boiling water. Put the honey, sugar, butter or oil in a small heavy saucepan, place over moderate heat and bring to the boil. Stir until golden, then add the almonds and the saffron liquid. Continue stirring for a further 3 minutes or until a little of the toffee sets when dropped onto a cold plate.

Put small knobs of the toffee on the greased baking tray, spacing them about ¼ inch/5 mm apart. Leave until cold, then remove with a palette knife.

Rice Crumbles

Nan-e-berenj

8½ oz/245 g aerated margarine or white cooking fat
6½ oz/185 g icing sugar, sifted
1 egg, separated
1 fl oz/25 ml rosewater
2 teaspoons ground cardamom, or to taste
18 oz/515 g rice flour
poppy seeds, to decorate

Preheat the oven to 325°F/170°C/gas mark 3 and grease a heavy, flat baking tray then dust with flour.

Melt the margarine or fat gently in the top of a double boiler, remove from the heat and leave to cool slightly. Add the sugar and beat with a wooden spoon until smooth, then add the egg yolk.

Stir in the rosewater and cardamom to taste, then gradually add the rice flour until you can gather the dough together in your hand.

Beat the egg white until stiff, then work into the dough with your hand or a wooden spoon. Knead with your hands until smooth. Take walnut-sized balls of dough and press to about ½ inch/1 cm thick between the palms of your hands.

Place the biscuits on the greased and floured tray, spacing them about ½ inch/1 cm apart to allow for spreading. Using the open end of a thimble, or similar object, press a pattern on top of each biscuit, then sprinkle over a few poppy seeds. Bake in the oven for about 10 minutes or until the biscuits are light golden and have risen. Remove from the oven, leave to cool slightly on the tray, then transfer to a plate and leave until cold. Store in an airtight tin.

Makes about 64.

YAZD, THE CITY OF DOMES

The city of Yazd is in the centre of Persia, surrounded by small scattered villages. This desert province, with its population of about sixty-six thousand, still has a large number of Zoroastrian inhabitants as well as Muslims, Jews and others.

Historically, there are several interesting buildings and ruins connected with the Zoroastrian religion, which has its roots in Yazd. The outskirts of the town are green and fertile as they are irrigated by purchased water from nearby Shirkooh, the mountain of milk. A special feature of the buildings is the 'domed' roofs. These are typical of old islamic architecture, some with tall 'ventilation' chimneys to catch the cool breeze.

Factories and local cottage industries produce top-quality woollen blankets and material for things such as suits. Copper jewellery is also produced in Yazd, but perhaps the most famous 'export' are the traditional sweets – *baghlava*, *ghotab* and *sohan*. My father once took me to the sweet factory near the famous Madan-e-Mirchaghmagh Square by the bazaar. The building was hundreds of years old and sweets were sent from there all over the world. It was, and is still, considered to be a very special treat if you receive one of these delicious sweets from the city of Yazd.

ﻣﻌﻨﯽ

Baklava

Baghlava

SYRUP
5 oz/140 g granulated sugar
2 tablespoons rosewater
1 teaspoon lemon juice

PASTRY
1½–1¾ oz/45–55 g plain white flour
¼ teaspoon baking powder
1 egg yolk
1 teaspoon oil
1 fl oz/25 ml milk
a few chopped almonds or unsalted pistachios, to decorate

FILLING
12 oz/345 g ground almonds
9 oz/206 g caster sugar
2 teaspoons ground cardamom
1¼ tablespoons rosewater
5 oz/140 g unsalted butter, clarified and cooled

First make the syrup: put the sugar in a small, heavy saucepan, add the rosewater and 3 tablespoons cold water and heat gently until the sugar has dissolved. Bring to the boil, add the lemon juice and boil for 2–3 minutes or until the syrup does not spread when a little is spooned on to a cold plate. Remove from the heat, pour into a bowl and leave to cool.

Prepare the pastry: sift the flour and baking powder together. Put the egg yolk in a bowl with the oil and milk. Stir with a fork, then gradually add the flour and stir with the fork for 3–4 minutes until a sticky mixture is formed. Place in a lightly greased polythene bag and leave to rest in a warm place for about 30–45 minutes.

Line an 11 × 7 × 1½ inch/28 × 18 × 4 cm baking tin with foil, making sure that the corners are neatly square and grease well. Divide the pastry in half and roll out each piece on a very well-floured surface to a 13 × 9 inch/32 × 23 cm rectangle. Brush off the excess flour. Place 1 of the rectangles in the tin. Leave to rest while making the filling.

Mix together the ground almonds, sugar and cardamom and pour over the pastry in the tin. Smooth out by pressing down firmly with the palm of your hand. Sprinkle over the rosewater, then 2 tablespoons of the cooled clarified butter.

Preheat the oven to 325°F/170°C/gas mark 3. Place the second rectangle of pastry over the filling and press down gently, making sure that the corners are neat. Pour over the remaining clarified butter and spread out evenly with the back of a spoon. Cut into diamond shapes with a sharp knife and sprinkle with almonds or pistachios. Bake in the coolest part of the oven for 20 minutes, then bake for a further 3 minutes in the centre until light golden.

Remove the *baghlava* from the oven and pour over the cooled sugar syrup. Cover the tray with a clean tea towel, tucking the ends carefully underneath. Leave undisturbed for at least 24 hours. To serve, lift out on the foil and cut through with a sharp knife. Store in an airtight tin in the refrigerator.

Makes about 30.

ﻣﻌﻨﯽ

Variation
Pistachio Baklava

Baghlava-ye-pesteh

Follow the method for BAKLAVA above, using 4 oz/115 g sugar, 3 tablespoons rosewater, 1 tablespoon water and 1 teaspoon lemon juice for the sugar syrup, the same ingredients for the pastry and the following ingredients for the filling: 9 oz/260 g unsalted shelled pistachios, ground almost to a paste, 8 oz/230 g ground almonds, 14 oz/400 g caster sugar, 1½ teaspoons ground cardamom, 1¼ tablespoons rosewater and 4 oz/115 g unsalted butter, clarified and cool.

ﻣﻌﻨﯽ

Cardamom, Rosewater and Nut Pasties

Ghotab

This famous Persian sweet originates from the city of Yazd, deep in central Persia. It was a custom amongst Zoroastrians to commemorate the birth of a new member of the family by purchasing, from the bazaar, a copper bowl or dish engraved with the new baby's name and date of birth. My mother used to use my engraved bowl to make the dough for *ghotab*, which would then be rolled out on an inverted copper tray outside the terrace. The whole family would join in the preparation, and great play was made of who could achieve the best original shape. I can still recall the scent of the spring flowers, the singing of the birds and the sound of the old-fashioned gramophone playing in the background.

8 oz/230 g plain white flour
1 teaspoon baking powder
3 egg yolks
3 fl oz/85 ml plain yoghurt
4 oz/115 g unsalted butter, clarified and cooled
icing sugar, for dusting
FILLING
6–7 oz/175–200 g ground almonds
2–3 oz/60–90 g icing sugar, sifted
2 teaspoons ground cardamom
1½ tablespoons rosewater
1 egg white, beaten

Sift the flour and baking powder together. Put the egg yolks in a bowl with the yoghurt and butter. Stir with a fork to mix. Add the flour and mix to a dough with one hand. Gather the dough together, but do not knead or this will cause the oil to separate from the pastry. Place in a lightly greased polythene bag and leave to rest in a warm place for about 20 minutes.

Meanwhile, make the filling: mix together the ground almonds, sugar, ground cardamom and rosewater, gathering the ingredients together with your hands to form a smooth, sticky dough.

Preheat the oven to 350°F/180°C/gas mark 4. Grease a heavy, flat baking tray and dust lightly with flour. Roll out the pastry on a lightly floured surface to ½ inch thickness and cut out circles with a 2 inch/5 cm plain pastry cutter. Brush with beaten egg white, then place a small almond-sized ball of filling in the centre of each circle. Bring the edges of the dough together over the filling and press to seal. Twist or crimp the edges.

Place the pasties on the greased and floured tray and bake in the oven for 10 minutes until risen and light golden. Transfer to a wire rack, leave to cool, then dust with icing sugar.

Makes about 30.

SISDAH BE DAR (THIRTEEN DAYS OUT)

The excitement of Nov Rooz lasted up to the 13th of Farvardeen (April 2nd); the day to be 'seen out'. The custom was to step gently into the green, newly grown wheat, walk for a short while, then sit on the grass and, with your hands behind your back, knot the green wheat and say this poem:

> Sisdah be dar/Thirteen days out,
> Chahrdah be too/Fourteen days in,
> Be haghe pire Kotkotoo/Trusting Kotkotoo the legendary saint,
> Sisdah ra kardim to kado/We put number 13 into a pumpkin
> Darash ra bastim ba judoo/And sealed it with glue
> Saleh digeh charghat be sar/Next year I wear the scarf (meaning to be married)
> Bacheh be baghal/And my baby in my arm.

Crispy Almond Bites

Haji badam

1 teaspoon ground cardamom
1½ oz/45 g icing sugar

1 oz soft margarine or butter

3 oz/90 g ground almonds

Preheat the oven to 350°F/180°C/gas mark 4. Grease a heavy, flat baking tray and dust with flour. Put the almonds in a mixing cardamom bowl, sift in the icing sugar and add the butter or margarine. Knead to a soft dough with your hands.

Place hazelnut-sized balls of the dough on the greased and floured tray and bake in the oven for 7–10 minutes until risen and golden. Remove from the oven and leave on the tray to cool slightly, then transfer to a wire rack and leave until cold. Store in an airtight tin.

Makes 20–30.

Rosewater Fondants

Noghl

5 oz/140 g granulated sugar

3 tablespoons rosewater

1⅛ teaspoons glucose powder

about 30 blanched almonds, split in half lengthways

Lightly grease a marble slab or heavy flat baking tray. Put the sugar in a small heavy saucepan, add the rosewater and glucose and heat gently until the sugar has dissolved. Bring to the boil and boil for 2½–3 minutes or until the syrup drops thickly from the tip of a spoon.

Pour the syrup immediately onto the greased slab or tray, leave to cool for 30–60 seconds, then gather together with a palette knife and when cooled a little knead well with your hands until cool.

Take chick-pea sized balls of dough and roll in the palms of your hands until smooth. Push 1 piece of almond into the side of each piece of dough, then continue rolling the dough in your hands until the nut is in the centre. Place the fondants on a plate and leave to set for 1–2 days before serving.

Makes about 60.

Pistachio Munchies

Shirini-e-pisteh

2 large egg yolks

2½ oz/75 g icing sugar, sifted

4 oz/115 g unsalted shelled pistachios or other nuts, ground to almost a paste

¼ teaspoon ground cardamom

1 egg yolk, to glaze

a few poppy seeds, to decorate

Preheat the oven to 350°F/180°C/gas mark 4. Grease a heavy, flat baking tray and dust with flour. Put the egg yolks and icing sugar in a bowl and beat until white. Add the ground nuts and cardamom and gather together with your hands to form a soft dough.

Take hazelnut-sized balls of the dough and press between your palms to flatten. Place on the greased and floured tray, spacing them well apart to allow for spreading. Brush in the yolk to glaze and sprinkle with poppy seeds. Bake in the oven for about 10–15 minutes until risen and light golden. Remove from the oven and leave to cool on the tray. Store in an airtight tin.

Makes about 36.

Raisin Crunchies

Shirini-e-keshmesh

2 oz/60 g margarine or butter, at room temperature

2 oz/60 g caster sugar

2½ oz/75 g plain white flour, sifted

2 teaspoons seedless raisins

Preheat the oven to 350°F/180°C/gas mark 4. Grease a heavy, flat baking tray and dust with flour. Put all the ingredients in a bowl and beat well until smooth.

Gather the dough together with your hands, then take hazelnut-sized balls and press into 2½ inch/6 cm rounds which are ¼ inch/5 mm thick. Place on the greased and floured tray and bake in the oven for 10–12 minutes until light golden. Transfer to a wire rack and leave to cool. Store in an airtight tin.

Makes 18–20.

Yazdi Cake

Cake-e-yazdi

2 eggs separated
5 oz sugar (granulated)
3 oz marge or butter
1 oz milk
1 oz rose water
1 teaspoon baking powder
1 teaspoon bicarbonate of soda
1 heaped teaspoon ground cardamon
2 oz chopped pistachio or any unsalted nuts desired
8 oz plain flour sieved
1 desertspoon ground unsalted pistachio nuts or any for garnishing

Beat the egg yolk with the sugar until white. Combine in the marge or butter, continue beating, add in the rose water and the milk, the baking powder and bicarbonate of soda, and the cardamon and beat, adding in the chopped nuts, slowly add in the flour and beat. Beat the egg white, until stiff, and with a wooden spoon add into the mixture, and slowly fold in with the dough. In the meantime set the oven to 350°/180°C. Place one desertspoon of the resulting mixture into individual cake cases and sprinkle on the nuts, place in the middle part of the oven on a baking tray and bake for approx 10/15 minutes until the cakes are risen and golden.

THE MOST IMPORTANT MONTH (RAMAZAN)

One of the most important Muslim festivals is that of Ramazan which is based on the Lunar calendar, a whole month of fasting and prayer when no music or entertainment is allowed.

As an exercise in self-denial, because their Holy Book, the *Quran*, was revealed to their prophet in this month, Muslims fast from sunrise to sunset, during which time not only are eating and drinking prohibited, but smoking and any form of physical pleasure. For Muslims who fast the days are dull and slow, until after sunset when activities begin again and shops and stores stay open until well after midnight. After sunset in Yazd, Muslim families would gather to break their fast, continuing their social life until the early hours of the next morning, right up to sunrise when you could hear the sound of Azan calling the faithful to pray.

It was a month I looked forward to as a child, with its appetising specialities such as Soft Syrup Fingers (*Bamya*) and Sweet Syrup Circles (*Zolubia*) piled high on large copper trays in their golden rosewater syrup. Placed at the entrance to shops in the evenings, the syrup would sparkle and glint in the lamplight.

Wheat and Cinnamon Meal-in-a-Bowl

Halim

4 oz/115 g whole wheat grains
8 oz/230 g boneless, lean lamb or beef, washed and cut into ½ inch/1 cm squares
1 large onion, peeled and chopped
salt and pepper
1 teaspoon ground cinnamon
1 teaspoon sugar

Wash the wheat, place in a bowl and cover with lukewarm water. Leave to soak overnight.

The next day, drain the wheat and grind in a food processor. Place in a 4 pint/2.25 litre heavy saucepan and add the meat, onion and salt and pepper to taste. Cover with about 2 pints/1.2 litres cold water and place over moderate heat until the froth rises. Immediately remove the pan from the heat to prevent boiling over, spoon off and discard the froth. Return the pan to the heat and bring to the boil, then reduce the heat to the lowest possible simmer. Partially cover the pan (to allow steam to escape and prevent boiling over) and cook for 1–2 hours until the meat is tender, stirring occasionally adding a little water if it is too dry. (The cooking time will vary according to the type, cut and quality of the meat used.) Remove from the heat and leave to cool.

Work the *halim* in a blender or food processor for 1–2 minutes until smooth. Return to the pan and reheat gently, then turn into warm individual dishes and sprinkle with the cinnamon and sugar.

Serve hot, with NAN.

Soft Syrup Fingers

Bamya

2½ tablespoons oil
2 oz/60 g plain white flour
1 egg, beaten
oil for deep frying
SYRUP
8 oz/230 g granulated sugar
3 fl oz/85 ml rosewater
2 tablespoons lemon juice

First make the syrup: put the sugar in a medium heavy saucepan, add a 4 fl oz/120 ml cold water and heat gently until the sugar has dissolved. Bring to the boil and cook for 3–4 minutes, or until the syrup does not spread when a little is spread onto a cold plate. Then add the rosewater and lemon juice and continue simmering for a further 2–3 minutes until the syrup is a little thickened. Remove from the heat and leave until cold.

Put the oil in a small heavy saucepan, add 3 fl oz/85 ml cold water and bring to the boil over high heat. Add the flour and stir with a wooden spoon to make a soft dough. Remove the pan from the heat, leave to cool slightly, then beat in the egg.

Heat the oil in a deep-fat fryer. Put the dough in a piping bag fitted with a fluted nozzle and pipe one or two 2 inch/5 cm lengths into the hot oil. Deep fry for 45–60 seconds until golden, then remove with a slotted spoon. Drain on kitchen paper for 1–2 minutes, then drop into the cold syrup. Leave for at least 5 minutes, then remove and place on a serving plate. Repeat with the remaining dough.

Sweet Syrup Circles

Zolubia

¼ oz/10 g dried yeast or ½ oz/15 g fresh
1 teaspoon sugar
7 oz/200 g plain white flour
pinch of salt
2 tablespoons plain yoghurt
oil for deep frying
SYRUP
1¼ lb/550 g granulated sugar
4 fl oz/120 ml rosewater
3 tablespoons lemon juice

First make the syrup: put the sugar in a large, heavy saucepan, add ½ pint/300 ml cold water and heat gently until the sugar has dissolved. Bring to the boil and cook for 3–4 minutes, then add the rosewater and lemon juice and continue simmering for 2–3 minutes until the syrup is quite thick. Remove from the heat and leave until cold.

Dissolve the yeast and sugar in 3 fl oz/85 ml warm water and leave in a warm place for 10–15 minutes until frothy. Sift the flour and salt into a large bowl. Make a well in the centre, add the frothing yeast and the yoghurt and stir with a fork in the bowl, gradually working in 3–5 fl oz/85–150 ml warm water to form a loose dough. Dust lightly with flour and cover with a damp cloth. Leave in a warm place until doubled in bulk.

Heat the oil in a deep-fat fryer. Put the dough in a piping bag fitted with a plain nozzle and pipe a circle of dough into the hot oil. Deep fry for 30–60 seconds on each side until golden, then remove with a slotted spoon. Drain on kitchen paper for 1–2 minutes, then drop into the cold syrup. Leave for at least 5 minutes, then remove and place on a serving plate. Repeat with the remaining dough.

Saffron and Nut Pudding

Sholeh zard

4 oz/115 g short grain or basmati rice
1 oz/30 g margarine or butter
2 oz/60 g blanched almonds or other nuts, finely chopped
6 fl oz/175 ml rosewater
1 generous teaspoon ground saffron
7 oz/200 g caster sugar
¼ teaspoon ground cinnamon and 1 teaspoon finely chopped nuts, to decorate

Clean, wash and soak the rice according to the general instructions on page 16.

Drain the rice into a sieve and rinse until the water runs clear. Melt the margarine or butter in a heavy saucepan, add the rice and 1 pint/600 ml cold water and bring to the boil. Reduce the heat and simmer for about 30 minutes, adding up to 1 pint/600 ml more water a little at a time whenever the pan becomes dry.

Stir in the nuts and rosewater. Dissolve the saffron in 1 fl oz/25 ml boiling water and stir into the rice.

Continue simmering until the mixture becomes thick, stirring all the time.

Stir in the sugar, remove the pan from the heat and leave to cool slightly. Transfer to a serving bowl, leave until completely cold, then cover and chill in the refrigerator for at least 2 hours.

Sprinkle with the cinnamon and nuts before serving.

Serve well chilled.

Elephant Ears

Goosh-e-fil

1 egg yolk
1 fl oz/25 ml milk
1 teaspoon oil
2 oz/60 g plain white flour
1 heaped teaspoon baking powder
a little beaten egg white, to seal
oil for deep frying
icing sugar and ground pistachios, to decorate

Put the egg yolk and milk in a bowl, beat with a fork, then stir in the oil. Sift the flour and baking powder together and stir into the egg mixture to form a sticky dough and beat for 3–4 minutes. Leave to rest in a warm place for 30 minutes to 1 hour.

Divide the dough into 15–18 pieces and roll into smooth balls in your hands. Roll out each ball on a floured surface to a circle about ⅛ inch/3 mm thick. Brush all the way round the edge of each circle with beaten egg white, then fold the circle over and press to seal.

Heat the oil in a deep-fat fryer to 350°F/180°C. Deep fry the elephant ears a few at a time for about 30 seconds until light golden, then remove with a slotted spoon. Drain on kitchen paper, then leave to cool. Sprinkle with icing sugar and nuts before serving.

Serve cold.

'COLD' IS A CURE FOR A COLD

A common belief amongst Persians was – and still is – that aches and pains were due to eating certain foods and therefore food could be used as a cure for certain ailments. For example, onion, garlic, rue, mint, tarragon, ripe grapes, melon, lamb and chicken are known as 'hot' foods, good for curing tummy aches and bad backs, whereas beef, cockerel, cucumber, tomatoes, watermelons, plums, unripe grapes, rice, barley and spinach are 'cold' foods, which are good for colds and 'flu.

During my childhood in Yazd, the neighbours would often seek each other's advice on what to cook if their children were sick, even when they had a doctor's prescription. If a baby was known to be unwell, neighbours would call at the house with a bowlful of food for the child, or if your own child was ill you might call on a friend asking for a little of a particular kind of soup. For example, a *nohodab*, a meat and chickpea soup, was known to be good for babies' colds, so if your baby had a cold you would ask around if any of your friends or neighbours were making it that day. In winter, if someone in our family had a cold or the 'flu, my mother used to prepare a dish of hot FERNY as a cure. At other times it made the most delicious cold pudding and was one of our family favourites.

ORTHODOX MUSLIM WEDDING IN YAZD

I was only six years old when my nanny Malog dressed me up to go to a Muslim wedding. I had to wear a *chador*, a long piece of cloth to cover my clothes and face with only my eyes showing. The bride was sitting on a hand-made mattress (*doshak*) in the corner of the paved garden, and the small patio area was packed with women dressed in different-coloured *chadors*, busy pouring tea (*chay*) out of the large brass samovar. Trays piled with various delicious sweets were offered to the guests.

The bride's bright red hands and nails had been coloured with henna the night before. She held a small mirror in front of her and when her future husband sat beside her on the *doshak* she slowly unveiled her face so that he could see her for the first time in the reflected glass. The sound of joy and cheering was heard amongst the guests, as the groom found her very attractive. He was of course delighted with his mother's choice.

Sweet Rice Sauce

Ferny

8 fl oz/225 ml milk
½ oz/15 g rice flour
2 fl oz/50 ml rosewater
½ oz/15 g caster sugar, or to taste

Put the milk and rice flour in a small heavy saucepan and bring to the boil over high heat, stirring constantly. Reduce the heat and stir in the rosewater and sugar to taste, then cook for 5–10 minutes until thick, stirring all the time.

Serve hot or cold.

Christian Festivals

CHRISTMAS

Christmas Pasties

Gata

10 oz/285 g plain flour
2 teaspoons baking powder
¼ teaspoon bicarbonate of soda
2 egg yolks
2 oz/60 g soft tub margarine or 2 fl oz/50 ml oil
2 oz/60 g caster sugar
2–3 fl oz/50–85 ml plain yoghurt
a little beaten egg white, to seal
FILLING
8 heaped teaspoons jam or marmalade
1½ oz/45 g ground almonds
1½ oz/45 g ground walnuts
2 oz/60 g caster sugar
1 teaspoon ground cardamom

Sift together the flour, baking powder and soda. Put one of the egg yolks in a large bowl, add the margarine or oil, the sugar and sifted flour mixture. Beat together, adding the yoghurt very slowly until a smooth (not sticky) dough is formed. Gather the dough in your hands to form a smooth ball. Chill in the refrigerator for 30 minutes to 1 hour.

Preheat the oven to 350°F/180°C/gas mark 4. Grease a heavy, flat baking tray and dust well with flour. Divide the dough into four. Roll out each quarter on a floured surface to a 6 inch/15 cm circle about ¼ inch/5 mm thick. Spread 2 heaped teaspoons jam or marmalade over each piece of dough, leaving a ½ inch/1 cm margin all round. Brush all the way round the edge of each circle with beaten egg white.

Mix together the ground nuts, sugar and cardamom and sprinkle 1½–2 teaspoons of this mixture over the jam on each piece of dough. Fold the circles over and press to seal. Twist or crimp the edges. Brush the pasties all over with the remaining egg yolk.

Place the pasties on the greased and floured tray and bake in the oven for 10–12 minutes or until risen and golden. Transfer to a wire rack and leave until cold.

≈≈≈≈≈

Stuffed Fried Fingers

Yokha

6 oz/175 g plain flour
1 heaped teaspoon baking powder
2 egg yolks
2 oz/60 g butter, melted and cooled or 2 fl oz/50 ml oil
2 fl oz/50 ml milk
oil for deep frying
FILLING
2–2½ oz/60–75 g ground almonds
2–2½ oz/60–75 g ground walnuts
2 oz/60 g caster sugar
1 teaspoon ground cardamom
about 1 tablespoon rosewater
icing sugar for dusting

Sift together the flour and baking powder. Put the egg yolks in a large bowl, add the butter or oil, the milk and the sifted flour and baking powder. Beat together, then gather the dough in your hands to form a smooth ball. Leave to rest in a warm place for 30 minutes to 1 hour.

Divide the dough into 24 pieces and roll into smooth balls in your hands. Roll out each ball on a floured surface to a triangle about ¼ inch/5 mm thick. Brush all the way round the edge of each triangle with beaten egg white.

Mix together the ground nuts, sugar and cardamom and moisten with rosewater. Place a small almond-size ball of the filling in the centre of each triangle, then gently roll the dough up around the filling to make a cigar shape. Seal with more egg white.

Heat the oil in a deep-fat fryer. Deep fry the rolls a few at a time for about 1 minute until light golden, then remove with a slotted spoon. Drain on kitchen paper, then dust with icing sugar.

Makes 24.

≈≈≈≈≈

Christmas Thin Rolls

Nazok

3 eggs
1 tablespoon rosewater
4 oz/115 g soft tub margarine
1 fl oz/25 ml milk
8 oz/230 g caster sugar
2 teaspoons baking powder
¼ teaspoon bicarbonate of soda
2 teaspoons ground cardamom or cinnamon
1 teaspoon ground mixed spice
4 fl oz/120 ml plain yoghurt
1½ lb/685 g plain flour, sifted
a little beaten egg white, to seal
2 teaspoons sesame seeds, to decorate
FILLING
12 heaped teaspoons jam or marmalade

5½ oz/155 g ground almonds
5½ oz/155 g ground walnuts
2 oz/60 g caster sugar
1 teaspoon ground cardamom

Put 2 of the eggs in a bowl, add the rosewater, margarine, milk, sugar, baking powder, soda and spices and beat together. Add the yoghurt very slowly with the flour until a smooth (not sticky) dough is formed. Gather the dough in your hands to form a smooth ball. Chill in the refrigerator for 30 minutes to 1 hour.

Preheat the oven to 350°F/180°C/gas mark 4. Grease a heavy, flat baking tray and dust well with flour. Divide the dough into 6 equal pieces. Roll out each piece on a lightly floured surface to a 9 × 5 inch/23 × 12.5 cm rectangle. Spread 2 heaped teaspoons jam over each piece of dough, leaving a 1 inch/2.5 cm margin all round. Brush all the way round the edges of each rectangle with beaten egg white.

Mix together the ground nuts, sugar and cardamom and sprinkle 3–4 teaspoons of this mixture over the jam on each piece of dough. Roll the rectangles up like Swiss rolls from one long end, then place on the greased and floured tray. Beat the remaining egg and brush over the pastries to seal. Sprinkle over the sesame seeds.

Bake the pastries in the oven for about 10–15 minutes until risen and golden. Remove from the oven, leave to cool on a wire rack, then cut each roll into 6 1½ inch/4 cm pieces.

Makes 36.

CHRISTMAS IN THE CITY

The Christmas celebration took place on January 5th, the date on which the Armenian Christians in Persia believed Christ was born. The snow over the chain of Alboerz mountains which overlooked Tehran was a continuous spread to the streets of the city, covering the naked branches of beech and plane trees bordering the boulevards and steep avenues along the water canals, now filled with frozen ice. Christmas was an international celebraiton, the shop windows colourfully decorated as in the West and busy with shoppers getting ready for the big celebration. Elo my Armenian friend asked me to accompany her to church on Christmas Eve. Every seat was taken and the burning candles at the altar gave a cosy, Christmas atmosphere. Traditional Christmas songs were sung and communion was received, many of the congregation taking home small pieces of bread to eat with wine before dinner as the head of the family conducted a small family service. I was fortunate to join Elo and her family for Christmas lunch after their return from church. The food was a repeat of the traditional Christmas Eve dinner – plain rice, smoked fish and Herb Savoury Cake, followed by a special sweet.

Star Rice

Berenj-e-setareh-ie

11 oz/315 g long grain rice
2 fl oz/50 ml oil
1 small onion, peeled and finely chopped
1 lb/455 g boneless chicken breasts, skin removed, washed and cut into 4 portions
salt
2 large or 4 small oranges
¼ oz/10 g caster sugar
1 oz/30 g sultanas, rinsed
1 oz/30 g blanched almonds, shredded
1 oz/30 g shelled unsalted pistachios, shredded
2 oz/60 g margarine or butter
¼ teaspoon ground saffron

Clean, wash and soak the rice according to the general instructions on page 16.

Heat the oil in a heavy frying pan, add the onion and fry gently until golden. Add the chicken and a little salt to taste, then pour in 1–2 fl oz/25–50 ml cold water. Cover the pan and simmer for 15–20 minutes until the chicken is just tender, then remove the lid and boil vigorously to evaporate excess liquid. Remove from the heat and set aside.

Remove the rind from the oranges with a zester or canelle knife. Place in a small, heavy saucepan with the sugar and 2 fl oz/50 ml cold water. Bring to the boil, reduce the heat and simmer for about 10 minutes until the rinds are soft. Set aside.

Parboil, drain and rinse the rice as in the recipe for CRISPY FISH AND DILL RICE (page 28). Put one-quarter of the rice in the bottom of a 4 pint/2.25 litre heavy saucepan and place the chicken breasts and their oil on top. Put the orange rind, sultanas and nuts in one corner of the pan and cover with some of the rice, then cover the chicken with the remaining rice.

Cut the margarine or butter into small pieces and dot all over the rice. Wrap the lid of the pan in a tea towel and *dam* for about 1 hour, as in the recipe for CRISPY FISH AND DILL RICE (page 28).

Transfer 1 ladleful of rice to a bowl with the orange rind, sultanas and nuts. Dissolve the saffron in 1 tablespoon boiling water and mix with the ladleful of rice. Turn the contents of the pan out onto a warm serving platter and garnish with the saffron mixture.

Serve hot, with any type of *khoresh*.

3

Dinner Party Dishes

STARTERS

.ᘓᘓᘓ.

Chicken hors D'œuvre

Pishghazay-e-morgh va badam

1½ lb/685 g boneless cooked chicken, skin removed
4 oz/115 g ground almonds
¼ pint/150 ml plain yoghurt
2 teaspoons finely chopped fresh dill
salt and pepper
a few almond flakes, toasted, to garnish

Mince the chicken and place in a large bowl with the ground almonds and yoghurt. Add the dill and a little salt and pepper to taste, then toss a few times until evenly mixed. Transfer to a serving dish and garnish with flaked almonds.

Serve at room temperature.

.ᘓᘓᘓ.

Melon Surprise

Pishghazay-e-kharbozeh

2 oz/60 g long grain rice
2 oz/60 g brown lentils
salt
3 dates, pitted and finely chopped
3 oz/90 g shelled walnuts, coarsely chopped
2 sprigs of fresh mint, finely chopped
2–3 sprigs of fresh tarragon, finely chopped
2 fl oz/50 ml oil
juice of 1 large lemon, or to taste
2 ogen melons
1 small potato, boiled, peeled and diced
a few lettuce leaves, to serve

Clean, wash and soak the rice according to the general instructions on page 16. Prepare and soak the lentils as in the recipe for PLUM AND MINT SOUP (page 11).

Drain the rice into a sieve until the water runs clear, then simmer in salted water for 8–10 minutes until tender. Drain and rinse under cold running water, then set aside to drain well. Simmer the lentils in their soaking water for about 20 minutes until they are cooked but not too soft. Drain and rinse under cold running water. Set aside to drain well.

Put the dates, nuts and herbs in a large bowl, add the rice and lentils, then stir in the oil and lemon juice. Add the diced potato and toss a few times until evenly mixed.

Cut the melons in half, scoop out and discard the seeds. Scoop out the flesh, taking care not to puncture the skin, then dice the flesh and add to the rice and lentil mixture. Toss gently a few times, then spoon into the melon cases.

Serve at room temperature on a bed of lettuce leaves.

.ᘓᘓᘓ.

Persimmon Hors D'œuvre

Pishghazay-e-khormaloo

4 firm ripe persimmons
6–8 oz/175–230 g feta cheese or PANIR (page 00), finely diced or mashed
1 tablespoon chopped toasted almonds or other nuts
1 teaspoon ground cinnamon
1 tablespoon plain yoghurt
1 heaped teaspoon icing or caster sugar
TO SERVE
a few flaked almonds, toasted
a few radicchio or lettuce leaves

Wash the persimmons, cut off a thin slice from the top of each fruit and reserve. Scoop out the pulp and reserve with the cases. Put the cheese in a bowl with the nuts. Add the cinnamon, yoghurt and sugar and toss a few times to mix. Dice some of the reserved persimmon pulp and add to the mixture, tossing gently to mix. Spoon into the cases, then arrange on individual plates with the reserved tops. Garnish the plate with radicchio or lettuce and sprinkle toasted almonds over the filling.

Serve at room temperature.

Spinach and Mortadella Hors D'œuvre

Pishghazay-e-esfenaj va kalbas

1 fl oz/25 ml oil
1 medium onion, peeled and chopped
2 garlic cloves, peeled and crushed
8 oz/230 g spinach leaves, washed and coarsely chopped
4 oz/115 g mortadella sausage, diced into ¼ inch/5 mm pieces
4 hard-boiled eggs, shelled and sliced

Heat the oil in a heavy saucepan, add the onion and fry gently until golden. Stir in the garlic and spinach, cover and simmer gently for about 10 minutes or until the spinach leaves are soft. Uncover the pan and increase the heat to evaporate most of the excess water (the ingredients should remain juicy).

Add the mortadella to the pan and toss a few times to mix and heat through. Turn the mixture onto a warm serving plate and garnish on top and around the plate with the sliced hard-boiled eggs.

Serve immediately with hot HUSHVA NAN.

Aubergine Starter

Kashk-o-Badimjan

Aubergine weighing approx 8/9 oz sliced ¼ inch thick
salt
oil for shallow frying
One large onion peeled and finely chopped
½ teaspoon turmeric
salt and pepper to taste
8 tablespoons plain yoghurt
Hot mint for garnishing

Place the aubergines on a tray or large plate, sprinkle with salt and leave for one hour, to degorge the black and bitter juice. Rinse under cold water and dab dry with the kitchen paper. Shallow fry in oil for two minutes on each side until golden. Remove the aubergines from the pan, fry the onions in 2/3 tablespoons of the oil from the pan until golden. Stir in the turmeric, salt and pepper to taste. Place one tablespoon of the plain yoghurt onto 4 individual large side plates, top up with some of the onion and turmeric mixture and place 2/3 slices of the fried aubergines on top. Pour over another spoon of the plain yoghurt and some more of the onion mixture. Garnish on top with hot mint. Serve with any type of nan.

For variations follow the recipe as above for COURGETTE, but it is not necessary to salt the slices before frying.

This dish is traditionally eaten with special dried cheese, (KASHK) but instead yoghurt can be used.

GHERKINS ALWAYS BREAK THE ICE

Hospitality was an important part of everyday life, whichever part of the country you lived in and whatever class of people you were. Proud housewives would make their homes colourful with large trays piled high with fresh fruit, often garnished with young gherkins. It was the custom for the host to peel a gherkin lengthways, leaving about an inch at the end to hold on to, then sprinkle the flesh with a little salt and pepper. The skin was then put back over the flesh so that it would not be touched by the fingers and placed on a side plate in front of the guest. This would 'break the ice' and the guest would then feel free to help himself.

※※※

Gherkin Hors D'œuvre

Pishghazay-e-khiyar

2 spring onions, trimmed and finely chopped
1 teaspoon chopped fresh mint
1 teaspoon chopped fresh tarragon
1 tablespoon oil
6 oz/175 g cheese or PANIR finely diced
2 teaspoons sultanas, well rinsed, or 1 teaspoon golden syrup
2 teaspoons chopped walnuts or other nuts
4 fat gherkins
salt and pepper
2 radishes, thinly sliced, to garnish

Put the spring onions and herbs in a large bowl, add the oil and toss well to mix. Add the cheese and sultanas (if using), then the nuts.

Cut the gherkins in half lengthways. Scoop out the pulp, taking care not to puncture the cases. Dice the pulp and add to the remaining ingredients with salt and pepper to taste. Spoon into the gherkin cases. If using golden syrup, trickle a little over each filling. Garnish with the sliced radishes.

Serve at room temperature, with hot HUSHVA NAN (page 135).

BRAVERY AND WALNUTS

A spring gushed out from underneath the mountains just outside our house in Manshad, making its way down for about a mile to a large pond which fed the walnut trees all around it. This pond and surrounding trees became a favourite meeting place for us local girls and boys as it was always shady in the heat of the midday sun. We used to swap stories and brag about who was the bravest in the group.

One day I decided to prove how brave *I* was, so I picked some walnuts from the lower branches of one of the trees, marked them with a knife and said I would take them from the house in the dead of night, go along the lonely steep road down to the pond and leave them under one of the trees. I was only thirteen at the time and tremendously excited about my forthcoming adventure.

I remember distinctly the *ash* we had for dinner that night, and how anxious I was that there should be no leftovers put outside the house for the wild fox! I chose to wear *giveh* on my feet and a long-sleeved, dark red dress with small white flowers on it. I put on a brave face and stepped out into the moonless night towards the pond.

The area was totally uninhabited. The stars were flickering, and the air was filled with the various sounds of crickets and croaking frogs, insects and the wild fox. I held very tight to my bag of walnuts and walked briskly down the wiggling road which was covered in pebbles. I kept slipping, but managed to keep control by singing my favourite song, which seemed to echo around the mountain. I could sense I was getting nearer as the sound of the spring got louder, and soon I was able to place the marked walnuts under the chosen tree.

Getting back home took longer because it was uphill, but once I could see the dim light from our house halfway up the mountain it helped me find my way. The next day everyone was most impressed by my bravery with the walnuts!

※※※

Meatballs in Walnut and Yoghurt sauce

Kaleh joosh

8 oz/230 g lean minced lamb or beef

1 large or 2 medium onions, peeled
5–7 tablespoons oil
1 teaspoon turmeric
1 teaspoon crushed dried mint
salt and pepper
TO SERVE
6 fl oz/175 ml plain yoghurt
2 oz/60 g shelled walnuts, ground

6–7 fl oz/175–200 ml oil
1½ lb/685 g minced lamb or beef
4 large or 2 medium onions, peeled
5–7 garlic cloves, peeled and crushed
1 teaspoon crushed dried mint
½ teaspoon ground saffron
6 fl oz/175 ml plain yoghurt
2 teaspoons flaked almonds or other nuts, toasted to garnish

Put the meat in a bowl. Grate 2 oz/60 g of the onion to a juice over the meat. Knead with your hands for about 5 minutes until the meat binds together. Form into smooth balls the size of hazelnuts.

Finely chop the remaining onion. Heat half of the oil in a large heavy saucepan, add the chopped onion and fry gently until golden. Add the remaining oil to the pan, then add the meatballs in batches and fry over moderate heat until browned on all sides. Add the turmeric, mint and a little salt and pepper, then add about 4 fl oz/120 ml cold water. Cover and simmer gently for about 10 minutes, then uncover the pan and increase the heat to evaporate any excess water though the ingredients should remain juicy.

Arrange the meatballs on individual serving plates, spoon over the yoghurt and sprinkle with the ground nuts.

Serve hot, with HUSHVA NAN (page 135).

MEAT AND VEGETABLE MAIN COURSES

Aubergine in Yoghurt and Saffron sauce

Borani-e-badimjan

1 lb/455 g aubergines, peeled and sliced into ¼ inch/5 mm rounds
salt and pepper

Put the aubergine slices on a tray or large plate. Sprinkle both sides with salt (about 2 teaspoons) and leave for 1 hour to extract the dark and bitter juices. Rinse under cold running water and pat dry with a clean tea towel. Heat the oil gently in a heavy frying pan, add the aubergine slices in batches and fry over gentle heat for 2 minutes on each side. Transfer to kitchen paper to drain while frying the remainder, then set aside.

Put the meat in a bowl. Grate 2 oz/60 g of the onion to a juice over the meat. Knead with your hands for about 5 minutes until the mixture binds together. Form into smooth balls the size of hazelnuts.

Finely chop the remaining onion and fry gently in the oil from the aubergines. Add the meatballs in batches and fry over moderate heat until browned on all sides. Transfer the meatballs and onion to a large casserole or heavy saucepan, leaving the oil behind in the frying pan. Sprinkle with salt and pepper to taste. Place the aubergines over the meatballs and pour in about 4 fl oz/120 ml cold water. Bring to the boil, then reduce the heat and cover and simmer gently for about 10 minutes. Do not stir.

Meanwhile, reheat 1 tablespoon of the aubergine oil in the frying pan, add the crushed garlic and stir for 1 minute. Stir in the mint and almost immediately remove from the heat. Set aside.

Uncover the casserole or saucepan and increase the heat to evaporate most of the excess water (the ingredients should remain juicy). Stir the saffron into the yoghurt. Place the meatballs and aubergines on a warm serving dish and spoon the saffron yoghurt over the top. Drizzle over the garlic and mint mixture and garnish with the toasted nuts.

Serve hot, with NAN (page 138) and a seasonal salad.

✿✿✿✿✿

Savoury Meat Cakes

Kotlet-e-shirin torsh

8 oz/230 g lean minced lamb or beef
1 medium onion, peeled
3 heaped teaspoons breadcrumbs
1 large egg, beaten
½ teaspoon ground cinnamon
salt and pepper
about 6 fl oz/175 ml oil for frying
2 heaped teaspoons sugar, preferably brown
3 tablespoons vinegar
few sprigs of fresh mint, to garnish

Put the meat in a bowl. Grate 1 oz/30 g of the onion to a juice over the meat, add the bread-crumbs, egg, cinnamon and salt and pepper to taste and knead with your hands for about 5 minutes until the mixture binds together. Dampen the hands slightly with water and form into balls the size of walnuts, then flatten each one until about ¼ inch/5 mm thick. Heat the oil in a deep, small frying pan. Add the *kotlet* in batches and fry over moderate heat for about 3 minutes on each side until brown.

Transfer the *kotlet* to a heavy or non-stick sauce-pan and pour over 3 tablespoons of the oil from the frying pan. Dissolve the sugar in the vinegar and pour into the pan. Bring to the boil, then reduce the heat and simmer for about 15 minutes until the liquid has evaporated and the *kotlet* are glazed. Remove the *kotlet* with a slotted spoon and drain off excess oil. Arrange on a warm serving dish and garnish with mint sprigs.

Serve hot or cold with salad.

✿✿✿✿✿

Stuffed shoulder of Lamb

Shaneh-e-bareh

1 shoulder of lamb weighing about 3 lb/1.5 kg, boned
4 oz/115 g dried apricots, soaked overnight and drained
1 teaspoon ground cinnamon
1 teaspoon sugar, preferably brown
STUFFING
4 oz/115 g long grain rice
salt and pepper
2 fl oz/50 ml oil
2 medium onions, peeled and finely chopped
4 oz/115 g minced lean lamb or beef
½ teaspoon ground cinnamon
¼ teaspoon turmeric
2 oz/60 g finely chopped fresh parsley or coriander
1 tablespoon chopped fresh dill
4 oz/60 g shelled walnuts or other nuts, finely chopped
2 oz/60 g seedless raisins or chopped sultanas, well rinsed

First make the stuffing: clean, wash and soak the rice according to the general instructions on page 16.

Drain the rice into a sieve until the water runs clear, then simmer in boiling salted water for 4 minutes. Drain, rinse under cold running water, then set aside. Heat the oil in a heavy pan, add the onions and fry gently until golden. Add the meat and stir for 2–3 minutes until browned, then stir in the spices. Transfer the mixture to a bowl and stir in the rice, herbs, nuts, raisins or sultanas and salt and pepper to taste.

Preheat the oven to 400°F/200°C/gas mark 6. Wash the lamb, pat dry with kitchen paper, then spoon the stuffing over the meat. Roll the meat up and tie with trussing thread or string. Place in a roasting tin, cover with foil and roast in the oven for 10 minutes. Reduce the temperature to 325°F/ 170°C/gas mark 3 and cook for a further 2½–3 hours until the meat is tender.

Meanwhile, put the apricots in a small pan, add the cinnamon and sugar and cover with 4–5 fl oz/ 120–150 ml cold water. Bring to the boil, then reduce the heat and simmer uncovered for about 20 minutes until the apricots are soft and a thick consistency is formed (it may be necessary to add more water from time to time). Remove from the heat, then mash with a fork to break up the apricots. Remove the lamb from the oven, take off the foil and pour over the apricot mixture. Return to the oven for a further 5–7 minutes.

Serve hot, with plain rice.

৵৽৻৶

Meatball Surprise

Koofteh tabrizi

3 oz/90 g split yellow lentils
½ oz/15 g basmati rice
salt and pepper
¼ teaspoon turmeric
1 lb/455 g minced lean lamb or beef
1 heaped tablespoon finely snipped chives or young part of a leek
3 garlic cloves, peeled and crushed (optional)
1 teaspoon ground cinnamon
1 large egg, beaten
oil for shallow frying
1 large onion, peeled and chopped
plain yoghurt and chopped fresh parsley or coriander, to garnish

STUFFING

2 teaspoons finely chopped walnuts
2 dried apricots, soaked overnight, drained and chopped
2–3 prunes, soaked overnight, drained, stoned and chopped
2 teaspoons sultanas, well rinsed
2 hard-boiled eggs, shelled

Prepare and soak the lentils as in the recipe for PLUM AND MINT SOUP (page 11). Clean, wash and soak the rice according to the general instructions.

Simmer the lentils in their soaking water for about 10–15 minutes until soft but not mushy. Drain and rinse under cold running water. Set aside until cold. Drain the rice into a sieve until the water runs clear, then simmer in salted water with the turmeric for 4 minutes. Drain well.

Put the meat in a bowl, add the lentils, rice, chives or leek, garlic (if using), cinnamon, beaten egg and salt and pepper to taste. Knead with your hands for about 5 minutes until the mixture binds together. Divide in half and place one portion in a small soup bowl. Make a well and place 1 of the eggs lengthways in the centre. Mix together the walnuts, apricots, prunes and sultanas and push half of the mixture around the egg. Turn out into your hands and smooth to make a neat ball. Make another ball in the same way with the remaining ingredients.

Heat the oil in a large, heavy saucepan, add the meatballs and fry gently for 3–4 minutes until browned on all sides. Gently remove from the pan. Fry the onion in the same oil until golden. Return the meatballs to the pan and cover with 4–6 fl oz/ 120–175 ml cold water. Bring to the boil, then reduce the heat, cover and simmer very gently for 45 minutes to 1 hour until the meat is cooked. Turn the meatballs carefully from time to time (to ensure even cooking) and add a little water if the pan becomes dry.

Remove the meatballs, cut into slices ¼–½ inch/5 mm–1 cm thick and place on a warm serving dish. Mix the onion and juices from the pan with a little yoghurt and use to garnish the meatballs, with parsley or coriander.

Serve hot, with any type of meal in a bowl.

৵৽৻৶

Roast and Fruit Pot

Tass kabab

1½ lb/685 g boneless chicken, skin removed, or lean lamb or beef (lamb fillet or frying steak), washed and sliced

1 large sweet Spanish onion, peeled and sliced into rings

1 medium potato, peeled and sliced into rings

1 small or medium quince, washed and sliced into rings

5–6 large prunes, soaked overnight, drained, stoned and chopped

¼ teaspoon ground saffron or ½ teaspoon turmeric

2 teaspoons tomato purée

juice of 1 small lemon, or to taste

Preheat the oven to 350°F/180°C/gas mark 4. Put a few pieces of the chicken or meat in a casserole and cover with layers of onion, potato, quince, prunes and spices. Repeat the layers until all the ingredients are used up. Dissolve the tomato purée in 2 fl oz/60 ml cold water, then pour into the casserole. Cover and cook in the oven until the meat is tender – about 45 minutes for chicken, up to 1½ hours for lamb or beef.

Hand lemon juice at the table to be added according to individual taste.

Serve hot, with plain rice or NAN (page 138).

Complete Meal-in-a-Bowl

Ash-e-sholeh ghalamkar

2 oz/60 g chick peas

2 oz/60 g black-eyed beans

1 oz/30 g red kidney beans

2 teaspoons pin barley

2 teaspoons cracked wheat (burghul)

1 oz/30 g brown lentils

2 oz/60 g mung beans

½ oz/15 g long grain rice

2 tablespoons oil

1 large onion, peeled and chopped

1 lb/455 g boneless chicken, skin removed, or lean stewing lamb or beef, washed and cubed

1 teaspoon turmeric

4 oz/115 g fresh spinach leaves, washed and coarsely chopped

2–3 sprigs of fresh mint, finely chopped

2–3 sprigs of fresh tarragon, finely chopped

1 oz/30 g each fresh parsley, coriander, leek, dill and fennel, finely chopped

1 teaspoon finely chopped fresh fenugreek

salt and pepper

4 fl oz/120 ml plain yoghurt or juice of 2–3 large lemons

Prepare and soak the pulses, barley and wheat as for the lentils in PLUM AND MINT SOUP (page 11). Clean, wash and soak the rice according to the general instructions.

Heat the oil in a 4 pint/2.5 litre casserole or heavy saucepan, add the onion and fry gently until golden. Add the meat and fry over gentle heat for 4–5 minutes until browned, then stir in turmeric. Drain the chick peas, black-eyed beans, kidney beans, barley and wheat, then add to the pan. Cover with 1½–2 pints/900 ml–1.2 litres cold water, bring to the boil and boil rapidly for 10 minutes, then reduce the heat to the lowest possible simmer. Partially cover the pan so that a little steam can escape (to prevent boiling over) and cook until the meat is tender – about 45 minutes for chicken, up to 2 hours for lamb or beef. If the pan becomes dry during this time, add a little extra water.

Twenty minutes before the end of cooking, drain the lentils and mung beans, then drain the rice into a sieve and rinse under cold running water. Add the lentils, mung beans and rice to the pan. Stir in the spinach, herbs and salt and pepper to taste. Cover and simmer again for 10 minutes, stirring occasionally to prevent the ingredients catching on the bottom of the pan. If using lemon juice, stir this in before serving. If using yoghurt, turn the *ash* into a warm serving dish and spoon over the yoghurt.

Serve hot, drizzled with HOT MINT (page 150) and NAN (page 138).

BAKHTI AND THE DARK TUNNEL

During cold winter evenings, when the snow had covered the cobbled area around the sunken gardens and filled the shallow octagonal pond in our open-style house in Yazd, dinner would be served around the cosy stove fire (*bokhari*). In between eating, daddy (*baba*) would tell us stories of his childhood days, keeping his bowl of *ash* warm on the red-hot iron stove.

One such story was about a young man called Bakhti who made a dare with his friends that in the dead of night he would go down the several hundred steps to the place where the women did their washing in the running stream. Even in the daytime it was dark, and the washerwomen had to carry oil lamps, but at night it was pitch black and Bakhti's friends were sure he wouldn't have the nerve to go even half-way without a light of some sort. As proof of his visit, therefore, Bakhti said he would hammer a nail into the ground at the bottom for all to see.

On the arranged night, Bakhti wore a creamy-coloured, long quilt coat, a Persian lamb hat and *giveh* on his feet. He found his way down the well-worn, slippery steps by feeling along the damp brick walls until he finally reached the water. He sat on the floor and hammered the nail in, but when he tried to stand up he found that someone was holding onto his coat and would not let him free. He shouted and begged to be let go, but there was no reply. The atmosphere was warm and steamy down there and Bakhti panicked until he fell back and lost consciousness. Luckily for him, his family and friends had become anxious when he hadn't returned after several hours, and a group of men descended the dark tunnel with their oil lamps. They found Bakhti lying unconscious, his coat nailed to the floor!

Mung Bean Meal-in-a-Bowl

Ash-e-mash

5 oz/150 g red kidney beans
4 oz/115 g mung beans
2 oz/60 g long grain rice
3 tablespoons oil
1 large onion, peeled and chopped
1 teaspoon turmeric
1 lb/455 g boneless chicken, skin removed, or lean stewing lamb or beef, washed and cubed
2 oz/60 g fresh coriander, finely chopped
2 oz/60 g fresh dill, finely chopped
1 small leek, washed and finely chopped
8 oz/230 g young turnips
salt and pepper

Prepare and soak the beans as for the lentils in PLUM AND MINT SOUP (page 11). Clean, wash and soak the rice according to the general instructions.

Heat the oil in a 4 pint/2.25 litre casserole or heavy saucepan, add the onion and fry gently until golden. Add the meat and fry over gentle heat for 4–5 minutes until browned, then stir in the turmeric. Drain the beans and add to the pan. Cover with water and bring to the boil, and then boil rapidly for 10 minutes. Add the drained mung beans and bring back to the boil, then simmer. Drain the rice into a sieve and rinse until the water runs clear. Add the beans and rice to the pan, cover with 1½–2 pints/900 ml–1.2 litres cold water and bring to the boil.

Boil rapidly for 10 minutes, then reduce the heat to the lowest possible simmer and partially cover the pan so that a little steam can escape (to prevent boiling over). Cook until the meat is tender – about 45 minutes for chicken, up to 2 hours for lamb or beef. If the pan becomes dry during this time, add a little extra water.

Add the herbs, leek, turnips and salt and pepper to taste. Cover and simmer again for 10–15 minutes or until the turnips are cooked, stirring occasionally to prevent the ingredients catching on the bottom of the pan.

Serve hot, with NAN.

ARDESHIR

Ardeshir was one of the oldest men in the community – my mother told me he was more than a hundred years old. He had a quiet manner and a holy face and was a familiar figure to everyone in the area with his felt hat, long jacket, brown trousers and thick shoes (*giveh*). He was almost always the first man to be out on the streets at dawn, and we used to hear his footsteps dragging along behind his mule through the narrow back streets of Yazd.

My mother told me the following story about Ardeshir. When he was a young man he was a bricklayer by trade, and on one occasion he had a bet with his fellow workmen that in one day he could eat a whole crate of grapes (weighing at least 20 kg!). He was a hard-working man, and it was his job to fetch and carry the bricks up and down the stairs. Each time he went down for a load of bricks he would bring a bunch of grapes back up with him, and while he was laying the bricks he would eat the grapes. He kept this up for the whole day, and so by the end of the day the crate of grapes was completely finished and he won his bet. I am still left wondering if it was the hard work that helped Ardeshir live to be 110 – or the amount of fruit he ate!

Grape Meal-in-a-Bowl

Ash-e-ab-e-ghooreh

The majority of Persians have vines in their gardens or *bagh*, and grapes are picked before they have ripened to make this special *ash*. If you have a friend or neighbour with a vine, ask for a bunch of unripened grapes so that you can try this very unusual dish.

3 oz/90 g black-eyed beans
1 oz/30 g split yellow lentils
1 oz/30 g long grain rice
5 tablespoons oil
1 large onion, peeled and chopped
1 teaspoon turmeric
1 lb/455 g minced chicken, lamb or beef
4 oz/115 g fresh spinach, washed and coarsely chopped
1 small leek, washed and finely chopped
2 oz/60 g fresh coriander, finely chopped
2 teaspoons crushed dried mint
a few green chillies, finely chopped, or pepper to taste
salt
8 oz/230 g unripe (sour) grapes

Prepare and soak the pulses as for the lentils in PLUM AND MINT SOUP (page 11). Clean, wash and soak the rice according to the general instructions.

Heat the oil in a 4 pint/2.25 litre casserole or heavy saucepan, add the onion and fry gently until golden. Stir in the turmeric. Drain the pulses. Drain the rice into a sieve and rinse until the water runs clear. Add the pulses and rice to the pan, cover with about 2 pints/1.2 litres cold water and bring to the boil.

Reduce the heat to the lowest possible simmer, then partially cover the pan so that a little steam can escape (to prevent boiling over). Form the minced meat into smooth balls the size of hazelnuts and drop into the simmering *ash*. Add the spinach, leek and herbs, cover again and simmer for 1–1½ hours until the *ash* is reduced to a thick consistency, stirring frequently.

Meanwhile, wash the grapes, place in a saucepan and cover with cold water. Bring to the boil and simmer for 10–15 minutes until soft. Tip the grapes and their liquid into a fine sieve placed over a bowl. Work with the back of a spoon to extract as much juice as possible, then discard the skin and pips. Stir the juice into the *ash*.

Serve hot.

꧁꧂

Golden Meal-in-a-Bowl

Ash-e-lapeh

3 oz/90 g split yellow lentils
1 oz/30 g pin barley
2 oz/60 g long grain rice
4 tablespoons oil
1 large onion, peeled and chopped
1 lb/455 g boneless chicken, skin removed, or lean stewing lamb or beef, washed and cubed
1 teaspoon turmeric
1 tablespoon each finely chopped leek, parsley and coriander
salt and pepper

Prepare and soak the lentils and barley as in the recipe for PLUM AND MINT SOUP (page 11). Clean, wash and soak the rice according to the general instructions .

Heat the oil in a 4 pint/2.25 litre casserole or heavy saucepan. Add the onion and fry gently until golden. Add the meat and fry over gentle heat for 4–5 minutes until browned. Drain the lentils, stir in with the onions for a few minutes to seal, stir in the turmeric. Drain the rice into a sieve and rinse until the water runs clear. Add the lentils, barley and rice to the pan, cover with about 2 pints/1.2 litres cold water and bring to the boil.

Reduce the heat to the lowest possible simmer, then partially cover the pan so that a little steam can escape (to prevent boiling over). Cook until the meat is tender – about 45 minutes for chicken, up to 2 hours for lamb or beef. If the pan becomes dry during this time, add a little extra water.

Add the leek, parsley, coriander and salt and pepper to taste. Cover and simmer again for 10 minutes.

Serve hot.

꧁꧂

Yoghurt-Meal-in-a-Bowl

Ash-e-mast

3 oz/90 g brown lentils
3 oz/90 g black-eyed beans
2 oz/60 g long grain rice
3 fl oz/85 ml oil
2 large onions, peeled and finely chopped
1 teaspoon turmeric
salt and pepper
1 lb/455 g lean tender lamb or beef, or chicken washed and cut into ½ inch/1 cm pieces
4 oz/115 g fresh parsley, finely chopped
2 oz/60 g leeks, washed and finely chopped
2 teaspoons crushed dried mint
3 garlic cloves, peeled and crushed
½ pint/300 ml plain yoghurt

Prepare and soak the lentils and beans as for the lentils in PLUM AND MINT SOUP (page 11).

Heat 2 fl oz/50 ml of the oil in a large, heavy saucepan, add the onions and fry gently until golden. Add the meat, toss and stir to mix with the onion for 4/5 minutes until brown, stir in the spices and stir for another minute. Drain the lentils, beans and rice. Add to the pan with the parsley, leek and half of the mint, then cover with about 1½ pints/900 ml cold water and bring to the boil.

Reduce the heat to simmer, then partially cover the pan so that a little steam can escape (to prevent boiling over). Cook until the meat is tender – at least 1 hour. If the pan becomes dry during this time, add a little extra water.

Heat the remaining oil in a small, heavy frying pan, add the garlic and stir quickly once or twice, then add the remaining mint. Immediately remove from the heat.

Uncover the *ash*. If there is too much liquid, increase the heat and boil to evaporate until thick. Remove the pan from the heat and stir in half of the yoghurt. Turn the *ash* into warm individual serving bowls, pour over the remaining yoghurt and garnish with the hot mint mixture.

Serve hot with TURMERIC AND CUMIN NAN (page 136)

A HAPPY TIME FOR THE LONELY WOMEN

My mother would often tell me stories about her early childhood in Yazd, one of which was about the social life of the lonely women of the community. Occasionally, to help pass the long, cold winter evenings, they would meet together in the local school and share in the preparation, cooking and eating of *ash*. Mahin, the eldest, usually brought the necessary ingredients, which were cooked in the large school copper saucepan. The preparation had to start very early in the evening because such a large quantity needed to be cooked and the school's paraffin burner was very slow. During the several hours it took to cook the *ash* everyone got busy with their knitting, crochet, embroidery and spinning, and the normally long winter evening would pass very quickly with the sound of knitting needles and spinning wheels filling the air. When the *ash* was served there was much fun and laughter, and afterwards the ladies would entertain themselves with singing, and telling stories and jokes.

Pomegranate Meal-in-a-Bowl

Ash-e-anar

2 oz/60 g chick peas
2 oz/60 g brown lentils
1 oz/30 g pin barley
1 oz/30 g long grain rice
5 tablespoons oil
1 large onion, peeled and chopped
1 lb/455 g boneless chicken, skin removed, or lean stewing lamb or beef, washed and cubed
1 teaspoon turmeric
4 oz/115 g fresh spinach, washed and coarsely chopped
1 small leek, washed and finely chopped
2 oz/60 g fresh coriander, finely chopped
2 teaspoons crushed dried mint
1–1½ pints/600–900 ml sweet and sour or sour pomegranate juice, or juice of 4–5 large lemons
sugar, to taste

Prepare and soak the pulses and barley as for the lentils in PLUM AND MINT SOUP (page 11). Clean, wash and soak the rice according to the general instructions.

Heat the oil in a 4 pint/2.25 litre casserole or heavy saucepan, add the onion and fry gently until golden. Add the meat and fry over gentle heat for 4–5 minutes until browned. Stir in the turmeric. Drain the pulses and barley. Drain the rice into a sieve and rinse until the water runs clear. Add the pulses, barley and rice to the pan, cover with about 2 pints/1.2 litres cold water and bring to the boil.

Reduce the heat to the lowest possible simmer, then partially cover the pan so that a little steam can escape (to prevent boiling over). Cook until the meat is tender – about 45 minutes for chicken, up to 2 hours for lamb or beef. If the pan becomes dry during this time, add a little extra water.

Add the spinach, leek, coriander and mint, then the pomegranate or lemon juice. (If adding lemon juice, you will need to add an equal quantity of water.) Cover the pan and simmer again for 10 minutes, stirring occasionally to prevent the ingredients catching on the bottom of the pan. Remove from the heat and add sugar to taste.

Serve hot.

Courgette Khoresh with Split Yellow Lentils

Khoresh-e-kadu

3 oz/90 g split yellow lentils
1 fl oz/25 ml oil
1 large onion, peeled and chopped
1½ lb/685 g chicken, skin removed and cut into serving pieces
½ teaspoon ground cinnamon
¼ teaspoon turmeric
salt and pepper
10 oz/275 g courgettes, cut into ½ inch/1 cm thick rings
chopped fresh parsley, to garnish

Prepare and soak the lentils as in the recipe for PLUM AND MINT SOUP (page 11).

Heat the oil in a 4 pint/2.25 litre casserole or heavy saucepan, add the onion and fry gently until golden. Add the chicken and fry over gentle heat for 4–5 minutes until browned, then stir in the cinnamon, turmeric and salt and pepper to taste. Drain the lentils, add to the pan and stir for a few minutes to seal. Add about ½ pint/300 ml cold water and bring to the boil. Reduce the heat to the lowest possible simmer, then cover the pan and cook for 45 minutes or until the chicken is tender.

Uncover the pan and place the courgette rings on top of the *khoresh*. Add up to 2 ladlefuls of water if the *khoresh* is too dry. Cover the pan and simmer again for 5–10 minutes or until the courgettes are just tender. If there is too much liquid at the end of cooking, uncover the pan, increase the heat and boil until reduced to a thick mixture. Sprinkle with parsley before serving.

Serve hot, with LENTIL AND SULTANA PILAF.

Mince and Potato Khoresh

Khoresh-e-kimeh ba sibizamini

3 tablespoons oil
1 large onion, peeled and chopped
1½ lb/685 g minced chicken, lamb or beef
1 teaspoon turmeric
¼ teaspoon ground cinnamon
salt and pepper
1 lb/455 g potatoes, peeled and quartered
2 teaspoons tomato purée

Heat the oil in a large, heavy saucepan, add the onion and fry gently until golden. Add the meat and fry over gentle heat, stirring until browned. Stir in the spices and salt and pepper to taste, then add the potatoes. Cover the ingredients with 8–10 fl oz/255–275 ml cold water and bring to the boil.

Reduce the heat to the lowest possible simmer, then cover the pan and cook for about 20 minutes or until the potatoes are tender. Dissolve the tomato purée in ¼ pint/150 ml cold water, stir into the pan and continue cooking until the *khoresh* has a thick consistency.

Serve with CRISPY POTATO RICE (page 86) or NAN (page 138).

Quince Khoresh

Khoresh-e-beh

2 fl oz/50 ml oil
1 large onion, peeled and chopped
1½ lb/685 g boneless chicken, skin removed, or lean tender lamb or beef, washed and cut into ½ inch/1 cm pieces
¼ teaspoon turmeric

| 2 quinces, total weight about 1 lb/455 g |
| 8 oz/230 g red plums |
| salt and pepper |
| 2 teaspoons crushed dried mint |

| 2 teaspoons sunflower seeds or chopped nuts |
| 2 teaspoons sultanas |

Heat the oil in a 4 pint/2.25 litre casserole or heavy saucepan, add the onion and fry gently until golden. Add the meat and fry over gentle heat for 4–5 minutes until browned. Stir in the turmeric, then add about ½ pint/300 ml cold water and bring to the boil.

Reduce the heat to the lowest possible simmer, then cover the pan and cook until the meat is tender – about 45 minutes for chicken, up to 2 hours for lamb or beef.

Meanwhile, wash the quinces and remove the hairy parts, cut into quarters, remove the seeds and the hard parts, then cut into ½ inch/1 cm pieces. Add to the pan and add more water if necessary. Bring to the boil, then reduce the heat and simmer for 5–10 minutes. Add the plums and mint, making sure there is still enough water, then add salt and pepper to taste. Cover and simmer again for 15 minutes or until the quinces and plums are soft. Stir in the mint before serving.

Serve hot, with plain rice.

Stuffed Mashed Potatoes

Kotlet-e-sibzamini

| 14 oz/400 g mashed potatoes |
| 2 eggs |
| 1 teaspoon ground cinnamon |
| salt and pepper |
| 1 tablespoon sesame seeds |
| oil for shallow frying |
| tomato slices, to garnish |
| FILLING |
| 2 tablespoons oil |
| 1 small onion, peeled and finely chopped |
| 4 garlic cloves, peeled and crushed |

Put the mashed potatoes in a bowl. Beat one of the eggs and knead into the potatoes with the cinnamon and salt and pepper to taste.

Make the filling. Heat the oil in a heavy frying pan, add the onion and fry gently until golden. Stir in the garlic and remove from the heat.

Dampen your hands and roll the potato mixture into small balls the size of tangerines. Make a well in the centre of each ball with your index finger and fill with a few sunflower seeds or nuts, sultanas and a little of the onion and garlic mixture. Cover the filling with potato so that it does not ooze out during cooking.

Beat the remaining egg in a shallow dish. Dip the potato balls in the egg, then roll in the sesame seeds until evenly coated. Shallow fry in hot oil for 30–60 seconds until golden, then drain on kitchen paper. Arrange on a warm serving platter and garnish with tomato slices before serving.

Serve hot.

Lentil Cutlets

Kotlet-e-adas

| 8 oz brown lentils soaked overnight or at least five hours before cooking |
| 1 oz onion grated almost to juice |
| 4 cloves of garlic pealed and crushed |
| 1 large egg |
| 2 heaped teaspoons fine Matzo meal or breadcrumbs |
| ¼ teaspoon ground coriander |
| salt and pepper to taste |
| 1 beaten egg |
| oil for frying |

Pour the water off the soaking lentils, and put into a small heavy pan. Cover with 8 oz cold water, bring to boil, lower the heat with the pan half covered, simmer gently for twenty minutes, or until the lentils are soft and the water has evaporated. Use a potato masher or a meat tenderiser and mash the lentils until smooth. Place into a large bowl, when sufficiently cold, add in the onion, garlic, and the egg with the spices and the Matzo meal or the breadcrumbs and knead for 5 minutes. Place approximately ½ inch deep oil into a small frying pan, dampen the hands with the beaten egg. Take a small ball (as big as a walnut) and press slightly in the palm of the hand to ½ inch thick and fry in the oil for approx one minute on each side until golden. Serve hot with plain rice and yoghurt.

Aubergines in Grape juice

Khoresh-e-badimjanba ab-e-angoor

10 oz/285 g aubergines, peeled and sliced lengthways, about ¼ inch/5 mm thick
salt and pepper
oil for shallow frying
1 large onion, peeled and chopped
1 lb/455 g lean lamb or chicken, washed and cut into 1 inch/2.5 cm cubes
½ teaspoon turmeric
½ teaspoon ground cinnamon
8–10 fl oz/225–300 ml white grape juice
a few flaked almonds, toasted, to garnish

Put the aubergine slices on a tray or large plate. Sprinkle both sides with salt (about 2 teaspoons) and leave for 1 hour to extract the dark and bitter juices. Rinse under cold running water and pat dry with a clean tea towel.

Heat shallow oil in a large heavy frying pan, add the aubergine slices in batches and fry over gentle heat for 2 minutes on each side. Transfer to kitchen paper to drain while frying the remainder, then set aside.

Pour 1–2 fl oz/25–50 ml of the oil into a large, heavy saucepan and heat through. Add the onion and fry gently until golden. Add the meat and fry over gentle heat for 4–5 minutes until browned, then stir in the turmeric, cinnamon and salt and pepper to taste.

Add the grape juice and bring to the boil. Reduce the heat to the lowest possible simmer, then cover the pan and cook for about 45 minutes or until the meat is tender. Place the aubergine slices on top of the *khoresh* 5–7 minutes before the end of cooking. Baste with the juices *but do not stir.* If there is too much liquid at the end of cooking, increase the heat and boil until reduced to a thick mixture. Sprinkle with toasted almonds before serving.

Serve hot, with CRISPY POTATO RICE (page 86).

Dill and Broad Bean Khoresh

Khoresh-e-shevid baghla

5–7 tablespoons oil
1 large onion, peeled and chopped
1½ lb/685 g lean lamb or chicken, washed and cut into 1 inch/2.5 cm cubes
½ teaspoon turmeric
salt and pepper
1 lb/455 g potatoes, peeled and coarsely diced
1 lb/455 g podded fresh or frozen broad beans
2 oz/60 g fresh dill, finely chopped

Heat the oil in a 4 pint/2.25 litre casserole or heavy saucepan, add the onion and fry gently until golden. Add the meat and fry over gentle heat for 4–5 minutes until browned, then stir in the turmeric and salt and pepper to taste. Add about 8–10 fl oz/225–300 ml cold water and bring to the boil.

Reduce the heat to the lowest possible simmer, then cover the pan and cook for about 45 minutes or until the meat is tender. Add more water from time to time if necessary.

Add the potatoes, cover and simmer again for 10 minutes. Add the broad beans and dill, toss a few times to mix and add more water if necessary (there should be 2–3 ladlefuls of liquid in the pan). Cover the pan and simmer again for 5–10 minutes or until the beans are tender. If there is too much liquid at the end of cooking uncover the pan, increase the heat and boil until reduced to a thick mixture.

Serve hot, with CRISPY YOGHURT RICE (page 86).

Okra Khoresh

Khoresh-e-bamya

1½ fl oz/37.5 ml oil
1 large onion, peeled and chopped
1 lb/455 g lean lamb or chicken, washed and cut into 1 inch/2.5 cm cubes
½ teaspoon turmeric
salt and pepper
1 large or 2 medium potatoes, peeled and quartered
2 heaped teaspoons tomato purée
8 oz/230 g okra, topped and tailed and cut in half if large
chopped fresh parsley, to garnish

Heat the oil in a 4 pint/2.25 litre casserole or heavy saucepan, add the onion and fry gently until golden. Add the meat and fry over gentle heat for 4–5 minutes until browned, then stir in the turmeric and salt and pepper to taste.

Add about 8 fl oz/225 ml cold water and bring to the boil. Reduce the heat to the lowest possible simmer, then cover the pan and cook for about 45 minutes or until the meat is tender. Add more water from time to time if necessary.

Add the potatoes, cover and simmer again for 10 minutes. Dissolve the tomato purée in 4 fl oz/120 ml cold water and stir into the pan. Place the okra on top of the *khoresh* and add more water if necessary (there should be 5–6 fl oz/150–175 ml liquid in the pan). Baste with some of the gravy from the pan. Cover the pan and simmer

again *without stirring* for about 10 minutes or until the okra are tender. If there is too much liquid at the end of cooking uncover the pan, increase the heat and boil until reduced to a thick mixture, taking care that the okra remain whole and do not become mushy. Sprinkle with parsley before serving.

Serve hot, with rice.

Rhubarb Khoresh

Khoresh-e-rivas

1 fl oz/25 ml oil
1 large onion, peeled and chopped
1 lb/455 g boneless chicken, skin removed and cut into serving pieces
1 teaspoon ground cinnamon
½ teaspoon turmeric
salt and pepper
1 lb/455 g rhubarb, trimmed and cut into 1 inch/2.5 cm pieces
the juice of a small lemon
2 teaspoons sugar, or to taste
a few flaked almonds, toasted, to garnish

Heat the oil in a 4 pint/2.25 litre casserole or heavy saucepan, add the onion and fry gently until golden. Add the chicken, stir for a few minutes until browned, then stir in the cinnamon and turmeric and salt and pepper to taste. Add about 8 fl oz/225 ml cold water and bring to the boil. Reduce the heat to the lowest possible simmer, cover the pan and cook for about 30–45 minutes or until the chicken is tender.

Add the rhubarb, lemon juice and sugar and continue simmering for 2–3 minutes or until the rhubarb is cooked but not too soft. Sprinkle with flaked almonds before serving.

Serve hot, with rice.

Carrot Khoresh

Khoresh-e-havij

1 fl oz/25 ml oil
1 large onion, peeled and chopped
1½ lb/685 g boneless chicken, skin removed, or lean stewing lamb or beef, washed and cut into ½ inch/1 cm pieces
¼ teaspoon ground saffron or ½ teaspoon ground cinnamon
salt and pepper
10 oz/275 g carrots, scraped and diced large.
8 oz/230 g red plums or 4 oz/115 g prunes, soaked overnight, drained and stoned
a few flaked almonds, toasted, to garnish

Heat the oil in a 4 pint/2.25 litre casserole or heavy saucepan, add the onion and fry gently until golden. Add the meat and fry over gentle heat for 4–5 minutes until browned. Stir in the saffron or cinnamon and salt and pepper to taste, then add about ½ pint/300 ml cold water and bring to the boil.

Reduce the heat to the lowest possible simmer, then cover the pan and cook until the meat is tender – about 45 minutes for chicken, up to 2 hours for lamb or beef.

Add the carrots, cover and simmer again for 10 minutes, then add the plums or prunes and continue simmering for 10–15 minutes until all the ingredients are cooked. If there is too much liquid at the end of cooking, increase the heat and boil until reduced to a thick mixture. Sprinkle with toasted almonds before serving.

Serve hot, with plain rice.

ॐॐॐ

Dill and Coriander Khoresh

Khoresh-e-shevid va geshnez

3 oz/90 g split yellow lentils

2 fl oz/50 ml oil
1 large onion, peeled and chopped
1 lb-455 g boneless chicken, skin removed, or lean stewing lamb or beef, washed and cut into ½ inch/1 cm pieces
1 teaspoon turmeric
salt and pepper
4 oz/115 g fresh coriander, finely chopped
4 oz/115 g fresh dill, finely chopped
1 large or 2 medium potatoes
lemon juice, to taste

Prepare and soak the lentils as in the recipe for PLUM AND MINT SOUP (page 11).

Heat the oil in a 4 pint/2.25 litre casserole or heavy saucepan, add the onion and fry gently until golden. Add the meat and fry over gentle heat for 4–5 minutes until browned. Drain the lentils, add to the pan and stir for a few minutes to seal, then add the spices. Add about 8 fl oz/225 ml cold water and bring to the boil.

Reduce the heat to the lowest possible simmer, then cover the pan and cook until the meat is tender – about 45 minutes for chicken, up to 2 hours for lamb or beef.

Uncover the pan and add the herbs and potatoes. Add more water if necessary – there should be at least 3 ladlefuls of liquid in the pan. Cover the pan and simmer again for 10–15 minutes until the potatoes are tender. If there is too much liquid at the end of cooking, increase the heat and boil until reduced to a thick mixture. Hand lemon juice at the table so that it can be added to individual taste.

Serve hot, with CRISPY POTATO RICE (page 86).

ॐॐॐ

Garden Pea Pilaf

Polov-e-lubia sabs

11 oz/315 g basmati rice
1 fl oz/25 ml oil

1 medium onion, peeled and finely chopped
¼ teaspoon ground cinnamon
¼ teaspoon turmeric
salt and pepper
1 lb/455 g very lean and tender lamb or beef, washed and cut into ½ inch/1 cm pieces
4 oz/115 g fresh or frozen shelled peas
1 fl oz/25 ml tomato purée
2 oz/60 g butter or margarine

Clean, wash and soak the rice according to the general instructions.

Heat the oil in a 4 pint/2.25 litre casserole or heavy saucepan, add the onion and fry gently until golden. Add the meat and toss over gentle heat for 2 minutes stir in the spices. Add 6–8 fl oz/175–225 ml cold water and bring to the boil.

Reduce the heat and simmer gently for about 45 minutes or until the meat is tender, adding the peas about halfway through cooking, according to whether fresh or frozen peas are used, together with the tomato purée dissolved in 2 fl oz/50 ml cold water.

Uncover the pan, increase the heat and boil vigorously until reduced but still juicy. Remove from the heat and turn into a bowl. Rinse the pan thoroughly.

Drain the rice, then parboil, drain and rinse according to the general instructions on page 00. Using both hands, sprinkle half of the rice into the rinsed-out pan. Cover with the meat and pea mixture, then sprinkle on the remaining rice. Cut the butter or margarine into small pieces and dot them all over the rice.

Wrap the lid of the pan in a tea towel according to the instructions on page 16, fit tightly on the pan and place over high heat for 1 minute until sizzling. Reduce the heat and *dam* for 45 minutes without lifting the lid. Turn the pilaf out onto a warm serving platter so that the crispy base (*tahdig*) is on top.

Serve hot, with plain yoghurt.

Lime Pilaf

Ghymeh polov

11 oz/315 g basmati rice
2 oz/60 g split yellow lentils
2 fl oz/50 ml oil
1 large onion, peeled and finely chopped
1½ lb/685 g very lean and tender boneless lamb, washed and cut into ½ inch/1 cm pieces
1 fl oz/25 ml tomato purée
1 teaspoon turmeric
juice of 2 limes or 1 large lemon
salt and pepper
3 oz/90 g butter or margarine

Clean, wash and soak the rice according to the general instructions on page 16. Prepare and soak the lentils as in the recipe for PLUM AND MINT SOUP (page 11).

Heat the oil in a 4 pint/2.25 litre casserole or heavy saucepan, add the onion and fry gently until golden. Add the lamb and toss over gentle heat for 2 minutes. Drain the lentils, add to the pan and stir for a few minutes to seal then stir in the turmeric. Add 6–8 fl 0z/175–225 ml cold water and bring to the boil.

Reduce the heat and simmer gently for about 45 minutes or until the lamb and lentils are tender. About half-way through cooking, add the tomato purée dissolved in 2–3 fl oz/50–85 ml cold water, the lime or lemon juice and salt and pepper to taste.

Uncover the pan, increase the heat and boil vigorously until reduced but still juicy. Remove from the heat and turn into a bowl. Rinse the pan thoroughly.

Drain the rice, then parboil, drain and rinse according to the general instructions on page 16. Using both hands, sprinkle half of the rice into the rinsed-out pan. Cover with the meat and lentil mixture, then sprinkle on the remaining rice. Cut the butter or margarine into small pieces and dot them all over the rice.

Wrap the lid of the pan in a tea towel according to the instructions on page 16, fit tightly on the pan and place over high heat for 1 minute until sizzling. Reduce the heat and *dam* for 45 minutes without lifting the lid. Turn the pilaf out on to a warm serving platter so that the crispy base (*tahdig*) is on top.

Serve hot, with a seasonal salad.

.ૡ૱ૠૡ.

Crispy Yoghurt Rice with Lamb or Chicken

Tahchin-e-bareh ya-morgh

---
12 oz/350 g basmati rice
1 fl oz/25 ml oil
1 medium onion, peeled and finely chopped
1½ lb/685 g boneless chicken, skin removed, or lean lamb, washed and cut into 1 inch/2.5 cm cubes
¼ teaspoon ground cinnamon
¼ teaspoon turmeric
salt and pepper
4 large egg yolks
3 tablespoons plain yoghurt
¼ teaspoon ground saffron
4 oz/116 g butter or margarine

Clean, wash and soak the rice according to the general instructions on page 16.

Heat the oil in a 4 pint/2.25 litre casserole or heavy saucepan, add the onion and fry gently until golden. Add the meat and toss over gentle heat for 2 minutes, then stir in the spices and salt and pepper to taste.

Add 6 fl oz/175 ml cold water and bring to the boil. Reduce the heat and simmer gently for about 45 minutes or until the meat is tender.

Uncover the pan, increase the heat and boil vigorously until reduced but still juicy. Remove from the heat, turn into a bowl and leave to cool.

Drain the rice, then parboil, drain and rinse according to the general instructions on page 16. Put the egg yolks, yoghurt and saffron in a bowl

and beat well to mix. Add half of the rice and stir a few times.

Preheat the oven to 350°F/180°C/gas mark 4. Melt the butter or margarine and pour half into a 2 inch/5 cm deep, 8 inch/20 cm square baking dish, making sure that it covers the bottom and sides well. Pour in the egg, yoghurt and rice mixture and smooth out with the back of a spoon. Cover with the meat mixture, then with the remaining plain rice. Pour over the remaining melted butter or margarine.

Cover the dish tightly with foil, ensuring that steam cannot escape, then bake just below the centre of the oven for 1 hour to 1½ hours or until the rice is cooked and the base is crispy. Loosen the edges with a palette knife, dampen a kitchen towel and dab around the dish to release the crispy base (*tahdig*), then turn out onto a warm serving platter.

Serve hot, with plain yoghurt.

.ૡ૱ૠૡ.

Berberry Pilaf

Zereshk polov

---
11 oz/315 g basmati rice
2 oz/60 g berberries, washed and drained several times until free of grit
2 teaspoons sugar
1½ lb/685 g boneless cooked chicken, skin removed and cubed
¼ teaspoon ground cinnamon
⅛ teaspoon cumin seeds
3 oz/90 g butter or margarine

Clean, wash and soak the rice according to the general instructions on page 16.

Drain the rice, then parboil, drain and rinse according to the general instructions on page 00.

Put the berberries and sugar in a heavy saucepan, add 2–3 fl oz/50–75 ml cold water and simmer gently for 10–15 minutes until soft.

Using both hands, sprinkle half of the rice into a 4 pint/2.25 litre casserole or heavy saucepan. Place the chicken on top and cover with the berberries.

Sprinkle with the cinnamon and cumin seeds, then sprinkle on the remaining rice. Cut the butter or margarine into small pieces and dot them all over the rice.

Wrap the lid of the pan in a tea towel according to the instructions on page 16, fit tightly on the pan and place over high heat for 1 minute until sizzling. Reduce the heat and *dam* for 45 minutes without lifting the lid. Turn the pilaf out onto a warm serving platter so that the crispy base (*tahdig*) is on top.

Serve hot, with plain yoghurt.

Crispy Potato Rice

Polov-e-sadeh ba sib zamini

14 oz/400 g basmati rice
salt
1 medium potato, peeled and sliced into ⅛ inch/3 mm rings
3 oz/90 g margarine or butter

Clean, wash and soak the rice according to the general instructions on page 16.

Bring 1½ pints/900 ml water to the boil with 2 teaspoons salt in a 4 pint/2.25 litre heavy saucepan. Drain the rice, add it to the boiling water and bring back to the boil. Immediately lower the heat to moderate and parboil for 4 minutes. Drain into a sieve and rinse under cold running water. Thoroughly wash the pan to remove all scum.

Place the slices of potato neatly in the bottom of the pan, then put the rice on top. Cut the margarine or butter into small pieces and dot all over the rice. Wrap the lid of the pan in a tea towel according to the instructions on page 16, fit tightly on the pan and place over high heat for 1 minute until sizzling. Reduce the heat and *dam* for about 45 minutes without lifting the lid. Carefully turn the rice out on to a warm serving platter so that the crispy potato slices are on top.

Serve hot, with any *khoresh* and plain yoghurt.

Lentil and Crispy Potato Rice

Addas polov ba sib zamini

8 oz/230 g basmati rice
4 oz/115 g brown lentils
½ teaspoon of cinnamon
2 oz/50 g sultanas
1 medium potato, peeled and sliced into ⅛ inch/3 mm thick rings
4 oz/115 g margarine or butter

Clean, wash and soak the rice according to the general instructions on page 16. Prepare and soak the lentils as in PLUM AND MINT SOUP (page 11).

Drain, parboil, drain and rinse the rice as in the recipe for CRISPY POTATO RICE (page 86). Bring the lentils to the boil in their soaking water, then simmer for about 5 minutes or until soft. Drain and rinse under cold running water.

Place the potato slices in the bottom of a 4 pint/ 2.25 litre heavy saucepan, then put one-quarter of the rice on top. Add the lentils and sultanas and the cinnamon, then the remaining rice. Cut the margarine or butter into small pieces and dot all over the rice, then continue with the method as for CRISPY POTATO RICE.

Serve hot, with plain yoghurt.

Aubergine and Tomato dish

Shekam pareh

3½ oz/100 g basmati or long grain rice
4 aubergines, each weighing about 6 oz/175 g
salt and pepper
7 tablespoons oil
1 large onion, peeled and chopped
8 oz minced chicken

5–7 garlic cloves, peeled and crushed
1 teaspoon crushed dried mint
1 teaspoon turmeric
2 teaspoons tomato purée
8 oz/230 g ground walnuts
2 teaspoons chopped fresh parsley

Clean, wash and soak the rice according to the general instructions on page 16.

Peel the aubergines at intervals of about 1 inch/ 2.5 cm. Cut lengthways through the middle, keeping the aubergine attached at the stem end. Carefully hollow out the centres of each half with a sharp-edged teaspoon, leaving about ¼ inch/ 5 mm flesh all round. Sprinkle the aubergines with salt and leave to dégorge for about 30 minutes.

Rinse the aubergines under cold running water, then pat dry with kitchen paper. Heat 5 tablespoons of the oil in a heavy frying pan, add the aubergines one at a time and fry for about 1 minute on each side until lightly coloured all over. Remove from the pan with a slotted spoon and set aside.

Add the onion to the oil in the pan and fry gently until golden, then add the chicken. Add the garlic, mint and turmeric. Dissolve the tomato purée in 5–6 fl oz/150–175 ml cold water. Add to the pan and stir well to mix, then cover and simmer gently for about 5 minutes. If there is too much water at the end of this time, uncover the pan, increase the heat and boil to evaporate.

Drain, parboil and rinse the rice according to the general instructions on page 16.

Preheat the oven to 350°F/180°C/gas mark 4. Combine the rice and onion mixture in a bowl with the nuts, parsley and salt and pepper to taste. Fill the aubergines with this mixture. Grease an ovenproof dish with 1 tablespoon oil, place the aubergines in the dish and pour over the remaining oil. Cover loosely with foil and bake in the oven for 30–45 minutes or until the aubergines are soft and tender.

Serve hot.

Spinach and Rice Mould

Tahchin-e-esfenaj

9 oz/260 g basmati rice
4 oz/115 g prunes
1 fl oz/25 ml oil
1 medium onion, peeled and finely chopped
8–10 large fresh spinach leaves, washed
4 large egg yolks
3 tablespoons plain yoghurt
¼ teaspoon ground saffron
3 oz/85 g margarine or butter

Clean, wash and soak the rice according to the general instructions on page 16. Soak the prunes in cold water for 5 hours or overnight.

Put the prunes and their soaking water in a small saucepan and simmer gently for 20–30 minutes or until soft. Drain, then remove the stones.

Heat the oil in a large heavy saucepan, add the onion and fry gently until golden. Add the spinach, cover and cook very gently for 5 minutes until all the leaves have wilted, then uncover the pan, and increase the heat to evaporate excess water. Remove from the heat and set aside.

Drain the rice, then parboil, drain and rinse according to the general instructions on page 16.

Preheat the oven to 350°F/180°C/gas mark 4. Beat the egg yolks in a bowl with the yoghurt and saffron, then add half of the rice and toss gently to mix. Melt the margarine or butter. Reserve 1–2 tablespoons. Pour the remainder into a 1½ pint/ 900 ml ring mould or a 2 inch/5 cm deep, 8 inch/ 20 cm square baking dish and swirl it around so that it greases the inside well. Arrange the spinach leaves lengthways in the bottom of the mould or dish. Put the rice and egg mixture over the spinach and press level with the back of a spoon. Arrange the prunes over the rice in a neat pattern, then top with the plain parboiled rice and press level again with the spoon. Pour over the reserved melted margarine or butter.

Cover with foil and bake in the oven for 1 hour, then reduce the temperature to 325°F/170°C/gas mark 3 and continue baking for a further 45 minutes, or until the rice is cooked. Loosen the edges with a palette knife and wrap wet kitchen paper around the base of the mould or tin to help release the base, then turn out on to a warm serving platter. Garnish with shredded lettuce and radicchio and lemon and lime slices, if liked.

Serve hot, with CARROT and OKRA SAVOURY CAKES (page 106) and plain yoghurt.

CHICKEN MAIN COURSES

Olivier Salad

Salad-e-olivier

2 medium potatoes, washed
salt and pepper
8 oz/230 g carrots, scraped
6 oz/175 g cooked fresh or frozen peas
2 lb/900 g boneless cooked chicken, skin removed and diced very small
4 hard-boiled eggs, shelled and diced very small
3 medium pickled cucumbers, diced very small
4 oz/115 g olives, stoned
juice of 1 large lemon, or to taste
about ½ pint/300 ml thick mayonnaise
radishes, to garnish

Cook the unpeeled potatoes in boiling salted water for about 20 minutes or until tender. Meanwhile, cook the carrots in a separate pan of boiling salted water for 10 minutes or until barely soft. Drain the potatoes and carrots. While the potatoes are still warm, peel off the skins with your fingers. Dice both the potatoes and carrots very small and place in a large bowl.

Add the peas, chicken, eggs and pickled cucumbers to the bowl. Toss gently to mix, then add the olives and lemon juice, salt and pepper to taste. Toss the salad several times, then add about half of

the mayonnaise very slowly and toss to mix. Spoon the salad onto an oval serving dish and spread the remaining mayonnaise over it with a palette knife. Garnish with radishes.

Serve at room temperature.

Roast Chicken in Honey and Cinnamon

Morgh-ba-darchin va asal

1 roasting chicken weighing about 3 lb/1.5 kg
1 small bunch of fresh mint
2 garlic cloves, peeled and crushed
½ teaspoon turmeric
½ teaspoon ground cinnamon
salt and pepper
2 teaspoons clear honey
few sprigs of fresh mint or parsley, to garnish

Preheat the oven to 325°F/170°C gas mark 3. Clean and wash the chicken thoroughly and pat it dry with kitchen paper. Place the bunch of mint inside the chicken (this will help to keep it moist). Rub the crushed garlic and spices over the chicken and place in a small roasting tin which is just large enough to hold it. Cover with foil.

Roast the chicken in the oven for 1–1½ hours or until tender. Fifteen minutes before the end of cooking, remove the foil and brush the honey over the chicken. Return to the oven until crisp and brown. Garnish with sprigs of mint or parsley before serving.

Serve hot, with plain rice.

OMAR-E-KHYAM

My Uncle Shari was a soldier in the army, and he often used to visit our house on his return from duty. We children used to listen to his conversations with father (baba) and the word games they used to play together. One of their favourite games was to think up sentences and poems starting with the last letter of the previous sentence. Sometimes these poems were recited in a sing-song voice, especially if they were by the poet Hakim Omar-E-Khyam, whose poems were about love, food and drink.

Much later in life, I fulfilled my wish to travel to the city of Neyshapur, to see the beautifully decorated minaret-style tomb of this great poet. The tomb was completely covered with his poems written with different coloured tiles all over the high building. Groups of people sat under the large apricot trees, shaded from the mid-June sun, resting their chins in the palms of their hands as they stared up at the high minaret, their moving lips whispering the poems to themselves. The atmosphere was one of utter tranquillity: the only sound that of the birds. Occasionally one of them would knock off a ripened fruit and it would land magically in our laps, ready to eat. It was one of the rare occasions in my life when I was lulled asleep by the hypnotic atmosphere, not realising that two hours had gone by. We had to run to catch the last bus home!

Stuffed Chicken with Apricots and Prunes

Morgh-e-porshodeh ba miveh va agil

1 roasting chicken weighing about 3 lb/1.5 kg	
1 fl oz/25 ml oil	
1 medium potato, peeled and cut into tiny 'chip' (french fry) shapes	
STUFFING	
2 fl oz/50 ml oil	
1 large onion, peeled and chopped	
2 garlic cloves, peeled and crushed	
4 oz/115 g shelled walnuts, chopped	

4 oz/115 g prunes, soaked overnight, drained, stoned and finely chopped	
3 oz/90 g dried apricots, soaked overnight, drained and finely chopped	
½ teaspoon ground cinnamon	
salt and pepper	
1 tablespoon POMEGRANATE PURÉE (page 150) or TAMARIND LIQUID (page 150), or 1 tablespoon lemon juice and 1 teaspoon sugar	

First make the stuffing: heat the oil in a small, heavy saucepan, add the onion and fry gently until golden. Stir in the garlic and walnuts, then the chopped fruit, cinnamon and salt and pepper to taste. Remove the pan from the heat and stir in the POMEGRANATE PURÉE, TAMARIND LIQUID or lemon juice and sugar.

Preheat the oven to 350°F/180°C/gas mark 4. Put the stuffing in the neck end of the chicken, then sew up with trussing thread or string. Pat the chicken thoroughly dry with kitchen paper, then place in a covered casserole or wrap well with foil and place in a roasting tin. Roast in the oven for 2–2½ hours or until the chicken is really tender and quite literally falls apart.

About 20 minutes before the chicken is ready, heat the remaining oil in a heavy frying pan, add the potatoes and fry until golden and tender. Arrange around the chicken on the serving dish.

Serve hot.

THE WATER INSPECTOR

At night, the way through the cobbled streets of Yazd to my grandfather's land (*bagh*) was lit by cottonseed oil lamps, set into niches in the walls. When you passed through the old wooden door and into the walled-in *bagh*, the sloping path led down to where he grew plants such as pulses, vegetables, herbs, melons and watermelons. These plots were divided into strips which were fed by irrigated water which my grandfather had to pay for, and around the edge were quince, pomegranate and all sorts of other fruit trees, which also relied on irrigated water. Only a few feet away there was a constant running stream and, like most people, my grandfather planted as many fruit trees as possible next to this stream, to take advantage of the free water!

We used to sit under one of the apricot trees with the batique cloth (*sofreh*) spread out for our lunchtime snack. Mr Sohrab the water inspector used to call by unexpectedly, knocking very loudly on the wooden door with a big piece of brick. His job was to make sure that no-one stole from the running stream to water the rest of their *bagh*, – and somehow, to our amusement, his inspection always seemed to coincide with our midday snack. Such perfect timing!

Chicken in Pomegranate Purée

Khoresh-e-fesenjan

At times when it is difficult to get fresh pumpkin, carrots may be substituted. Work them to a pulp in a food processor before adding them to the pan.

2 tablespoons oil
1 medium onion, peeled and chopped
2 lb/900 g boneless chicken breasts, skin removed, and washed
8 oz/230 g pumpkin, peeled, washed and grated
4 oz/115 g shelled walnuts, ground
1 teaspoon ground cinnamon
8–10 oz/230–275 g POMEGRANATE PURÉE (page 150), according to taste

Heat the oil in a flameproof casserole or heavy saucepan, add the onion and fry gently until golden. Add the chicken to the pan and cook for a few minutes until golden on all sides.

Add the pumpkin, walnuts and cinnamon and stir well to mix with the chicken. Dissolve the POMEGRANATE PURÉE in 8–12 fl oz/225–350 ml cold water and stir into the pan.

Cover and simmer for 30–35 minutes or until the chicken is tender. Uncover the pan, increase the heat and continue simmering until the sauce is thick.

Serve hot, with plain rice.

Chicken in Plum and Herb sauce

Khoresh-e-naana jaafary

1 fl oz/25 ml oil
1 large onion, peeled and chopped
1½ lb/685 g chicken, skin removed, cut into serving pieces and washed
1 teaspoon turmeric
salt and pepper
2 oz/60 g fresh mint, finely chopped
2 oz/60 g fresh parsley, finely chopped
8 oz/230 g red plums

Heat the oil in a flameproof casserole or heavy saucepan, add the onion and fry gently until golden. Add the chicken to the pan and cook for a few minutes until golden on all sides. Add the turmeric and salt and pepper to taste, cover with 8–10 fl oz/225–300 ml cold water and bring to the boil.

Reduce the heat to the lowest possible simmer, then cover the pan. Cook until the chicken is tender – about 45 minutes.

Add the herbs and plums, cover and simmer again for about 5 minutes or until the plums are soft. If there is too much liquid at the end of cooking, increase the heat and boil until reduced to a thick mixture.

Serve hot, with plain rice.

Chicken in Orange, Saffron and Nut sauce

Morgh ba zaafaran va agil

1 fl oz/25 ml oil
1 large onion, peeled and chopped
2 lb/900 g chicken, washed and cut into serving pieces
4 medium carrots, scraped or peeled and diced

3 large oranges

1 teaspoon sugar

2 teaspoons rice flour or plain flour

⅛ teaspoon ground saffron or ½ teaspoon
ground cinnamon

about 30 shelled pistachios or other nuts

a few flaked almonds, toasted, to garnish

Heat the oil in a 4 pint/2.25 litre flameproof casserole or heavy saucepan, add the onion and fry gently until golden. Add the chicken to the pan and cook for a few minutes until golden on all sides. Add the carrots and 3–4 fl oz/85–120 ml cold water and bring to the boil. Reduce the heat to the lowest possible simmer, then cover the pan and cook for about 20 minutes.

Meanwhile, remove the outer rind from the oranges with a zester or canelle knife and place in a small saucepan with the sugar. Add 2 fl oz/50 ml cold water, bring to the boil and simmer uncovered for 5 minutes. Halve the oranges and squeeze the juice. Mix the juice with the flour and the saffron or cinnamon.

Stir the flour mixture into the chicken with the orange rind and liquid and the nuts. Cover and continue cooking for a further 25 minutes or until the chicken is tender and the sauce is thick. Sprinkle with toasted almonds before serving.

Serve hot, with plain rice.

ൠൠ

Chicken in Plum and Lentil sauce

Khoresh-e-alu

3 oz/90 g split yellow lentils

1 fl oz/25 ml oil

1 large onion, peeled and finely chopped

½ lb/685 g chicken, skin removed, washed
and cut into serving pieces

¼ teaspoon ground saffron or 1 teaspoon
ground cinnamon

1 lb/455 g red plums

sugar

salt and pepper

a few flaked almonds, toasted, to garnish

Prepare and soak the lentils as in the recipe for PLUM AND MINT SOUP (page 11).

Heat the oil in a 4 pint/2.25 litre flameproof casserole or heavy saucepan, add the onion and fry gently until golden. Add the chicken to the pan and cook for a few minutes until golden on all sides. Drain the lentils, add to the pan and stir for a few minutes to seal. Add the saffron or cinnamon and about 8 fl oz/225 ml cold water and bring to the boil.

Reduce the heat to the lowest possible simmer, then cover the pan and cook until the chicken is tender – about 45 minutes. Add more water from time to time if necessary, to prevent the lentils sticking on the bottom of the pan.

Add the plums, sugar and salt and pepper to taste, with more water if necessary. Cover and simmer again for 10–15 minutes or until the plums are soft. If there is too much liquid at the end of cooking, increase the heat and boil until reduced to a thick mixture. Sprinkle with toasted almonds before serving.

Serve hot, with plain rice.

ൠൠ

Chicken Drumsticks with Orange sauce

Ran-e-morgh ba ab-e-porteghal

1 small onion, peeled and grated

½ teaspoon ground cinnamon, cardamom,
turmeric and paprika, mixed together

6 large or 12 small chicken drumsticks
(total weight 2–2½ lb/900 g–1.25 kg),
skin removed and washed

2 oz/60 g margarine or butter

3 large oranges

2 teaspoons sugar

1 teaspoon rice flour or plain flour

salt and pepper

a few flaked almonds, toasted, to garnish

Preheat the oven to 350°F/180°C/gas mark 4. Rub the grated onion and spices all over the chicken drumsticks. Melt the margarine or butter in a large flameproof casserole, add the drumsticks and toss to coat. Cover and cook in the oven for about 1 hour or until tender.

Meanwhile, remove the outer rind from the oranges with a zester or canelle knife and place in a small saucepan with half of the sugar. Add 2 fl oz/50 ml cold water. Bring to the boil and simmer uncovered for 7–10 minutes until the rind is sticky and the pan has become almost dry. Remove from the heat.

Remove the drumsticks from the casserole with a slotted spoon, cover and keep warm. Slowly pour the cooking liquid into a clean saucepan, leaving behind any fat. Halve the oranges and squeeze the juice. Mix the flour, the remaining sugar and the orange juice together, stir into the cooking liquid and simmer gently until thick. Add salt and pepper to taste.

Arrange the chicken on warm dinner plates and coat with the sauce. Sprinkle the glazed orange rind and the toasted almonds on top before serving.

Serve hot, with CRISPY POTATO RICE (page 86).

SIDE DISHES

Stuffed Courgettes

Dolmeh-e-kadu

3 oz/90 g long grain rice, preferably basmati
2 fl oz/50 ml oil
1 medium onion, peeled and finely chopped
½ teaspoon ground cinnamon
⅛ teaspoon cumin seeds
4 oz/115 g minced chicken, lean lamb or beef
6 fat courgettes, total weight about 1½ lb/685 g
a few flaked almonds, toasted, to garnish

Clean, wash and soak the rice according to the general instructions on page 16.

Heat 1 fl oz/25 ml of the oil in a heavy saucepan, add the onion and fry gently until golden. Add the spices and meat and fry, stirring, for 3–4 minutes until browned. Remove from the heat and set aside.

Bring ½ pint/300 ml water to the boil in a clean saucepan. Drain the rice, add to the water and bring back to the boil. Immediately reduce the heat and simmer gently for 4 minutes.

Pour into a sieve and rinse under cold running water to remove the froth, then add to the meat mixture and toss well to combine.

Preheat the oven to 350°F/180°C/gas mark 4. Cut a ¼ inch/5 mm slice off the stem end of each courgette and reserve. Using an apple corer or sharp-edged teaspoon, hollow out the centres, taking care not to puncture the skin. Discard the pulp.

Fill the courgettes with the meat and rice mixture, then place them in a baking dish into which they will just fit neatly, side by side. Replace the caps and secure with wooden cocktail sticks. Spoon any leftover stuffing in the corners of the dish and pour over 1 tablespoon of the remaining oil. Cover with foil and bake in the oven for about 30–35 minutes or until the courgettes are soft. Meanwhile, heat the remaining oil in a small frying pan, add the reserved courgette pulp and fry for a few minutes or until the courgettes are soft.

Arrange the courgettes on a warm serving platter and garnish with the almonds.

Serve hot, with plain yoghurt.

Stuffed Onions

Dolmeh-e-piaz

2 oz/60 g long grain rice
4 onions weighing each approx 8 oz/240 g (sweet Spanish)
2 oz/60 g oil

3 oz/90 g lean lamb, beef or chicken, (minced)
¼ level teaspoon ground cinnamon
¼ level teaspoon ground turmeric
little salt and pepper to taste
1 desertspoon cleaned, washed and finely chopped dill leaves
1 desertspoon cleaned, washed and finely chopped coriander leaves
few sprigs of fresh mint and tarragon

Clean, wash and soak the rice overnight or five hours before cooking. Peel the onion carefully. And take a neat slice off the top and reserve. Use an apple corer and gently hollow the middle until only two rings are showing. Reserve the centres. Place them in a saucepan and fill up with water, place on high heat bring to boil and cook moderately for about 3/4 minutes or until barely soft. Drain off the water and leave to cool, chop the reserved pulps from one onion discard the rest and fry in 1 oz of the oil until golden, add the meat stir in the spices and the herbs toss them a few times and remove the pan from the heat set aside to cool. Fill a pan ¼ full with water bring to boil. Pour the water off from the soaking rice and add in to the pan. Simmer gently for 4 minutes, drain in a sieve and rinse with cold water to remove any scum. Place the semi-cooked rice in a large bowl and add the cooked and the cooled meat mixture. Set the oven to gas mark 4/180°C/350°F fill the onion cases with the mixture replace the reserved caps and place them side by side in a small oven-proof dish. Pour over the reserved 1 oz oil place any left over ingredients in the corner of the dish and cover with a piece of foil and place in the middle shelf and cook for approx 20/30 minutes or until the veg are soft. Remove the dolmehs into a serving dish, garnish with few sprigs of mint and fresh tarragon.

Stuffed Vine Leaves

Dolmeh-e-barg-e-mov

This recipe gives instructions for preserved vine leaves which are easy to obtain at supermarkets. If you are lucky enough to have fresh vine leaves, then so much the better. Simply soak them in boiling water for about 20 minutes until they become limp. They are then ready for stuffing.

8 oz/230 g packet vine leaves preserved in brine
3 oz/90 g long grain rice
2 oz/60 g split yellow lentils
6 fl oz/175 ml oil
1 large onion, peeled and finely chopped
8 oz/230 g lean minced lamb or beef
4 garlic cloves, peeled and crushed
2 heaped tablespoons finely chopped fresh dill
2 teaspoons crushed dried mint
½ teaspoon turmeric
salt and pepper

Put the vine leaves in a large bowl, pour over boiling water to cover and leave for about 20 minutes. Drain into a colander and rinse under cold running water, then pour boiling water over them. Return to the bowl, cover with cold water and leave to soak overnight. Clean, wash and soak the rice according to the general instructions on page 00. Prepare and soak the lentils as in the recipe for PLUM AND MINT SOUP (page 11).

The next day, taste the water in which the vine leaves are soaking. If it is salty, rinse the leaves several times in boiling water. Parboil, drain and rinse the rice as in the recipe for STUFFED COURGETTES (page 92). Drain the lentils, place them in a saucepan of boiling water and simmer for about 5–7 minutes until half cooked. Drain and set aside.

Heat 1 fl oz/25 ml of the oil in a heavy saucepan, add the onion and fry gently until golden. Add the meat and fry, stirring, for 3–4 minutes until browned, then stir in the garlic, dill, mint, turmeric and salt and pepper to taste. Cook for a few minutes more, then remove from the heat, add the rice and lentils and toss well to combine. Set aside. Drain the vine leaves well and choose the best ones for stuffing. Reserve any torn leaves to line the pan.

Place 1 vine leaf at a time on a flat surface, vein

side facing towards you. Put 1 heaped teaspoon of the stuffing near the stem end, then roll the leaf up tightly around the stuffing and tuck in the edges to make a neat cigar shape.

Swirl 1 fl oz/25 ml of the remaining oil over the inside of a large heavy saucepan, then line with the reserved torn vine leaves. Place the *dolmeh* side by side in one layer in the pan, pressing them down well with the back of your hands to ensure that they are packed in firmly. Pour over the remaining oil and 8 fl oz/225 ml cold water and bring to the boil. Reduce

the heat, cover and simmer gently for about 2 hours until the leaves are very soft, adding 3–4 fl oz/85–120 ml cold water every 30 minutes or whenever the pan becomes dry.

Serve hot, with plain yoghurt.

Stuffed Aubergines

Dolmeh-e-badimjan

Peeling the aubergines at intervals to give a stripey effect not only makes them look more attractive when served, it also helps keep them intact during cooking.

3 oz/90 g long grain rice, preferably basmati
4 aubergines, each weighing about 6 oz/175 g
salt
7 tablespoons oil
1 large onion, peeled and finely chopped
7 garlic cloves, peeled and crushed
8 oz/230 g minced chicken, lean lamb or beef
2 teaspoons tomato purée
2 teaspoons sultanas, well rinsed
1 teaspoon crushed dried mint
salt and pepper

Clean, wash and soak the rice according to the general instructions on page 16.

Peel the aubergines at ½ inch/1 cm intervals,

then cut a ½ inch/1 cm slice off the stem ends and reserve.

Using an apple corer or sharp-edged teaspoon, hollow out the centres, leaving the cases about ¼ inch/5 mm thick all round. Sprinkle the insides with a little salt, place on a tray or large plate and leave for 1 hour to extract the dark bitter juices.

Meanwhile, heat 2 tablespoons of the oil in a heavy saucepan, add the onion and fry gently until golden. Stir in the garlic, then add the meat and fry, stirring, for 3–4 minutes until browned. Dissolve the tomato purée in 3 fl oz/85 ml cold water and add to the pan with the sultanas, mint and salt and pepper to taste. Stir well to combine and increase the heat to evaporate excess liquid – the mixture should be firm but juicy. Remove from the heat and set aside.

Parboil, drain and rinse the rice as in the recipe for STUFFED COURGETTES (page 92), add to the meat mixture and toss well to combine.

Preheat the oven to 350°F/180°C/gas mark 4. Rinse the aubergine cases under cold running water and pat dry with kitchen paper. Fill with the meat and rice mixture, replace the caps and secure with wooden cocktail sticks.

Heat 2 tablespoons of the remaining oil in a heavy frying pan, add the aubergines and fry gently until lightly coloured on all sides. Transfer them to a baking dish into which they will just fit neatly, side by side. Spoon any leftover stuffing in the corners of the dish and pour over the remaining oil. Cover loosely with foil and bake in the oven for 45 minutes to 1 hour or until the aubergines are soft. (The cooking time will vary according to how thinly you have hollowed out the aubergines.)

Serve hot, with plain yoghurt.

Stuffed Tomatoes

Dolmeh-e-govjeh

4 oz/115 g long grain rice, preferably basmati
2 fl oz/50 ml oil

1 onion, peeled and finely chopped	1 medium onion, peeled and finely chopped
5 oz/150 g minced chicken, lean lamb or beef	3 oz/90 g minced chicken, lean lamb or beef
1 teaspoon ground cinnamon	1 teaspoon ground cinnamon
1 tablespoon finely chopped fresh dill	1 oz/30 g almonds or other nuts, finely chopped
¼ teaspoon crushed dried mint	a few sultanas, well rinsed
¼ teaspoon dried tarragon	salt and pepper
salt and pepper	6 crisp eating apples, each weighing about 4 oz/115 g
4 large tomatoes, each weighing about 8 oz/230 g	a few flaked almonds, toasted, to garnish
sprigs of fresh herbs, to garnish	

Clean, wash and soak the rice according to the general instructions on page 16.

Heat 1 fl oz/25 ml of the oil in a heavy saucepan, add the onion and fry gently until golden. Add the meat and fry, stirring, for 3–4 minutes until browned, then stir in the herbs and salt and pepper to taste. Cook for a few minutes more then stir in the cinnamon. Remove from the heat and set aside.

Parboil, drain and rinse the rice as in the recipe for STUFFED COURGETTES (page 92), add to the meat mixture and toss well to combine.

Preheat the oven to 350°F/180°C/gas mark 4. Carefully slice the top (stalk end) off each tomato and reserve. Scoop out the centres with a sharp-edged teaspoon and discard. Fill the tomato cases with the meat and rice mixture, replace the caps, then place the tomatoes side by side in a baking dish. Spoon any leftover stuffing in the corners of the dish and pour over the remaining oil. Cover loosely with foil and bake in the oven for 20 minutes or until the tomatoes are cooked. Garnish with herbs before serving.

Serve hot, with meat.

Clean, wash and soak the rice according to the general instructions on page 16.

Heat the oil in a heavy saucepan, add the onion and fry gently until golden. Add the meat and fry, stirring, for 3–4 minutes until browned, then stir in the cinnamon, nuts, sultanas and salt and pepper to taste and cook for a few minutes more. Remove from the heat and set aside.

Parboil, drain and rinse the rice as in the recipe for STUFFED COURGETTES (page 92), add to the meat mixture and toss well to combine.

Preheat the oven to 350°F/180°C/gas mark 4. Carefully slice the top (stalk end) off each apple and reserve. Using an apple corer, hollow out the centres and discard. Fill the apples with the meat and rice mixture, replace the tops, then place the apples side by side in a baking dish. Spoon any leftover stuffing in the corners of the dish and pour over the remaining oil. Cover loosely with the foil and bake in the oven for about 30 minutes or until the apples are soft. Garnish with toasted almonds before serving.

Serve hot, with meat dishes.

Stuffed Apples

Dolmeh-e-sib

3 oz/90 g long grain rice, preferably basmati
2 fl oz/50 ml oil

Stuffed Peppers

Dolmeh-e-felfel

5 oz/150 g long grain rice, preferably basmati
1 oz/30 g split yellow lentils

| 4 green peppers, each weighing about 8 oz/230 g |
| 2 fl oz/50 ml oil |
| 1 large onion, peeled and finely chopped |
| 5 oz/150 g minced chicken, lean lamb or beef |
| 1 tablespoon chopped fresh dill |
| ¼ teaspoon crushed dried mint |
| ¼ teaspoon dried tarragon |
| 1 teaspoon ground cinnamon |
| ¼ teaspoon turmeric |
| salt and pepper |

Clean, wash and soak the rice according to the general instructions on page 16. Prepare and soak the lentils as in the recipe for PLUM AND MINT SOUP (page 11).

Carefully slice the top (stalk end) off each pepper and reserve, then scoop out the seeds and gently peel off the membranes inside. Blanch the pepper cases in boiling water for 3–4 minutes until barely soft. Drain and rinse under cold running water, then set aside.

Heat 1 fl oz/25 ml of the oil in a heavy saucepan, add the onion and fry gently until golden. Add the meat and fry, stirring, for 3–4 minutes until browned, then stir in the herbs, spices and salt and pepper to taste and cook for a few minutes more. Remove from the heat and set aside.

Parboil, drain and rinse the rice as in the recipe for STUFFED COURGETTES (page 92). Drain the lentils, place them in a saucepan of boiling water and simmer for about 5–7 minutes until half cooked but not too soft. Drain, then add to the meat mixture with the rice and toss well to combine.

Preheat the oven to 350°F/180°C/gas mark 4. Fill the peppers with the meat and rice mixture, then place them in a baking dish into which they will just fit neatly, side by side. Replace the caps. Spoon any leftover stuffing in the corners of the dish and pour over the remaining oil. Cover loosely with foil and bake in the oven for about 30 minutes or until the peppers are soft.

Serve hot, with plain yoghurt.

ﬔﬔ

Rosewater Ice Cream

Bastany

The more you beat this ice cream during freezing the smoother the texture will be. If you have an electric ice cream machine it will give your ice cream a velvety consistency.

| 4 oz/115 g granulated sugar |
| 2 tablespoons rosewater |
| 2 teaspoons lemon juice |
| ½ pint/300 ml double cream |
| 2 oz/60 g blanched almonds or other nuts, finely chopped |

Put the sugar, rosewater and lemon juice in a small heavy saucepan, add 1 tablespoon cold water and heat gently until the sugar has dissolved. Bring to the boil and boil for 3–4 minutes or until the syrup sets into a ball when a little is spooned onto a cold plate. Remove from the heat, pour into a bowl and leave to cool.

Whip the cream until it will stand in soft peaks. Fold in the nuts, then slowly stir in the cooled sugar syrup. Put the mixture in a freezer container and freeze for at least 4 hours, beating the mixture every 45 minutes. Cover the container and freeze overnight.

Allow to soften in the refrigerator for about 15 minutes before serving.

ﬔﬔ

Rosewater Melon Dessert

Deser-e-kharbozeh

| 2 ripe ogen melons |
| 5–6 oz/150–175 g black and white grapes, halved and seeded |
| ½ teaspoon granulated sugar |
| juice of 1 small lemon |
| 2 oz/60 g blanched almonds or unsalted |

shelled pistachios or other nuts, finely chopped

---

5 tablespoons rosewater

½ pint/300 ml whipping or double cream

---

2 teaspoons flaked almonds, toasted, to decorate

Cut the melons in half and scoop out and discard the seeds. Scoop out the flesh with a spoon or melon baller, taking care not to puncture the skin. If using a spoon, cut the flesh into small pieces.

Put the melon in a bowl with the grapes. Dissolve the sugar in the lemon juice and add to the bowl with the nuts and rosewater. Fold gently to mix.

Whip the cream until it will stand in soft peaks. Spoon the fruit salad into the melon cases and top with the whipped cream. Chill in the refrigerator for at least 1 hour before serving, then sprinkle with the toasted almonds.

Serve chilled.

Fruit Salad

Salad-e-miveh

---

2 large oranges, peeled and segmented

---

4 tangerines, peeled and segmented

---

3 eating apples, peeled, cored and diced

---

2 bananas, peeled and sliced

---

6 oz/175 g black and white grapes, halved and seeded

---

1 teaspoon caster or brown sugar (optional)

---

juice of 2 large oranges

---

6 tablespoons rosewater

½ pint/300 ml plain yoghurt or lightly whipped cream

---

1 tablespoon ground unsalted pistachios

Put all the prepared fruit in a bowl and fold gently to mix. If using sugar, dissolve it in the orange juice. Add the orange juice to the fruit salad with the rosewater and toss gently to mix.

Transfer the fruit salad to a serving bowl and spoon over the yoghurt or cream. Sprinkle with the ground pistachios just before serving.

Serve at room temperature or chilled.

THE STORY OF GIVEH

When Uncle Shari came on a visit, his favourite sitting place was under the large fig tree at the bottom of our garden, well shaded by the branches laden with sweet black figs. I would always be the first to run to him, asking for stories to be read from the heavy *Shahmameh* (*The Book of Kings*). When I was about six years old he read me the story about shoes and how they came to be called *giveh*. The story went like this. . . .

One of the ancient Persian kings, Kaykavous, married a young girl after his wife's death. The girl's name was Soodabeh, and she quickly fell in love with the king's son, Prince Siyavash. The prince was a loyal son and ignored his stepmother's advances – so much so that she became angry with him and told tales about him to her husband. As a punishment for his son and also to prove his innocence, Kaykavous ordered Siyavash to ride through fire on horseback.

The son obeyed his father and rode through the fire. He escaped unharmed, but was so angry with his father that he did not turn back. He rode straight on until he eventually reached Tooran, which is north of Khorasan, now in Soviet territory. Afrasiyab, the king of Tooran, welcomed Siyavash and arranged for him to marry his daughter Farangis, making him heir to the throne. But the king's brother naturally became jealous of Siyavash and told tales about him to the king. Afrasiyab became so suspicious that he ordered Siyavash to be beheaded.

The king of Persia heard the tragic news of his son's death, and that his daughter-in-law Farangis was expecting his grandchild. He sent a strong warrior called Giv to look for her and bring her to him. So Giv set off on his long journey. He walked for many days, until eventually his footwear fell to pieces and his feet hurt. Giv knew that he still had a long way to travel. He hit upon the idea of making stronger footwear by compressing old cloth and leather together, passing leather through the sole of the shoes to strengthen them and sewing the top with strong cotton.

Giv's invention worked, and from that day on this type of footwear was called *giveh* after Giv.

Fruit Salad with Yoghurt sauce

Salad-e-miveh ba mast

3 large oranges, peeled, segmented and chopped
3 large eating apples, peeled, cored and diced
4 oz/115 g shelled walnuts or other nuts, coarsely chopped
6 oz/175 g dried figs, well rinsed and chopped
1 teaspoon ground cinnamon
6–8 fl oz/175–225 ml plain yoghurt or soured cream
1 tablespoon flaked almonds, toasted, to decorate

Put all the prepared fruit in a bowl, add the cinnamon and fold gently to mix. Add the yoghurt or soured cream and fold the salad gently again, until the fruit and sauce are evenly mixed. Transfer to a serving bowl and sprinkle with the toasted almonds.

Serve at room temperature or chilled.

Stuffed Melon Dessert

Deser-e-kharbozeh-e-poushodeh

1 large ogen melon
2–2½ oz/60–75 g black cherry, strawberry or raspberry jelly
2 oz/60 g black and white grapes, halved and seeded

about 20 unsalted shelled pistachios or other nuts, coarsely chopped
whipped cream, to serve

Cut a 3 inch/7.5 cm slice off the top of the melon and scoop out the seeds from the centre. Put the jelly and 4 tablespoons hot water in the top of a double boiler and stir until the jelly has dissolved. Remove from the heat and leave to cool slightly.

Add the grapes and pistachios to the jelly and chill in the refrigerator until just on the point of setting. Fill the centre of the melon with this mixture and smooth the top with a palette knife. Return to the refrigerator until set.

Peel the melon, then cut it crossways into slices. Arrange the slices on a serving plate. Hand whipped cream separately at the table.

Serve chilled.

Cardamom and Nut Pudding

Halva berenj ba agil

4 oz/115 g basmati or short grain rice
1 oz/30 g margarine or butter
10–12 fl oz/300–350 ml milk
1 oz/30 g shelled unsalted pistachios or other nuts, chopped
1 oz/30 g blanched almonds or other nuts, chopped
1 teaspoon ground cardamom
1 oz/30 g sultanas, well rinsed
2–3 oz/60–90 g granulated sugar
2 teaspoons ground pistachios or other nuts, to decorate

Clean, wash and soak the rice according to the general instructions on page 16.

Drain the rice into a sieve and rinse under cold running water until the water runs clear. Melt the margarine or butter in a non-stick or heavy saucepan, add the rice and cover with cold water. Bring to the boil, then reduce the heat, cover and simmer for 35–40 minutes, stirring frequently to prevent the rice catching on the bottom of the pan.

Add the milk and continue simmering for a further 5 minutes, then add the chopped nuts and ground cardamom and stir until the consistency is thick. Stir in the sultanas, cook for a further 1–2 minutes, adding a little extra milk or water if the mixture is too dry. Finally stir in sugar to taste. Pour into individual bowls or into one large bowl, cover and chill in the refrigerator for 1–2 hours. Sprinkle with the ground nuts just before serving.

Serve chilled.

MIMI MY CAT

My family were never without pets and at one time I had five cats to look after. Mimi, my last and favourite, would beat the alarm clock to wake me up, patting my hair with her little paws as I slept. She would mew softly in my ear telling me to get up as I was late for school, or, more likely, that she

was impatiently waiting for her breakfast. She was a very spoilt kitten, starting breakfast with a saucer of fresh milk, followed by *memeh's* homemade cookies and a little *panir* (cheese). Mimi always used to meet me from school near the house, dressed in the little clothes I had made especially for her. Everyone admired her and passed comments as they went by.

THE SURPRISING CITY

The 500-mile journey from Yazd was coming to an end; the blue and white coach with its tired-looking passengers approached the city of Tehran. My body suddenly woke up and I raised myself in my seat. The city took me by surprise: completely the wrong image for an eastern city. Looking through the window, misty with the road dust, I stared, amazed, as the coach drove along endless avenues and boulevards. There were government offices and monuments surrounded by colourful gardens and fountains. Bustling crowds wearing the latest fashions were shopping in self-service supermarkets and going into restaurants. Others were queuing up to see the latest film at a cinema matinée. There were children just starting school in their smart uniforms, playing in the modern school grounds. Avenues and pavements looked spotlessly clean, just sprinkled with the late autumn leaves from the high beech and plane trees on each side of the avenue. Each had been nurtured by a steady stream of melted snow running down from the Alborz mountains that shadowed our coach on its journey through the heavy traffic. I was deep in thought, knowing Yazd was many many miles away, when the coach drove into the terminus where my eldest brother Kumars was waiting for me. It was a short drive to his apartment in Shahreza Avenue, a modern flat on the third floor with four rooms and a large hall acting as a family sitting room. It had a modern, fully-fitted kitchen and the table was already laid with various dishes. There I discovered relatives and close friends waiting – it was a surprise party! That was the way Kumars would always welcome his family, even from a short journey.

4

Outdoor Meals and Picnics

SOFREH IN THE PARK

A Persian *sofreh* in the park looked as colourful as the table at home. Approaching the park with its trees covered in blossom, you could see families and friends sitting in groups with the large cloth (*sofreh*) spread out between them on the vivid green grass. The cloth would be set with various foods in aluminium containers (*ghablemeh*), triangular pieces of bread (*nan*), and tea in small *estekan* glasses from the teapot (*ghoori*) which brewed over the brass samovar nearby. The same hospitality would be extended to guests as it was back home, and you would constantly hear the word *'befarmaied'*, meaning 'please help yourself', or 'after you'. It was only a matter of minutes before you had a long list of new friends in your notebook.

ଌୡୄଌ

Minced Kebabs

Kabab-e-koobideh

Somagh powder is available in Persian supermarkets; it is brown in colour with a spicy sharp taste and is traditionally used for garnishing rice. If you cannot obtain it, use paprika instead. If you are worried that the meat may fall off the skewers, bind it with a beaten egg before kneading.

1½ lb/685 g lamb fillet, minced
1 medium onion, peeled
pepper
¼ teaspoon bicarbonate of soda
TO SERVE
1 egg yolk
11 oz/315 g plain rice, cooked according to the general instructions
somagh powder or paprika
grilled tomatoes
slices of raw Spanish onion

Put the meat in a large bowl. Grate the onion to a juice over the meat, add pepper to taste and knead with your hands for at least 5 minutes until the mixture becomes sticky. Cover the bowl and leave the meat to stand in a cool place for about 15 minutes.

Dissolve the bicarbonate of soda in a little warm water. Dip your hands in the water, then take a walnut-sized ball of the meat and press around a flat metal skewer with your hands until smooth. Repeat with more balls of meat, pressing them immediately next to each other until 4–5 inches/ 10–12.5 cm of skewer is covered. Repeat with more skewers until all the meat is used.

Cook the kebabs over a preheated barbecue or on a rack under a preheated hot grill for 5–6 minutes, turning frequently.

To serve, mix the egg yolk into the centre of the hot rice, then spread out on a warm serving platter and sprinkle with somagh powder or paprika. Arrange the kebabs on top and garnish with the tomatoes and onion.

Serve hot, with YOGHURT DRINK (page 144).

ONE OF MANY RESTAURANTS

The capital city of Tehran, with its nightclubs and restaurants, was most impressive. I had many favourite restaurants, but one in particular was situated on the lower slopes of the mountain in a suburb called Shemiran. The setting for this restaurant was one of the most magnificent I have ever seen, and I well remember eating out in the open there under the blue sky with millions of stars. You could hear the sound of a waterfall gushing from the nearby mountain, adding a special cool breeze to the warm atmosphere of the night. It was a totally different feeling from eating out on the flat roof of our home in Yazd, but both experiences were equally enjoyable.

A GOOD HEALTH DRINK FROM A GHERKIN

Late spring in Yazd was the 'first season' for gherkins. My father (*baba*) would pick the gherkins fresh from our garden to offer his male guests as a late afternoon snack. I would sit in the warm sunshine and watch as they first ate the pistachio nuts then sliced the gherkins lengthways, carefully loosening and quartering the flesh. They would eat the flesh from the centre, then carefully scrape every last bit of flesh from the skin with a spoon. Finally, they would pour *aragh* (a spirit similar to vodka) into the empty cases and drink to each other's good health.

ᒷᑌᐯᒷᒷᑌᕲ

Lamb Kebabs

Kabab-e-barg

If liked, you can thread squares of red, yellow and green pepper in between the pieces of meat. Fillet of beef can also be cooked in this way, but it should be brushed with a little more oil before cooking to prevent drying out.

1½ lb/685 g boneless leg of lamb, trimmed of fat and cut into 1½ × 1 inch/ 4 ×2.5 cm pieces
1 large onion, peeled and finely chopped
pepper
TO SERVE
1 egg yolk
11 oz/315 g plain rice, cooked according to the general instructions
slices of raw Spanish onion

Pound the meat a few times to tenderise it, then place in a bowl with the onion and pepper to taste. Stir well to mix, then cover the bowl and leave to marinate in the refrigerator overnight.

Thread the pieces of meat lengthways onto metal kebab skewers. Cook over a preheated barbecue or on a rack under a preheated hot grill for 5–6 minutes, turning every 2–3 minutes.

To serve, mix the egg yolk into the hot rice, then spread out on a warm serving platter. Arrange the kebabs on top and garnish with onion.

Serve hot, with YOGHURT DRINK (page 144).

ᒷᑌᐯᒷᑌᕲ

Kebabs in a Pan

Kabab-e-boshghabi

These kebabs are traditionally cooked over a primus stove on picnic outings.

2 lb/900 g lean lamb or beef, minced
1 medium onion, peeled
salt and pepper
TO SERVE
rings of raw onion and tomato
sprigs of fresh mint
somagh powder (see MINCED KEBABS On page 102)

Put the meat in a large bowl. Grate the onion to a juice over the meat, add salt and pepper to taste and knead with dampened hands for about 5 minutes.

Heat a frying pan or griddle. Take tangerine-sized balls of meat and flatten between the palms of your hands until about ¼ inch/5 mm thick. Place in the pan and cook for 7–10 minutes, tossing several times until browned on both sides and cooked through. Increase the heat to evaporate any liquid in the pan, then place the kebabs on a warm serving dish. Garnish with onion, tomato and mint and sprinkle over a little somagh powder.

Serve hot, with plain rice and yoghurt.

PERSEPOLIS

The history of Persia and its kings was a fascinating subject to me at school and I well remember my visit to Takht-e-Jamishid (Persepolis), the ancient capital of the Persian Empire. It was in mid June when our tour bus left Shiraz on its fifty mile journey to Persepolis. We travelled through rocky, barren land along an asphalt road which wound deeper and deeper into the desert plain. Stepping down from the bus the midday sun was almost unbearable, but our discomfort soon vanished as the vast expanse of this historical site met our eyes, covering many hundreds of square yards right to the foothills of the nearby mountains. A monumental double staircase, with carved bas-reliefs depicting emissaries from foreign lands paying tribute and homage to the king, led up to the Apandana, the king's audience chamber. Buried into the mountain sides were the tombs of Artaxerxes II and Artaxerxes III. Representatives of the many countries which made up the Persian Empire were engraved on the front entrance to these tombs, with bas-reliefs of the king standing in front of the fire altar after paying tribute to Ahuramazda.

Only a short distance away was Pasargadae, a rural community set on a treeless plain which was the ancient site of the burial place of Cyrus the Great. Also not very far away was Naghsh-e-Rostam or 'the valley of the kings', where several Achaemenian kings were interred. Tombs included those of Xerxes and Darius the Great, and the symbols on many of the bas-reliefs emphasised the importance of the Zoroastrian religion in these ancient times.

We returned to Shiraz by way of the outskirts of Persepolis, where the late Shah of Iran held his coronation. Colourful tents, gorgeous furniture and drapes were on display to the public, just the setting for a magnificent banquet. Rather a contrast to our lunch from an ice box at the back of the coach!

Chicken Kebabs

Jujeh kabab

4 boneless chicken breasts, each weighing 8 oz/230 g
1 large onion, peeled and finely grated
6 tablespoons plain yoghurt
1 tablespoon lemon juice
1 teaspoon ground saffron or turmeric

Cut the chicken breasts in half (leaving the skin on) and place in a shallow dish. Mix together the remaining ingredients and pour over the chicken. Cover the dish and leave to marinate in the refrigerator overnight.

Thread the pieces of chicken onto long metal kebab skewers. Cook over a preheated barbecue or on a rack under a pre-heated hot grill for 5–10 minutes, turning frequently.

Serve hot, with lime juice and a seasonal salad.

Savoury Fish Cakes

Kotlet-e-mahi

1¼ lb/550 g minced white fish
1 small onion, peeled
1 egg, beaten
1 tablespoon fine matzo meal or fine dried breadcrumbs
2 teaspoons finely chopped fresh coriander
salt and pepper
oil for shallow frying

Put the fish in a large bowl. Grate the onion to a juice over the fish, add the egg, matzo meal or breadcrumbs, coriander and salt and pepper to taste and knead to a soft, dough-like consistency.

Heat about ½ inch/1 cm oil in a heavy frying pan. Take walnut-sized balls of the fish mixture and flatten between the palms of your hands until about ½ inch/1 cm thick. Shallow fry in the hot oil for 2–3 minutes on each side until golden. Drain and leave to cool on kitchen paper.

Serve cold, with plain yoghurt and a seasonal salad.

THE LOUD ALARM

At dawn in our holiday home in Manshad, the singing cockerel from the downstairs terrace sounded a regular natural alarm clock. Mattresses (*doshak*), eiderdowns and Persian rugs were folded and piled high in the corner of the largest room, then the long white cloth (*sofreh*) was laid along the white-washed balcony. Freshly laid eggs were served with different kinds of home produce – *sabzi khordan* (a salad of spring onions, mint and tarragon), grapes, melon, *panir* (cheese), *nan* (bread), honey and walnuts. The brass tea urn (*samovar*) bubbled in the corner with the *ghoorie* (teapot) brewing on the top, making a warm welcome for early visitors from down in the valley.

ᘓᘐᘍᘓᘐ

Savoury Pastries

Pirashki

7 oz/200 g plain white flour
½ teaspoon baking powder
2 oz/60 g butter or margarine, softened
1 teaspoon caster sugar
1 large egg, beaten
1 tablespoon plain yoghurt
FILLING
2 tablespoons oil
1 small onion, peeled and finely chopped
4 oz/115 g minced chicken, lean lamb or beef
1 medium potato, peeled and finely diced
½ teaspoon turmeric
½ teaspoon ground cinnamon
salt and pepper

Make the pastry. Sift the flour and baking powder together. Beat the butter or margarine with the sugar until white, then beat in the egg, yoghurt and flour. Gather together with your hands to make a smooth dough. Chill in the refrigerator for about 30 minutes while making the filling.

Heat the oil in a heavy saucepan, add the onion and fry gently until golden. Add the meat and fry for 3–4 minutes, stirring, until browned. Add the potato, spices and salt and pepper to taste, then stir in 2–3 fl oz/50–85 ml cold water. Bring to the boil, then reduce the heat, cover and simmer until

the potatoes are soft, adding a little more water from time to time if the pan becomes dry. Increase the heat at the end of cooking to evaporate any excess liquid, then set aside to cool.

Divide the pastry into about 9 equal balls. Roll out each one on a lightly floured surface to a 5–6 inch/12.5–15 cm circle. Brush all around the edge of each circle with water. Place 2 teaspoons of the filling in the centre of each pastry, bring up the edges to seal, then twist or crimp them.

Heat the oil in a deep-fat fryer to 350–375°F/180–190°C. Deep fry the *pirashki* a few at a time for about 4 minutes or until golden. Remove with a slotted spoon and drain on kitchen paper.

Serve hot, with DATE AND TAMARIND CHUTNEY (page 143).

Makes about 9.

ᘓᘐᘍᘓᘐ

Variation

Vegetarian Pirashki

Make the pastry as for the chicken *pirashki* above, but use the following filling: fry 1 small onion, peeled and finely chopped, in 3 tablespoons oil until golden. Add 4 oz/115 g potato, peeled and finely diced, 2 oz/60 g young leek, finely chopped, 1 heaped tablespoon finely chopped fresh dill or parsley, 2 oz/60 g carrots, peeled and finely chopped or coarsely grated, 1 oz/30 g PANIR (page 150) or other cheese (grated if hard), 1 oz/30 g sunflower seeds or chopped nuts and salt and pepper to taste. Cover with 2–3 fl oz/50–60 ml cold water and cook as for the chicken filling above.

THE EVIL EYE AND THE EGG

A traditional belief amongst Persian ladies is that a sick person can be cured with a raw egg. First hold the egg in its shell in your hand and wave it around the patient's head in a clockwise direction. Repeat this three times, then draw a circle on the shell for each person you know, starting at the top with close family, relations and then friends, and working your way round and down the egg until there is no space left. The circles symbolise the eyes of the people you know and traditionally they were drawn in coal, but nowadays you can use a black felt tip pen.

Once the egg is covered, fill a large bowl one-quarter full with cold water and get a second person to hold it over the patient's head. Break the egg vigorously into the water (thus breaking the 'evil eyes'), then throw the water and egg out of the house.

Another custom is to put the egg in the middle of a small fire lit away from the house. The louder the noise when the egg cracks, the more effective the cure.

❧❧❧

Carrot Savoury Cake

Kuku-ye-havij

5 tablespoons oil
1 large onion, peeled and finely chopped
8 oz/230 g grated carrots
4 large eggs
1 heaped teaspoon self-raising flour
2 tablespoons plain yoghurt
2 oz/60 g shelled walnuts or other nuts, ground
⅛ teaspoon ground saffron or ¼ teaspoon ground cinnamon
salt and pepper

Heat 3 tablespoons of the oil in a heavy saucepan, add the onion and fry gently until golden. Stir in the carrots, then pour in 3–4 fl oz/85–120 ml cold water and bring to the boil. Reduce the heat, cover and simmer for about 3 minutes until the carrots are semi-cooked. Remove the lid, increase the heat and cook until all the liquid has evaporated. Do not cook the carrots too dry – they should be juicy at this stage. Remove from the heat and set aside to cool.

Preheat the oven to 350°F/180°C/gas mark 4.

Pour the remaining oil into a 2 inch/5 cm deep, 8 inch/20 cm square baking dish. Place in the oven, on the shelf above centre, for 5–7 minutes until hot.

Meanwhile, beat the eggs with the flour and yoghurt (preferably using an electric mixer), then beat in the ground nuts, saffron or cinnamon and salt and pepper to taste. Finally beat in the cooled carrot and onion mixture.

Remove the baking dish from the oven and pour in the *kuku*. Return to the oven and bake for 15 minutes or until risen. Cut into squares while still hot, then leave to cool in the dish.

Serve cold, with plain yoghurt and a seasonal salad.

❧❧❧

Variations

Potato Savoury Cake

Kuku-ye-sib zamini

Fry 1 medium onion, peeled and finely chopped, and 4 garlic cloves, peeled and crushed, in 3 tablespoons oil. Set aside. Beat 4 large eggs in a bowl with 2 teaspoons self-raising flour, 2 tablespoons plain yoghurt, 2 teaspoons sunflower seeds, ¼ teaspoon cumin seeds and salt and pepper to taste. Combine with the onion and garlic mixture, 8 oz/230 g mashed potatoes and 2 teaspoons sultanas. Pour into an oiled dish as for CARROT SAVOURY CAKE above, sprinkle the top with 1 teaspoon sunflower seeds tossed in a little flour and bake as for CARROT SAVOURY CAKE.

❧❧❧

Courgette Savoury Cake

Kuku-ye-kadu sabz

Fry 1 medium onion, peeled and finely chopped, and 4 garlic cloves, peeled and crushed, in 3 tablespoons oil. Add 8 oz/230 g courgettes, grated, and 3 oz/90 g split yellow lentils, cooked and mashed, then pour in 3 fl oz/85 ml cold water, cover and simmer for 10 to 15 minutes. Uncover the pan to evaporate excess liquid, then set aside to cool. Beat 4 large eggs in a bowl with 2 teaspoons self-raising flour, 3 tablespoons plain yoghurt, ½ teaspoon ground cinnamon and salt and pepper to taste. Combine with the courgette and lentil mixture, then bake in an oiled dish as for CARROT SAVOURY CAKE above.

Chicken Savoury Cake

Kuku-ye-morgh

Fry 1 large onion, peeled and finely chopped, in 1 fl oz/25 ml oil, remove from the heat and stir in ½ teaspoon ground saffron or cinnamon. Beat 4 large eggs in a bowl with ¾ oz/25 g self-raising flour, then beat in the fried onion, 8 oz/230 g diced cooked chicken and salt and pepper to taste. Bake in an oiled dish as for CARROT SAVOURY CAKE above.

Aubergine Savoury Cake

Kuku-ye-badimjan

Peel 10 oz/285 g aubergines, slice them thinly lengthways, then sprinkle with salt and leave to dégorge for about 30 minutes. Rinse and dry, then fry in hot shallow oil for 2 minutes on each side. Drain, chop finely and set aside. Fry 1 medium onion, peeled and chopped, in 3 tablespoons oil from the pan, stir in 6 garlic cloves, peeled and crushed, and 1 teaspoon crushed dried mint. Remove from the heat and stir in the chopped aubergines. Beat 4 large eggs in a bowl with 1 teaspoon self-raising flour, 2 oz/60 g chopped walnuts, 2 teaspoons sultanas and salt and pepper to taste. Combine with the aubergine mixture, then bake in an oiled dish as for CARROT SAVOURY CAKE above.

Dill and Broad Bean Savoury Cake

Kuku-ye-shevid baghla

Cook 8 oz/230 g frozen broad beans in boiling water for 5–7 minutes or until tender. Drain and leave to cool. Fry 1 large onion, peeled and finely chopped, in 3 tablespoons oil, stir in 6 garlic cloves, peeled and crushed, the broad beans and ¼ teaspoon turmeric. Set aside to cool. Beat 4 large eggs in a bowl with 1 teaspoon self-raising flour, 1 tablespoon finely chopped fresh dill and salt and pepper to taste. Combine with the cooled broad bean mixture, then bake in an oiled dish as for CARROT SAVOURY CAKE above.

Pumpkin Savoury Cake

Kuku-ye-kadu zard

Fry 1 medium onion, peeled and finely chopped, in 3 tablespoons oil, add 9 oz/260 g grated pumpkin flesh, cover and cook gently for 2–3 minutes until soft. Set aside to cool. Beat 4 large eggs in a bowl with 1 teaspoon self-raising flour, 4 oz/115 g shelled unsalted pistachios (or other nuts), coarsely chopped, ⅛ teaspoon ground saffron or ½ teaspoon ground cinnamon and salt and pepper to taste. Combine with the pumpkin mixture, then bake in an oiled dish as for CARROT SAVOURY CAKE above.

Okra Savoury Cake

Kuku-ye-bamya

Fry 1¼ lb/550 g okra, topped and tailed, sliced into thin rings, in fairly hot shallow oil for about 1 minute. Remove with a slotted spoon and set aside to cool. Add 1 large onion, peeled and finely chopped, to the oil in the pan, then add ½ teaspoon turmeric, ⅛ teaspoon cumin seeds and salt and pepper to taste. Stir well to mix and set aside to cool. Beat 4 large eggs in a bowl with 1 teaspoon self-raising flour, then combine with the cooled okra and onion mixture. Bake in an oiled dish as for CARROT SAVOURY CAKE above.

THE WINTER WAIT

During the cold winter months, the vast arid land around the province of Yazd was covered in snow and ice. Temperatures could reach several degrees below zero. The cultivated fields were already ploughed, ready to be seeded in early spring, and the farmers had put away their gardening tools. Wrapped in creamy-coloured sheepskin coats (*pustin*), hand-knitted hats, gloves and matching socks with heavy footwear (*giveh*), the farmers would sit on their wooden stools on the corners of the cobbled streets enjoying the pale winter sun, exchanging a few words with their friends about last autumn's harvest. Wheat was their major crop. Vegetables such as beets and potatoes were stored deep in their own garden earth to use during the harsh winter months. These would make a wonderful variety of hot dishes with dried herbs from the previous summer.

SNACK IN THE STREET

Approaching early evening when the yellow globe of sun began to sink behind the Shirkuh mountain and the day's housework was over, a small group of ladies met near each other's homes in the narrow backstreets of Yazd. They sat on their small hand-made mattresses (*doshak*) busy knitting, crocheting or finishing their embroidery in the dim light, enjoying the summer's evening breath. Passing round roasted melon and watermelon seeds from their hand-made silk bags, they devoted these hours to gossiping, telling jokes and occasionally singing together. The evening would finish with a neighbour providing a tray of ready-made *ash* while they waited for their husbands to return from a long day's work.

5

Light Entertainment

The Persians have always been known for their hospitality (*meham navazi*), welcoming unexpected guests with open arms. The best room in the house is invariably reserved for visitors – relations and close friends, those they hardly know, and even those they have never met before.

Persian food is designed not to keep guests waiting. Many of the dishes can be made from just a few vegetables from the garden or whatever happens to be in the house, and within ten minutes the table can be set and food prepared, looking as though several hours have been spent working in the kitchen.

The recipes in this chapter are uncomplicated to prepare and cook, perfect for spontaneous entertaining when friends drop by, for informal suppers rather than sophisticated, pre-planned dinner parties, and for help-yourself buffet-style meals.

KOOFTEH

Literally translated, *koofteh* means 'minced meat', but it is a word used to describe many different kinds of meatballs, both large and small. *Koofteh* are usually prepared with herbs and are quite subtle in flavour, but spices can be added to individual taste. They are economical to make if you are entertaining on a budget, and are just the thing for an informal evening supper party with friends, especially on a cold winter's day. They are usually served simply, with plain yoghurt and a plain bread such as *nan*, but if you have the time to make a sweet chutney sauce such as DATE AND TAMARIND CHUTNEY (page 143) to go with them, they will taste even better.

The following two recipes for *koofteh* are both based on minced meat and rice but are very different in flavour, and KOOFTEH-E-SABZI BA MIVEH VA AGIL are given extra interest by being stuffed before cooking.

Stuffed Herb Meatballs

Koofteh-e-sabzi ba miveh vaagil

4 oz/115 g basmati rice
8 oz/230 g minced lamb or beef
1 large onion, peeled
2 teaspoons each finely chopped fresh dill, coriander, chives and parsley
1 teaspoon finely chopped fresh fenugreek leaves
1 egg, beaten
salt and pepper
2 teaspoons sultanas
2 teaspoons sunflower seeds or finely chopped nuts
1 fl oz/25 ml oil
1 teaspoon turmeric
2 medium potatoes, peeled and quartered

Clean, wash and soak the rice according to the general instructions on page 16.

Drain the rice into a sieve and rinse until the water runs clear. Shake to remove as much water as possible, then place in a bowl with the meat. Grate 2 oz/60 g of the onion to a juice over the meat and rice. Add the herbs, egg and salt and pepper to taste, then knead with your hands for at least 8–10 minutes. Form into smooth balls the size of small tangerines and make a hole in the centre of each with your index finger. Fill the hole with sultanas and sunflower seeds or nuts, then smooth the meat mixture around the stuffing to enclose it. Finely chop the remaining onion. Heat the oil in a large, heavy saucepan, add the chopped onion and fry gently until golden. Add the turmeric and stir well, then add 1½ pints/900 ml cold water and bring to the boil.

Drop the meatballs into the pan, cover and simmer gently for 45 minutes to 1 hour, adding more water from time to time if the pan gets too dry. Twenty minutes before the end of cooking, add the quartered potatoes and stir gently to combine with the meatballs. Cover and simmer again for 7–10 minutes or until the potatoes are tender and the liquid is thick but still juicy.

Serve hot.

🙟🙝

Spicy Meatballs in-a-bowl

Koofteh-e-berenji

1 oz/30 g split yellow lentils
3 oz/90 g basmati rice
8 oz/230 g minced lamb or beef
1 large onion
1 fl oz/25 ml oil
½ teaspoon turmeric
2 teaspoons finely chopped fresh coriander
1 teaspoon cumin seeds
1 egg, beaten
salt and pepper
2 teaspoons tomato purée

Prepare and soak the lentils as in the recipe for PLUM AND MINT SOUP (page 11). Clean, wash and soak the rice according to the instructions on page 16.

Drain the lentils and place in a small saucepan half full of boiling water. Simmer for 5–6 minutes until semi-soft, but not mushy. Drain and set aside to cool.

Drain the rice into a sieve and rinse until the water runs clear. Shake to remove as much water as possible, then place in a bowl with the meat. Grate 2 oz/60 g of the onion to a juice over the meat and rice. Add the lentils, coriander, cumin, egg and salt and pepper to taste, then knead with your hands for at least 8–10 minutes. Form into smooth balls the size of small tangerines.

Finely chop the remaining onion. Heat the oil in a large, heavy saucepan. Add the chopped onion and fry gently until golden. Add the turmeric and stir well, then add 1½ pints/900 ml cold water and bring to the boil. Dissolve the tomato purée in 4 fl oz/120 ml cold water and stir in to the pan.

Drop the meatballs into the pan, cover and simmer gently for 45 minutes to 1 hour, adding more water from time to time if the pan gets too dry.

Serve hot.

🙟🙝

Basic Soup

Abgoosht

3 oz/90 g chick peas
2 lb/900 g lean stewing lamb or beef, washed and cut into large serving pieces
1 large onion, peeled and quartered
1 teaspoon turmeric
salt and pepper
2 large or 4 medium potatoes, peeled and quartered

Prepare and soak the chick peas as for the lentils in PLUM AND MINT SOUP (page 11). Put the meat in a large, heavy saucepan. Cover with about 1½–2 pints/900 ml–1.2 litres cold water and place over moderate heat until the froth rises. Spoon off and discard the froth. Drain the chick peas and add to the pan with the onion, turmeric and pepper to taste.

Reduce the heat to the lowest possible simmer, cover the pan tightly and cook for 1–2 hours, until both meat and chick peas are tender. Add the potatoes and salt to taste, cover and simmer again for 7–10 minutes or until the potatoes are tender.

Serve hot, with NAN (page 138) or HUSHVA NAN (page 135).

🙟🙝

Minced Meat and Chick Pea Soup

Abgoosht-e-goosht-e-koobideh

3 oz/90 g chick peas
2 lb/900 g lean minced lamb or beef

1 teaspoon cumin seeds
1 fl oz/25 ml oil
1 large onion, peeled and finely chopped
1 teaspoon turmeric
salt and pepper
1 large or 2 medium potatoes, peeled and cut into cubes
1 lb/455 g tomatoes, skinned and quartered

Put the chick peas in a sieve and rinse under cold running water until the water runs clear. Drain well, then grind coarsely in a food processor or nut grinder. Place in a bowl, add the meat and cumin seeds and knead with your hands for at least 8–10 minutes. Form into smooth balls the size of small tangerines.

Heat the oil in a large, heavy saucepan. Add the onion and fry gently until golden. Add the turmeric and salt and pepper to taste, stir well, then add 1½ pints/900 ml cold water and bring to the boil.

Drop the meatballs into the pan, cover and simmer gently for 1–1½ hours until the meatballs are tender, adding more water from time to time if the pan gets too dry. About 10 minutes before the end of cooking, add the potatoes and tomatoes. Stir gently to combine with the meatballs, cover and simmer again for 7–10 minutes or until the potatoes are tender, adding more water if necessary.

Serve hot, with TURMERIC AND CUMIN NAN (page 136).

Lime and Lentil Soup

Abgoosht-e-limoo

4 oz/115 g brown lentils
3 oz/90 g black-eyed beans
2 lb/900 g lean stewing lamb or beef, washed and cut into large serving pieces
1 teaspoon turmeric
salt and pepper

1 small onion, peeled and quartered
1 medium uncooked beetroot, peeled and cut into ½ inch/1 cm cubes
1 lb/455 g spinach leaves, washed and coarsely chopped
1 teaspoon dried mint
juice of 4–5 limes or lemons

Prepare and soak the pulses as for the lentils in PLUM AND MINT SOUP (page 11). Put the meat in a large, heavy saucepan. Cover with about 2 pints/1.2 litres cold water and place over moderate heat until the froth rises. Spoon off and discard the froth. Drain the pulses and add to the pan with the turmeric and pepper to taste.

Reduce the heat to the lowest possible simmer and add the onion and beetroot. Cover the pan and cook for 1–2 hours, until both meat and pulses are tender. Add the spinach, mint, lime juice and salt to taste; cover and simmer again for a further 10 minutes.

Serve hot.

Lime and Tomato Soup

Abgoosht-e-limoo va govjeh

3 oz/90 g chick peas
3 oz/90 g black-eyed or butter beans
2 lb/900 g lean stewing lamb or beef, washed and cut into large serving pieces
1 large onion, peeled and quartered
1 teaspoon turmeric
salt and pepper
1 large or 2 medium potatoes, peeled and quartered
1 lb/455 g tomatoes, skinned and quartered
juice of 2–3 limes or lemons

Prepare and soak the pulses as for the lentils in PLUM AND MINT SOUP (page 11). Put the meat in a large, heavy saucepan. Cover with about 2 pints/1.2 litres cold water and place over moderate heat until the froth rises. Spoon off and discard the froth. Drain the pulses and add to the pan with the onion, turmeric and pepper to taste.

Reduce the heat to the lowest possible simmer, cover the pan and cook for 1–2 hours, until both meat and pulses are tender.

Add the potatoes, tomatoes and salt to taste, cover and simmer again for 7–10 minutes or until the potatoes are tender. Stir in the lime juice before serving.

Serve hot.

Potato and Yoghurt Salad

Salad-e-sib zamini ba mast

1 lb/455 g small or medium potatoes, washed
5 oz/140 g fresh or frozen peas, cooked and drained
10 oz/285 g celery, trimmed and cut into ¼ inch/5 mm dice
2 tablespoons finely chopped fresh dill
2 fl oz/50 ml olive oil
4 oz/115 g shelled walnuts or other nuts, chopped
juice of 1 lemon
salt and pepper
10 fl oz/300 ml plain yoghurt
2 medium cooked beetroots, peeled and diced small

Put the potatoes into a saucepan of cold water and bring to the boil. Lower the heat, cover and simmer for about 20 minutes until tender. Drain, leave until cool enough to handle, then peel off the skins with your fingers.

Cut the potatoes into ¼ inch/5 mm dice and place in a large bowl. Add the peas, celery and dill and toss to combine, then add the oil, nuts, lemon juice and salt and pepper to taste. Toss again, then slowly mix in the yoghurt. Divide the salad equally between individual dishes. Garnish with the beetroot just before serving.

Serve at room temperature, with NAN (page 138) or TUMERIC AND CUMIN NAN (page 136).

Rice Salad

Salad-e-berenj

For a pretty garnish, make radish 'roses'. Trim both ends off the radishes, then make thin cuts around each one to form petal shapes. Soak in iced water while preparing the salad so that the petals open out slightly.

5 oz/140 g chick peas
5 oz/140 g basmati rice
8 oz/230 g celery, trimmed and cut into ¼ inch/5 mm dice
3–4 fl oz/90–120 ml olive oil
4 hard-boiled eggs, shelled and chopped
salt and pepper
10–12 radishes

Prepare and soak the chick peas as for the lentils in PLUM AND MINT SOUP (page 11). Clean, wash and soak the rice according to the general instructions.

Drain the chick peas and place in a saucepan half full of boiling water. Simmer for 30 minutes or until soft. Meanwhile, drain and rinse the rice, then cook in a separate saucepan of boiling water for 8–10 minutes until soft but not mushy. Drain and rinse under cold running water, then drain again.

Drain the chick peas; leave to cool, then place in a bowl with the rice and celery. Toss to combine, then slowly add the oil, toss again and add salt and pepper to taste. Gently fold in the chopped eggs. Divide the salad equally between individual dishes and garnish with the radishes.

Serve as room temperature, with NAN (page 138).

Apple and Walnut Salad in Cream Sauce

Salad-e-sib ba gerdu

6 oz/175 g basmati rice
8 oz/230 g celery, trimmed and cut into ¼ inch/5 mm dice
5 eating applies, peeled, cored and cut into ½ inch/1 cm dice
5 oz/140 g shelled walnuts, roughly chopped
4 oz/115 g sultanas
10 fl oz/300 ml single cream
¼ teaspoon ground cinnamon
salt and pepper
flaked almonds, to garnish

Clean, wash and soak the rice according to the general instructions.

Drain and rinse the rice, then cook in a saucepan of boiling water for 8–10 minutes until soft but not mushy. Drain and rinse under cold running water, then drain again. Place in a bowl with the celery, applies, walnuts and sultanas. Toss to combine, then add the cream, cinnamon and salt and pepper to taste and toss again. Divide the salad equally between individual dishes and sprinkle flaked almonds over the top.

Serve at room temperature.

Red Kidney Bean Salad

Salad-e-lubia ghermez

5 oz/140 g red kidney beans
2 small or 1 medium potato, washed
3 hard-boiled eggs, shelled and chopped
3 fl oz/90 ml olive oil
juice of 2 large lemons
finely chopped fresh parsley
salt and pepper

1 large Spanish onion, peeled and cut into rings

Prepare and soak the kidney beans as for the lentils in PLUM AND MINT SOUP (page 11).

Drain the beans and place in a large saucepan. Cover with plenty of cold water, bring to the boil and boil rapidly for 10 minutes. Reduce the heat, cover the pan and simmer for 1 hour or until tender.

Meanwhile, cook, peel and dice the potato(es) as in the recipe for POTATO AND YOGHURT SALAD (page 113).

Drain the kidney beans and leave to cool, then place in a large bowl with the potatoes and chopped eggs. Toss to combine, then slowly add the olive oil, lemon juice, parsley and salt and pepper to taste and toss again. Transfer to a deep salad bowl and garnish with the onion rings.

Serve at room temperature.

Brown Lentil and Sultana Salad

Salad-e-addas

5 oz/140 g brown lentils
4 oz/115 g basmati rice
1 small Spanish onion, peeled and finely chopped
2 oz/60 g sultanas
3 fl oz/90 ml olive oil
juice of 1 small lemon
salt and pepper
a little chopped fresh parsley, to garnish

Prepare and soak the lentils as in the recipe for PLUM AND MINT SOUP (page 11). Clean, wash and soak the rice according to the general instructions.

Place the lentils and their soaking liquid in a saucepan and bring to the boil. Lower the heat and simmer for 15–20 minutes until tender but not too soft.

Meanwhile, drain and rinse the rice, then cook in a separate saucepan of boiling water for 8–10 minutes until soft but not mushy. Drain and rinse under cold running water, then drain again.

Drain the lentils, leave to cool, then place in a bowl with the rice, onion and sultanas. Toss to combine, then slowly add the oil and lemon juice. Toss again and add salt and pepper to taste. Transfer to a deep salad bowl or divide equally between individual dishes. Garnish with parsley.

Serve at room temperature, with plain yoghurt and NAN (page 138).

Chicken and Herb Salad

Salad-e-morgh ba sib zamini

2 small or 1 medium potato, washed
5 oz/140 g runner beans, topped and tailed
6 oz/175 g fresh or frozen peas, cooked and drained
1½ lb/685 g boneless chicken, skin removed, and diced
1 tablespoon finely chopped fresh dill
2 teaspoons finely chopped fresh parsley
1 teaspoon finely chopped fresh tarragon
1 teaspoon chopped fresh mint
juice of 1 lemon
salt and pepper
4 fl oz/120 ml mayonnaise
2 medium cooked beetroots, peeled and finely diced

Cook, peel and dice the potato(es) as in the recipe for POTATO AND YOGHURT SALAD (page 113).

Cook the runner beans in boiling water for about 7 minutes, then drain and cut into ¼ inch/5 mm dice. Put the potato and beans in a large bowl, add the peas and chicken and toss to combine. Add the herbs, lemon juice and salt and pepper to taste and toss again. Slowly add the mayonnaise, toss again, then transfer to a large bowl or divide equally between individual dishes. Garnish with the beetroot just before serving.

Serve at room temperature, with NAN (page 138).

KHORESH

Khoresh is a typical Persian stew made with meat or poultry and vegetables, sometimes with fruit and nuts added. It is served as a main meal for lunch or dinner, with either *POLOV* or *chelou* rice, or with *nan*. Although exotically flavoured, *khoresh* does not contain strong or hot spices such as curry powder or chilli, and so it is suitable for the most fastidious or delicate palate or stomach.

It is important to remember that *khoresh* must be cooked over very gentle heat. Do not add the vegetables until after the meat has become tender or they will overcook, and do not stir too vigorously or too often after the vegetables have been added or they will lose their shape. During cooking water should be added a little at a time and when ready to serve the gravy should be thick and not watery. If there is too much gravy, simply increase the heat, uncover the saucepan and boil to evaporate the extra liquid.

For vegetarian *Khoresh*, simply omit the meat and replace the water with vegetable stock.

Dill and Bean Khoresh

Khoresh-e-bozmocheh

3 oz/90 g red kidney beans
2 fl oz/50 ml oil
1 large onion, peeled and chopped
1½ lb/685 g boneless chicken, skin removed, or lean stewing lamb or beef, washed and cut into ½ inch/1 cm pieces
1 teaspoon turmeric
1 large or 2 medium potatoes, peeled and cut into 2 inch/5 cm pieces
1 large bunch of fresh dill, weighing 2–3 oz/60–90 g, finely chopped
salt and pepper

Prepare and soak the kidney beans as for the lentils in PLUM AND MINT SOUP (page 11).

Drain the beans and place in a large saucepan. Cover with plenty of cold water, bring to the boil and boil rapidly for 10 minutes. Reduce the heat, cover the pan and simmer for 1 hour or until tender.

Meanwhile, heat the oil in a large, heavy saucepan, add the onion and fry gently until golden. Add the meat and turmeric, stir for 5 minutes then add spices and then cover with 1–1½ pints/600–900 ml cold water and bring to the boil.

Reduce the heat to the lowest possible simmer, then cover the pan. Cook until the meat is tender – about 45 minutes for chicken, up to 2 hours for lamb or beef.

Add the potatoes, cover and simmer again for 7–10 minutes or until the potatoes are tender. Drain the cooked beans and add to the pan with the dill and salt and pepper to taste. Continue cooking until the liquid is reduced to a thick mixture.

Serve hot with crispy potato rice.

ᏋᏨᎬᏋ

Cauliflower Khoresh

Khoresh-e-gol-e-kalam

4 oz/115 g split yellow lentils
1 fl oz/25 ml oil
1 large onion, peeled and finely chopped
1 teaspoon ground cinnamon
¼ teaspoon turmeric
2 lb/900 g boneless chicken, skin removed, or lean stewing lamb or beef, washed and cut into ½ inch/1 cm pieces
12 oz/345 g cauliflower florets
salt and pepper
1 heaped tablespoon finely chopped fresh parsley

Prepare and soak the lentils as in the recipe for PLUM AND MINT SOUP (page 11).

Heat the oil in a large, heavy saucepan, add the onion and fry gently until golden. Drain the lentils and add to the pan with the cinnamon and turmeric. Stir for 2–3 minutes, then add the meat and stir for a further 1–2 minutes. Add about 12 fl oz/350 ml cold water and bring to the boil.

Reduce the heat to the lowest possible simmer, cover the pan and cook until the meat is tender – about 45 minutes for chicken, up to 2 hours for lamb or beef. If the pan becomes dry during this time, add a little extra water.

Add the cauliflower and salt and pepper to taste, with a little more water if necessary. Cover and simmer again for 7 minutes or until the cauliflower is tender but still with a crunchy bite. If there is too much liquid at the end of cooking, increase the heat and boil until reduced to a thick mixture. Sprinkle with the parsley before serving.

Serve hot, with a rice dish.

ᏋᏨᎬᏋ

Celery Khoresh

Khoresh-e-karafs

2 fl oz/50 ml oil
1 large onion, peeled and chopped
1 lb/455 g boneless chicken, skin removed, or lean stewing lamb or beef, washed and cut into ½ inch/1 cm pieces
1 teaspoon turmeric
8 oz/230 g celery, trimmed and cut into ½ inch/1 cm dice
1 medium potato, peeled and cut into ½ inch/1 cm pieces
1 heaped tablespoon finely chopped fresh parsley
juice of 1 large lemon, or to taste
salt and pepper

Heat the oil in a large, heavy saucepan, add the onion and fry gently until golden. Add the meat and stir for 3–4 minutes until browned on all sides, then add the turmeric and toss to coat the meat evenly. Add 10 fl oz/300 ml cold water and bring to the boil.

Reduce the heat to the lowest possible simmer, cover the pan and cook until the meat is tender – about 45 minutes for chicken, up to 2 hours for lamb or beef. If the pan becomes dry during this time, add a little extra water.

Add the celery, potato and parsley, with a little more water if necessary. Cover and simmer again for 10–15 minutes until the vegetables are just tender. Add lemon juice and salt and pepper to taste. If there is too much liquid at the end of cooking, increase the heat and boil until reduced to a thick mixture.

Serve hot.

Garden Pea Khoresh

Khoresh-e-lubia sabz

2 fl oz/50 ml oil
1 large onion, peeled and chopped
1 lb/455 g boneless chicken, skin removed, or lean stewing lamb or beef, washed and cut into ½ inch/1 cm pieces
1 lb/455 g fresh or frozen peas
2 teaspoons finely chopped fresh parsley
2 teaspoons tomato purée
salt and pepper

Heat the oil in a large, heavy saucepan, add the onion and fry gently until golden. Add the meat and stir for 3–4 minutes until browned on all sides, then add 10 fl oz/300 ml cold water and bring to the boil.

Reduce the heat to the lowest possible simmer, cover the pan and cook until the meat is tender – about 45 minutes for chicken, up to 2 hours for lamb or beef. If the pan becomes dry during this time, add a little extra water.

Add the peas and the parsley. Dissolve the tomato purée in 4 fl oz/120 ml cold water and stir into the pan. Add salt and pepper to taste, cover and simmer again for 3–4 minutes until the peas are semi-soft. If there is too much liquid at the end

of cooking, increase the heat and boil until reduced to a thick mixture.

Serve hot, with a rice dish.

Turnip Meal-in-a-Bowl

Ash-e-shalgham

4 oz/115 g long grain rice
1 lb/455 g lean minced lamb or beef
1 large onion, peeled
4 oz/115 g mung beans
1 teaspoon cumin seeds
1 lb/455 g turnips, topped and tailed and cut in halves or quarters if large
2 teaspoons each finely chopped fresh dill, parsley and coriander
1 small leek, washed thoroughly and finely chopped
salt and pepper

Clean, wash and soak the rice according to the general instructions on page 16.

Put the meat in a bowl. Grate 1 oz/30 g of the onion to a juice over the meat. Knead with your hands for at least 5 minutes until the meat binds together. Form into smooth balls the size of hazelnuts.

Finely chop the remaining onion. Rinse the rice and mung beans until clean. Put the rice and mung beans in a large, heavy saucepan, add the onion and 2 pints/1.2 litres cold water and bring to the boil.

Reduce the heat to the lowest possible simmer, then partially cover the pan so that a little steam can escape (to prevent boiling over). Cook for 1–1½ hours until the mung beans are tender. If the pan becomes dry during this time, add a little extra water.

Drop the meatballs into the pan and add the cumin seeds and extra water if necessary. Add the turnips, herbs, leek and salt and pepper to taste, cover and simmer again for 15 minutes or until all the ingredients are well cooked and the liquid is reduced to a thick mixture.

Serve hot with nan.

Stir in the herbs, cover and simmer again for 10 minutes, then add the plums and continue simmering for a further 10 minutes. If there is too much liquid, increase the heat and boil until reduced to a thick mixture.

Serve hot, with TURMERIC AND CUMIN NAN (page 136).

Plum and Herb Meal-in-a-Bowl

Ash-e-alu

4 oz/115 g long grain rice
3 oz/90 g split yellow lentils
1 fl oz/25 ml oil
1 large onion, peeled and chopped
salt and pepper
1 lb/455 g boneless chicken, skin removed, or lean fillet of lamb or beef frying steak, washed and cut into ½ inch/1 cm pieces
3 oz/90 g fresh coriander, finely chopped
1 teaspoon turmeric
1 oz/30 g each fresh parsley and leek or chives, finely chopped
1 oz/30 g fresh mint, chopped, or 2 teaspoons dried mint
1 lb/455 g red plums, washed

Clean, wash and soak the rice according to the general instructions on page 16. Prepare and soak the lentils as in the recipe for PLUM AND MINT SOUP (page 11).

Heat the oil in a large, heavy saucepan, add the onion and fry gently until golden. Add salt and pepper to taste, then the meat. Drain the rice into a sieve and rinse until the water runs clear. Drain the lentils. Add the rice and lentils to the pan, cover with 1½–2 pints/900 ml–1.2 litres cold water and bring to the boil.

Reduce the heat to the lowest possible simmer, then partially cover the pan so that a little steam can escape (to prevent boiling over). Cook until the meat is tender – about 45 minutes for chicken, up to 2 hours for lamb or beef. If the pan becomes dry during this time, add a little extra water.

Barley Meal-in-a-Bowl

Ash-e-jo

5 oz/140 g brown lentils
2 oz/60 g pin barley
1 fl oz/25 ml oil
1 large onion, peeled and chopped
1 lb/455 g boneless chicken, skin removed, or lean stewing lamb or beef, washed and cut into ½ inch/1 cm pieces
5 garlic cloves, peeled and crushed
1 teaspoon turmeric
salt and pepper
4 oz/115 g fresh spinach, washed and finely chopped
2 oz/60 g fresh parsley, finely chopped
2 oz/60 g chives, snipped, or 1 small leek, washed and finely chopped
juice of 3 large lemons
sugar to taste

Prepare and soak the lentils and barley as for the lentils in PLUM AND MINT SOUP (page 11).

Heat the oil in a large, heavy saucepan, add the onion and fry gently until golden. Add the meat, toss and stir to mix with the onion, then add the garlic, turmeric and salt and pepper to taste. Wash the lentils and barley. Add to the pan, cover with about 2 pints/1.2 litres cold water and bring to the boil.

Reduce the heat to the lowest possible simmer, then partially cover the pan so that a little steam can escape (to prevent boiling over). Cook until the meat is tender – about 45 minutes for chicken, up to 2 hours for lamb or beef. If the pan becomes dry during this time, add a little extra water.

Add the spinach and herbs and simmer again for 10 minutes, stirring occasionally to prevent the ingredients catching on the bottom of the pan. Add lemon and sugar to taste.

Serve hot, drizzled with HOT MINT (page 150).

White Meal-in-a-Bowl

Ash-e-safid

3 oz/90 g long grain rice
2 oz/60 g chick peas
1½ lb/685 g boneless chicken, skin removed, or lean tender lamb or beef, washed and cut into ½ inch/1 cm pieces
1 small bunch of fresh coriander, weighing about 2 oz/60 g, finely chopped
1 large onion, peeled and coarsely chopped
¼ teaspoon cumin seeds
salt and pepper

Prepare and soak the chick peas as for the lentils in PLUM AND MINT SOUP (page 11).

Put the rice into a sieve and rinse until the water runs clear. Drain the chick peas. Place both rice and chick peas in a large, heavy saucepan. Add the remaining ingredients with pepper to taste, cover with about 2½ pints/1.6 litres cold water and bring to the boil.

Reduce the heat to the lowest possible simmer, then partially cover the pan so that a little steam can escape (to prevent boiling over). Cook until the meat is tender – about 45 minutes to one hour for chicken, up to 2 hours for lamb or beef. If the pan becomes dry during this time, add a little extra water. Add salt to taste before serving.

Serve hot with nan.

Courgette Fritters

Shami-e-kadu

2 large eggs
1 tablespoon self-raising flour
¼ teaspoon baking powder
9 oz/260 g courgettes, washed and grated
8 garlic cloves, peeled and crushed
1 teaspoon ground cinnamon
salt and pepper
oil for shallow frying

Break the eggs into a bowl and beat with a fork. Sift in the flour and baking powder, beat into the eggs, then beat in the courgettes, garlic, cinnamon and salt and pepper to taste.

Heat ½ inch/1 cm oil in a heavy frying pan. Drop dessertspoonfuls of the mixture into the hot oil (as many as the pan will comfortably hold), flatten slightly with the back of the spoon and fry for 2–3 minutes on each side until golden. Remove with a fish slice and drain on kitchen paper.

Serve hot, with fish, plain yoghurt and rice.

Potato Fritters

Shami-e-sib zamini

1 egg
¼ teaspoon ground cinnamon
salt and pepper
4 garlic cloves, peeled and crushed
9 oz/260 g raw potatoes, peeled and finely grated to a pulp
1 teaspoon self-raising flour
¼ teaspoon baking powder
oil for shallow frying

Break the egg into a bowl and beat with a fork. Stir in the cinnamon and salt and pepper to taste, then the garlic. Drain the potatoes well to remove excess water, then add to the egg mixture with the flour and baking powder. Mix well with a fork.

Heat ½ inch/1 cm oil in a heavy frying pan. Drop dessertspoonfuls of the mixture into the hot oil (as many as the pan will comfortably hold), flatten slightly with the back of the spoon and fry for 1 minute on each side until golden. Remove with a fish slice and drain on kitchen paper.

Serve hot, with SPICED MEAT CAKE or any type of rice or salad and tararind chutney

Aubergine Fritters

Shami-e-badimjan

1 aubergine, weighing about 6 oz/175 g, peeled and sliced lengthways ⅛ inch/3 mm thick
salt
oil for shallow frying
1 large egg
1 heaped teaspoon self-raising flour
4–5 garlic cloves, peeled and crushed
½ teaspoon crushed dried mint
1 teaspoon sugar
¼ teaspoon baking powder

Put the aubergine slices on a tray or large plate. Sprinkle both sides with salt (about 1 teaspoon) and leave for 1 hour to extract the dark and bitter juices. Rinse under cold running water and pat dry with a clean tea towel. Heat shallow oil gently in a heavy frying pan, add the aubergine slices and fry over gentle heat for 2 minutes on each side. Transfer to kitchen paper to drain, then mash with a fork.

Break the egg into a bowl and beat with a fork. Stir in the flour, garlic, mint, sugar and baking powder, then the aubergine pulp. Mix well with a fork.

Heat ½ inch/1 cm oil in the frying pan. Drop dessertspoonfuls of the mixture into the hot oil (as many as the pan will comfortably hold), flatten slightly with the back of the spoon and fry for 1 minute on each side until golden. Remove with a fish slice and drain on kitchen paper.

Serve hot, with rice, and plain yoghurt.

Chicken and Yoghurt Fritters

Shami-e-morgh

4 large eggs
8 garlic cloves, peeled and crushed
¼ teaspoon ground cinnamon
salt and pepper
4 tablespoons plain yoghurt
4 teaspoons self-raising flour
9 oz/260 g boneless cooked chicken, skin removed and diced
oil for shallow frying

Break the eggs into a bowl and beat with a fork. Stir in the garlic, cinnamon and salt and pepper to taste, then the yoghurt and flour. Beat vigorously until smooth, then stir in the chicken.

Heat ½ inch/1 cm oil in a heavy frying pan. Drop dessertspoonfuls of the mixture into the hot oil (as many as the pan will comfortably hold), flatten slightly with the back of the spoon and fry for 1 minute on each side until golden. Remove with a fish slice and drain on kitchen paper.

Serve hot, with ORANGE RICE (page 48) and a salad, and DATE AND TAMARIND CHUTNEY (page 143).

Aubergine and Garlic Delight

Mirza ghasemi

2 aubergines, each weighing about 8 oz/230 g
3 fl oz/85 ml oil
6 garlic cloves, peeled and crushed
2 large tomatoes, each weighing about 8 oz/230 g, skinned and roughly chopped

4 eggs

salt and pepper

a few mint sprigs, to garnish

Preheat the grill to hot. Put the aubergines on the grill rack and grill for about 10 minutes until the skins are soft, turning them frequently. Remove from the heat, peel off the black skins and discard, then chop the flesh finely.

Heat the oil in a large heavy frying pan, add the garlic and fry for 1 minute until brown. Add the aubergines and tomatoes, stir well to mix, then simmer uncovered for 4–5 minutes, stirring occasionally. If there is too much liquid, increase the heat and boil to evaporate until the mixture is thick.

Push the mixture to one side of the pan. Beat the eggs in a bowl with salt and pepper to taste, pour into the empty part of the pan, then toss to mix with the aubergine and tomato mixture. Garnish with mint sprigs before serving.

Serve hot, with NAN (page 136) and a seasonal salad.

Pumpkin Meal-in-a-Bowl

Ash-e-kadu halvaie

3 oz/90 g brown lentils

2 oz/60 g long grain rice

3 fl oz/85 ml oil

2 large onions, peeled and chopped

¼ teaspoon ground cinnamon

¼ teaspoon turmeric

1 lb/455 g peeled pumpkin flesh, cubed

juice of 2–3 large lemons, to taste

sugar, to taste

HOT MINT

Prepare and soak the lentils as in the recipe for PLUM AND MINT SOUP (page 11). Clean, wash and soak the rice according to the general instructions

Heat 2 fl oz/50 ml of the oil in a large, heavy saucepan, add the onions and fry gently until golden. Stir in the cinnamon and turmeric.

Drain the lentils and rice. Add to the pan, cover with 8–10 fl oz/250–300 ml cold water and bring to the boil. Reduce the heat to the lowest possible simmer, add the pumpkin and cook until the ingredients are soft – about 10–15 minutes. Add lemon juice and sugar to taste, pour into a warm deep serving bowl and garnish with HOT MINT.

Serve hot, with NAN (page 138).

6

Little Gifts of Entertainment

LITTLE GIFTS OF ENTERTAINMENT

Fresh fruit is the traditional end to a meal in Persia; sweetmeats are served throughout the day whenever visitors call – as a symbol of friendship and happiness. They are also traditionally served at *Norooz*, the Persian New Year. These sweetmeats also make ideal gifts to take when visiting your friends in their homes, or hotels. None is difficult to prepare, but they will certainly be something a little bit different for most of your friends – and no doubt a great conversation piece.

SWEET COMINGS AND GOINGS

Did-o-baz-did is a Persian custom. When someone is arriving from, or leaving for a journey, relations and friends pop in to give them boxes of sweets, biscuits and flowers. Sometimes the person can end up with twenty different boxes, which are shared and offered round to other friends and relations as they come to visit (*di-dani*).

Sweets, biscuits, cakes and even breads are made, and in this chapter you will find a typical selection.

NUTS

A Persian house is never without nuts. There are always separate bowls of pistachios, roasted almonds, pumpkin seeds and large water melon seeds set out on the tables, and as you sit and chat it is quite easy to nibble at them without stopping, for hours.

My mother used to 'roast' nuts herself by putting them into a frying pan, covering them completely with salt and cooking them until they were brown. She would then remove the nuts from the pan and dust off the excess salt. They were at their best when freshly cooked, preferably while still warm.

Chick peas were everyone's favourite – usually eaten with sultanas. To this day they always remind me of our Nanny, whose name was Malog. She was a Muslim, but religion did not affect our relationship. One of Malog's duties was to weed some nearby land, and I used to go with her to sit in the shade of the large mulberry or apricot tree while she worked. Malog would give me bunches of freshly pulled-up branches of chick peas. I would pop each one, peel it and then quickly eat it. On the way home Malog would keep me entertained with funny stories, and she always had her share of chick peas to take back for her family.

Chick Peas

Nokhodchi

---
4 oz/115 g chick peas

Prepare and soak the chick peas as for the lentils in PLUM AND MINT SOUP (page 11).

Cook the chick peas in their soaking liquid for 3–4 minutes, then drain and pat dry with kitchen paper. Preheat the oven to 300°F/150°C/gas mark 2. Spread the chick peas out on a baking tray and roast in the oven for 45 minutes. Serve in small bowls.

LEARNING TO BURN

Our school classrooms were built around a large central playground and on the other side of the buildings there were trees in sunken gardens. I loved the scent of the pines, and the pistachio trees looked so beautiful with their green branches and bright red nuts.

When the pistachios were ripe, the outer shell would open to release the nut which would split open ready to be picked, and during break we were allowed to pick them and eat them. There were also almond trees heavy with nuts. These were too hard for us to crack at break time, although it was these that were used for our first cookery lesson. Getting the ingredients ready for this lesson was a great excitement, although I remember being a bit worried in case I got lower marks than my friends. I needn't have worried: the next day, I proudly presented my Aunt Pari with the sweets which I had made.

CHICKEN DRUMSTICKS WITH ORANGE SAUCE

AUBERGINE AND TOMATO DISH (top); MEATBALL SURPRISE (Bottom)

PERSIMMON HORS D'OEUVRE AND MEATBALLS IN WALNUT AND YOGHURT SAUCE

COURGETTE KHORESH, LENTIL & CRISPY POTATO RICE & SPICY MEATBALLS (main dish); WITH SPICED MEAT CAKES, DATE CHUTNEY & PICKLED GRAPES

SPINACH AND RICE MOULD; CARROT SAVOURY CAKE AND OKRA SAVOURY CAKE
(top)

DELICACIES FOR AN INFORMAL GATHERING, INCLUDING PISTACHIO MUNCHIES, COCONUT DROPS, CHICK PEA TEARS AND YAZDI CAKES

MINCED BEEF KEBABS AND LAMB KEBABS; LAVASH NAN AND TURMERIC AND CUMIN NAN; STUFFED MELON DESSERT

SHIRIN DISPLAYS A TYPICAL PERSIAN BUFFET MADE OF TANTALISING LIGHT DISHES

Burnt Sugar Almonds

Badam sookhteh

4 oz/115 g granulated sugar
2 oz/60 g blanched almonds, shredded

Grease a flat, heavy baking tray. Put the sugar in a small, non-stick or heavy frying pan. Place over gentle heat until the sugar has melted and is turning a caramel colour, then add the almonds and stir once or twice until completely coated in the toffee mixture.

Remove the pan from the heat. With a teaspoon, immediately put small blobs of the mixture on to the greased tray, spacing them well apart to allow for spreading. Leave until cold and hard, then transfer to greased foil. Eat as soon as possible or the almonds will become very sticky.

NIGHT TIME TREATS

The flat roof of our house was joined to my Aunt Pari's, and so on summer evenings we used to get together on the roof with our cousins to play games, discuss school homework and exchange gossip. One game we often played was pointing out the pictures formed by the constantly changing shapes of the clouds. When they dispersed the clear night sky would be visible and we would study the starlit heavens. Even as a little girl I knew the star constellations. They often seemed near enough to touch and I felt they were almost joining in our conversation.

My mother and Aunt Pari both used to cook different things for dinner, making sure that the dishes complemented each other so that we could share our meals together on the roof. As my mother liked to play cards after the meal, she always encouraged as many people as she could to join us. Time passed quickly during these family parties and sometimes we would chat and joke right through the night until the early morning – nibbling away all the time at my mother's home-made sweets.

Almond Treats

Shirini-e-badam

2 large egg whites
4 oz/115 g caster sugar
1 teaspoon almond essence
6 oz/175 g ground almonds
almond flakes, to decorate

Preheat the oven to 300°F/150°C/gas mark 2. Grease a flat, heavy baking tray and dust well with flour.

Whisk the egg whites until stiff. Gently fold in the sugar with a large metal spoon, then gently fold in the almond essence and ground almonds until evenly incorporated.

Place ½ teaspoonfuls of the mixture on the greased and well floured tray, spacing them about 2 inches/5 cm apart to allow for spreading. Place 1 almond flake in the centre of each. Bake in the oven for 10–11 minutes until risen and light golden. Remove from the tray with a palette knife while still hot and transfer to a plate. Leave until cold, then store in an airtight tin.

Makes about 50.

MULBERRY TIME

March 21 is the beginning of spring and the Persian New Year. Forty days later (April 29) is the beginning of the fruit season heralded by the ripening of the mulberry. There is a legend that the birds love the mulberries (*toot*) so much that they sing *chehelom-chehelom-toot to delom*, which means 'the fortieth day the berries are in my tummy'.

We all look forward to going to the orchard (*bagh*) with its trees full of fruit, one of which was a very large, high mulberry tree. Five or six of us would hold a sheet of strong material right beneath the branches laden with ripe berries, then one of the men would climb into the tree. With one foot carefully secured, he would shake the branch with the other foot so that the berries came cascading down into our waiting sheet. We then sorted the berries out and, as the little creamy coloured *toot* looked so enticing, we used to wash a few and eat them then and there, then dry what was left to save for winter use.

I still receive *toot* regularly from Persia.

Marzipan and Rosewater Mulberries

Toot

3 oz/90 g ground almonds
2½ oz/75 g icing sugar
1 tablespoon best-quality rosewater
about 48 thin strips of pistachio nut or blanched almond

Put the ground almonds in a bowl with 1½ oz/45 g of the icing sugar and stir well to mix. Slowly blend in the rosewater with a fork, to form a sticky mixture. With slightly damp hands, roll out small amounts of dough between your palms until slightly larger than a pea. Taper each one slightly at the end, then roll in the remaining icing sugar until evenly coated. Insert a strip of nut into the thicker end to resemble a mulberry stalk. Place well apart on a flat plate and leave uncovered in a cool place for at least 1 hour. Store in a single layer in an airtight tin.

Makes about 48.

FOOD FOR THOUGHT

My father's knowledge of English was very good, and he would often read stories to us children, translating them from English into Persian. Although there were several years between my three brothers, my sister and myself, we would all gather round my father in the corner of the garden at Yazd to listen eagerly to his reading in the warm, soft autumn sunlight. He would read with great feeling, and he made every new story as exciting as the last. My mother contributed to these treats with trays of milk and a dash of tea or coffee, served with her homemade sweets. We looked forward to this part of the family evening as eagerly as to the stories, and she seemed to always manage to produce something different.

BUSTLE AND SMELLS

Khiyabane Pahlavi (Pahlavi Avenue) was about ten miles long – one of the longest roads in Tehran – and I loved it; it had so much character. Starting from the main railway station you passed lots of different shops and many cafés. Firooz would take me there. I never tired of walking along that avenue, looking at the many different designs of Persian rugs and carpets hanging on the street walls and lying on the pavements – the tiny shops were far too small for potential customers to measure the carpets inside.

Large, high beech trees formed miles of arcade along the avenue, beside which ran a canal from the Shemiran mountain region. Students would stroll along with piles of books, and everyone would be vying for a seat in one of the many cafés which had tables and chairs by the water, out of the sun's heat. The smell of confectionery from these cafés was so enticing!

Coconut Drops

Ghatreh-e-nargil

2 large egg whites
3 oz/90 g icing sugar
¼ teaspoon vanilla essence
3 oz/90 g desiccated coconut

Preheat the oven to 300°F/150°C/gas mark 2. Grease a flat, heavy baking tray and dust well with flour or line with non-stick baking parchment.

Whisk the egg whites until stiff. Gently fold in the icing sugar with a large metal spoon, then gently fold in the vanilla essence and coconut until a sticky mixture is formed.

Place ½ teaspoonfuls of the mixture on the greased or lined tray, spacing them ¼ inch/5 mm apart to allow for slight spreading. Bake in the oven for 10 minutes until risen and golden. Remove from the tray with a palette knife while still hot and transfer to a plate. Leave until cold, then store in an airtight tin.

Makes about 45.

TRADITIONAL SIGHTS AND TASTES

A very ancient, pre-Islamic tradition was to visit the Zurkhaneh (House of Strength). This beautifully decorated circular building has a high central dome, beneath which are circular rows of seats. Well-built, athletic men, often with tattoos, used to perform there, showing off their strength and other skills such as juggling with weighted clubs. These men could toss their heavey clubs right up to the apex of the ceiling and dome, and I shall never forget the day my English husband and I visited this unique show. We were so engrossed in watching the acts that we nibbled our way through a whole box of SHIRINI-E-GERDU BA ZAN-JAFIL!

Walnut Ginger Nibbles

Shirini-e-gerdu ba zanjafil

7 tablespoons oil
2 oz/60 g icing sugar
1 heaped teaspoon ground ginger
2 oz/60 g shelled walnuts, finely chopped
4 oz/115 g plain flour
1 egg yolk, beaten, to glaze
a few chopped nuts, to decorate

Have ready an ungreased flat baking tray. Pour the oil into a bowl, add the icing sugar and mix with a fork until smooth. Add the ginger and walnuts, then the flour. With your hands, gather the dough together until well blended and smooth. Wrap in foil and chill in the refrigerator for 30 minutes. Meanwhile, preheat the oven to 350°F/180°C/gas mark 4.

Take hazelnut-sized balls of the dough and roll until smooth. Gently press to ¼ inch/5 mm thick in the palms of your hands and place on the ungreased tray. Brush with the beaten egg yolk to glaze, then sprinkle with a few chopped nuts. Bake in the oven for about 16 minutes until golden and lightly risen. Leave to cool on the tray, then store in an airtight tin.

Makes about 32.

SNEEZES AND SPICES

BISCUIT-E-DARCHIN were my sister's favourites. One day, just after she got married, she came to visit my parents and while sitting chatting and munching a plateful of these biscuits, she told us she had lost all her sense of smell – even for these spicy favourites.

Some while later, on another visit, she suddenly sneezed – and dislodged a large water melon seed that had got stuck some years earlier when she was eating melon. She immediately recognised the familiar spicy aroma of the biscuits, and realised that from that moment her sense of smell had returned.

Sweet Spice Biscuits

Biscuit-e-darchin

6 tablespoons oil
1½ oz/45 g icing sugar
1 heaped teaspoon best-quality ground cinnamon
3 oz/90 g plain flour
1 egg yolk, beaten, to glaze
poppy seeds, to decorate

Pour the oil into a bowl, add the sugar and cinnamon and mix with a fork until smooth. Stir in the flour, then knead to a smooth dough with your hands. Chill in the refrigerator for 15–20 minutes. Meanwhile, preheat the oven to 350°F/180°C/gas mark 4 and have ready an ungreased flat baking tray.

Take hazelnut-sized balls of the dough and roll until smooth. Gently press to ¼-inch/5 mm thick in the palms of your hands and place on the ungreased tray. Brush with the beaten egg yolk to glaze, then sprinkle with poppy seeds. Bake in the oven for 10 minutes. Remove from the tray when slightly cool and transfer to a plate. Store in an airtight tin.

Makes about 26.

MOONSHINE

One of the most interesting things I learned from my father was that winter moonshine is the same as summer sunshine.

I can remember quite vividly waking up one winter's night, looking out of my window and seeing the ground covered in white. I was delighted: the snow was so deep that I wouldn't have to go to school the next day. I went back to a warm bed and contented sleep.

It seemed just a few moments later that my mother called me saying that I'd be late for school. I opened my eyes sleepily, puzzled that I was expected to go to school in such thick snow. Then I realised that what I had seen had been bright moonshine and not snow!

When the heavy snow really did fall and there was a full moon and a clear sky it was easy to imagine the garden was bathed in summer sunshine.

ᘓᘖᘇᘖᘒ

Moonshine Surprises

Shirini-e-mah

½ teaspoon ground saffron

1½ heaped teaspoons freshly ground cardamom

---

2 fl oz/50 ml oil, plus 1 teaspoon

---

3 oz/90 g icing sugar

---

1 large egg, beaten

---

6 oz/175 g rice flour (*not* ground rice)

---

about 30 shelled pistachio nuts or 15 blanched almonds, halved

---

poppy seeds, to decorate

Put the saffron in a bowl, add 1 tablespoon boiling water and stir well to mix. Add the cardamom, 2 fl oz/50 ml oil and the icing sugar. Mix until smooth, then blend in the egg and rice flour. Knead with your hands to a soft dough, cover the bowl and chill in the refrigerator for 15–20 minutes. Meanwhile, preheat the oven to 300°F/150°C/gas mark 2 and grease a flat, heavy baking tray.

Moisten your hands with 1 teaspoon oil. Take hazelnut-sized balls of the dough and roll until smooth. Make a small hole in the centre of the balls and insert 1 pistachio or almond in each. Close up the hole, then press in the palms of your hand to about ¼ inch/5 mm thickness. Place on the greased and floured tray. Using the open end of a thimble, or similar small object, press a pattern on top of each ball of dough, then sprinkle over a few poppy seeds. Bake at the bottom of the oven for about 15 minutes or until the moons have risen. Remove from the oven, leave to cool on the tray, then store in an airtight tin.

Makes about 30.

SWEET WELCOME

One evening, I was sitting chatting with some friends, and our hostess brought in some delicious-looking coffee. I had not yet tasted mine when I noticed several of the others pulling strange faces. Just as I was about to take a sip, a number of my friends burst out laughing . . . our hostess had mistakenly used salt instead of sugar!

All was forgiven when she produced some fresh coffee, with sugar – and plates of delicious GHAND-E-SHEKOOFEH. These biscuits are so called because they crack open slightly during baking and look a little like flowerbuds.

꧁꧂

Flower Bud Biscuits

Ghand-e-shekoofeh

6½ tablespoons oil
2 oz/60 g caster sugar
½ teaspoon baking powder
4 oz/115 g plain flour
1 egg white, beaten, to glaze
poppy seeds, to decorate

Pour the oil into a bowl, add the sugar and baking powder and mix with a fork until smooth. Stir in the flour, then knead to a smooth dough with your hands. Cover the bowl and chill in the refrigerator for 15–20 minutes. Meanwhile, preheat the oven to 350°F/180°C/gas mark 4 and have ready an ungreased flat baking tray.

Take hazelnut-sized balls of the dough and roll until smooth. Gently press to ¼ inch/5 mm thick in the palms of your hands and place on the ungreased tray, spacing them slightly apart to allow for spreading. Brush with the beaten egg white to glaze and sprinkle with poppy seeds. Bake in the oven for 16–18 minutes. Remove from the oven, leave to cool on the tray, then store in an airtight tin.

Makes about 26.

SECRET GREED

As a child I loved reading novels and my favourite place on hot summer days was the cool cellar (*ziramin*), to which I would retreat and get immersed in a good story. I remember one particular day when I got a scolding from my mother. I had got so engrossed in my book, munching BISCUIT-E-NARGIL, that I had forgotten all about my school homework. Not only that, but by the time my mother realised where I was I had eaten all the biscuits, and left none for the rest of the family!

꧁꧂

Coconut Biscuits

Biscuit-e-nargil

7 tablespoons oil
2 oz/60 g icing sugar
2 oz/60 g desiccated coconut
3 oz/90 g plain flour
1 egg white, beaten, to glaze
poppy seeds, to decorate

Pour the oil into a bowl, add the sugar and mix with a fork until smooth. Stir in the coconut and flour, then knead to a soft dough with your hands – at first it will be crumbly, but continue gathering the dough together with both hands and kneading between your palms until soft. Cover the bowl and chill in the refrigerator for 15–20 minutes. Meanwhile, preheat the oven to 350°F/180°C/gas mark 4. Grease a flat, heavy baking tray and dust well with flour.

Take hazelnut-sized balls of the dough and roll until smooth. Gently press to ¼ inch/5 mm thick and place on the greased tray. Brush with the beaten egg white to glaze and sprinkle with poppy seeds. Bake in the oven on the shelf just above centre for 8–10 minutes until risen and light golden. Remove from the oven, leave to cool slightly on the tray, then transfer to a plate and leave until cold. Store in an airtight tin.

Makes about 36.

POLITE DISAPPOINTMENT

My parents were living in Esfahan and had made some very good friends, when my aunt came to visit from Shiraz. My mother took my aunt with her on a visit to some of her new friends, who welcomed them both with trays full of beautiful sweets. My mother declined them, insisting that as they had just had lunch they really didn't want a thing to eat. My aunt said nothing and the trays were duly removed.

As soon as they got back to my parents' house, however, my aunt exclaimed that she was very upset, as she had longed to taste one of the sweets!

To this day the story is repeated in our family as a warning not to refuse what you are offered – particularly on someone else's behalf!

ᏝᏬᎨᏕᏕ

Date and Cinnamon Rolls

Shirini-e-khorma va darchin

PASTRY

6 oz/175 g self-raising flour
1 heaped teaspoon ground cinnamon
3 oz/90 g butter or margarine, cut into small pieces
2 teaspoons lemon juice

FILLING

5 oz/140 g stoned dates, soaked overnight in 6 fl oz/175 ml cold water
½ oz/15 g butter or margarine
1 heaped teaspoon ground cinnamon
juice of 1 large lemon
1 oz/30 g ground almonds
icing sugar, for dusting

Prepare the pastry: sift the flour and cinnamon into a bowl. Add the butter or margarine and rub in with the fingertips until the mixture is crumbly. Add the lemon juice and about 1½ fl oz/37.5 ml ice-cold water to make a soft dough. Cover the bowl and chill in the refrigerator for 15–20 minutes.

Meanwhile, put the dates and their soaking liquid in a small, heavy saucepan. Bring to the boil, then reduce the heat to moderate and simmer until soft and creamy, stirring with a wooden spoon. Add the butter or margarine, cinnamon, lemon juice and ground almonds. Stir well to mix, remove from the heat and stir in a further 1 fl oz/25 ml cold water if the mixture is too dry. Set aside to cool.

Preheat the oven to 350°F/180°C/gas mark 4 and have ready an ungreased flat baking tray. Divide the dough into 2 equal portions. Roll out 1 portion on a very lightly floured board to a 13 × 5 inch/32.5 × 12.5 cm rectangle. Spread the cooled filling to within ½ inch/1 cm of the edges. Roll the pastry over like a Swiss roll, then cut into ten 1 inch/2.5 cm pieces with a very sharp knife.

Lift the pieces carefully onto the ungreased tray, spacing them ½–1 inch/1–2.5 cm apart. Repeat with the second portion of dough. Bake in the oven for 12–15 minutes until risen and light golden. Remove the tray from the oven, dust the rolls with icing sugar, then transfer to a wire rack and leave to cool. Store in an airtight tin.

Makes about 20.

ᏝᏬᎨᏕᏕ

Chick Pea Tears

Nan-e-nokhodchi

---

2 oz/60 g butter, softened
1½ oz/45 g icing sugar
1 heaped teaspoon freshly ground cardamom
2¾ oz/80 g chick pea flour

Preheat the oven to 300°F/150°C/gas mark 2 and have ready an ungreased flat baking tray. Put the butter in a bowl, add the sugar and cardamom and whisk with an electric mixer until creamy. Sift in the chick pea flour and whisk again until a creamy consistency (don't worry if the dough crumbles at first – this is as it should be).

Gather the dough together with your hands and immediately roll out to ½ inch/1 cm thickness. Cut out 'tear' shapes with a small aspic cutter. Place on the ungreased tray and bake on the bottom shelf of the oven for 15 minutes. Leave to cool on the tray, then remove and store in an airtight tin.

Makes about 37.

FRESH DATES

As a child in Yazd I would hold Memeh's skirt as we went through the long dark bazaar to the parts that were bright with lights. In summer, water was sprayed to cool the air and in most shops there was a bubbling samovar. Every shop was different. I could hardly take my eyes off the large sacks of dates shining under the bright lights, and I seldom went home without Memeh treating me to some.

7

Baking

A BIT TOO TEMPTING

To this day I really can't forgive myself for letting my mother down in front of her guests. My sister and I had discovered one of our favourite cakes, CAKE ZORATI, carefully packed in a tin, awaiting the arrival of some very special friends. So when no-one was in sight, we two naughty children lifted each square of cake and pinched a taste from the bottom, replacing the thinner layer. A couple of days later my mother opened the tin – and offered her friends slices of half-eaten cake! She didn't think it was funny, but as well as keeping a sharper eye on us after that, she always made an extra CAKE ZORATI when visitors were expected.

ಒಂ೫ಿ೭.

Rosewater Cake

Cake zorati

SYRUP
2 oz/60 g granulated sugar
2 fl oz/50 ml rosewater
1 teaspoon lemon juice
¼ teaspoon freshly ground cardamom

CAKE
3 large eggs
5 fl oz/150 ml oil
5 fl oz/150 ml yoghurt
1½ heaped teaspoons baking powder
¼ heaped teaspoon freshly ground cardamom
8 oz/230 g semolina
4 oz/115 g caster sugar
about 2 teaspoons almond flakes, to decorate

Make the syrup: put the sugar in a small, heavy saucepan, add 2 fl oz/50 ml cold water and bring to the boil until beginning to thicken – about 5–7 minutes. Add the rosewater and lemon juice cardamom and bring back to the boil. Boil vigorously for 3 minutes or until a thin syrup is formed. Test by dropping a little syrup onto a cold plate: if it doesn't spread it is ready. Remove the pan from the heat and leave the syrup to cool.

Meanwhile, prepare the cake. Preheat the oven to 350°F/180°C/gas mark 4. Grease an 11 × 7 inch/ 28 × 18 cm cake tin with a *solid* base, 1½ inches/4 cm deep. Dust well with flour. Beat the eggs in a bowl with the oil, yoghurt, baking powder and cardamom. Beat in the semolina and sugar to form a runny consistency, then pour into the prepared tin. Roll the flaked almonds in a little flour and sprinkle over the cake.

Bake the cake in the oven for 17–20 minutes until risen and golden. Remove from the oven, cut into 1½ inch/4 cm squares or diamonds, but do not remove from the tin. Spoon on the cooled rosewater syrup, then leave to cool completely. Transfer the cake to a plastic container (not metal). Store in the refrigerator and eat within a few days.

AN ABUNDANCE OF CITRUS

Friends from the citrus area of Shiraz and the northern part of Persia would give us large boxes of fruit. The juice would be squeezed to use in cakes and the rind dried for ORANGE RICE later in the year. Everyone in the family was willing to help prepare the fruit.

ಒಂ೫ಿ೭.

Yoghurt Citrus Cake

Cake morabiyat

4 eggs, separated
6 oz/175 g caster sugar
finely grated rind of 1 lemon or orange
10 fl oz/300 ml oil
1½ heaped teaspoons baking powder
4 fl oz/120 ml plain yoghurt
8 oz/230 g plain flour
almond flakes, to decorate

Preheat the oven to 400°F/200°C/gas mark 6. Grease a 7 inch/18 cm square cake tin with a removable base and dust with flour. Beat the egg yolks with the sugar until creamy and white, then beat in the lemon or orange rind, the oil, baking powder and yoghurt. Slowly sift in the flour and beat until smooth.

Whisk the egg whites in a separate bowl until stiff, then fold into the flour mixture with a large metal spoon until thoroughly blended. Pour into the prepared tin and sprinkle with flaked almonds. Bake in the oven for 20 minutes, then reduce the heat to 350°F/180°C/gas mark 4 and bake for a further 20 minutes. Remove the tin from the oven, turn the cake out on to a wire rack and leave to cool. Store in an airtight tin for up to 1 week.

CAKE OR BREAD?

KOMACH is a wonderful sweet yeast bread, a cross between a bread and a cake recipe, which has been passed down through families of Zoroastrians for hundreds of years.

When we went on a picnic, mother would make the dough at home then take it with us in a copper saucepan. After cooking the lunchtime *kabab*, she would bury the KOMACH in its covered copper pan under the hot charcoal. By the time the glow had completely died, the KOMACH would be perfectly cooked in time for tea.

ﻼﺧﻤﺎﭺ

Zoroastrian Cake

Komach

¼ oz/10 g dried yeast or ½ oz/15 g fresh
2 oz/60 g brown sugar
1 lb/455 g plain wholemeal flour
½ teaspoon salt
1 heaped teaspoon ground cinnamon
2 oz/60 g sultanas
1 heaped teaspoon freshly ground cardamom
2 oz/60 g chopped walnuts
2 oz/60 g chopped blanched almonds
2 large eggs, beaten
2 fl oz/50 ml milk
1½ fl oz/37.5 ml rosewater
1 heaped teaspoon baking powder
4 fl oz/120 ml oil

Dissolve the yeast and 1 teaspoon of the sugar in 2 fl oz/50 ml warm water. Leave in a warm place for 5–10 minutes until frothy. Mix the flour and salt together in a large bowl. Make a well in the centre and add the remaining sugar, the cinnamon, sultanas, cardamom, nuts and eggs. Add the frothing yeast, mix well and add the milk and rosewater, then slowly add about 4–5 fl oz/120–150 ml warm water to form a soft bread dough.

Dampen your hands with warm water. Knead the dough in the bowl for 10 minutes, then cover with a damp cloth and leave in a warm place until doubled in bulk. Remove the cloth and add the baking powder. Dampen your hands again with warm water and knead the dough for a further 4–5 minutes. Cover and leave in a warm place again until doubled in bulk.

Preheat the oven to 350°F/180°C/gas mark 4. Pour the oil into a 2 inch/5 cm deep, 8 inch/20.5 cm square dish. Place in the oven to heat for 7–10 minutes. Place the risen dough in the hot oil, taking care to disturb it as little as possible. Bake in the oven for 35–40 minutes until risen and golden. Leave to cool in the dish so that the oil is absorbed, then remove and cut into squares to serve.

CASTING AWAY A BAD DREAM

A charming Zoroastrian custom, which is still in practice today, is the casting away of a bad dream. On waking from a bad dream you must cast it away by telling the story of the dream to three pieces of bread. Then you throw the three pieces of bread out of the house. The birds will then come and take the bread (and the dream) away.

DAILY BREADS

You will always find at least three different varieties of *nan* (bread) in any Persian household. *Nan* is part of every meal – breakfast, lunch, dinner, picnics and even dinner parties – and is usually made fresh every day.

BARBARY is only eaten at breakfast time, still hot from the nearby bakery where you can see it being made; LAVASH is a bread so thin that you can see through it. Traditionally it is wrapped in a cloth or tin, and should be kept in the refrigerator. It is eaten with kabab and PANIR VASABSI (page 151).

One of the traditional Persian breads is sangak, which is made by spreading the dough over pebbles then baking it in a clay oven (*tanoor*). I do not have a recipe for *sangak*, but HUSHVA NAN, a Zoroastrian bread eaten with KABAB and other main courses, is very similar.

CRISPY MILK BREAD AND CINNAMON TEA

One of my most nostalgic memories is of coming home while the autumn sun was still shining, to join the family gathering and dipping milk bread into sweet cinnamon tea . . . even if it did some-times spoil my appetite for dinner.

 දිම්දිම්

Crispy Milk Bread

Nan-e-shir

6 oz/175 g plain flour
1 teaspoon baking powder
⅛ teaspoon salt
2 oz/60 g caster sugar
½ teaspoon vanilla essence
2–3 fl oz/50–90 ml milk
extra plain flour for dusting

Preheat the oven to 300°F/150°C/gas mark 2 and dust a heavy, flat baking tray lightly with flour. Sift the flour, baking powder and salt into a bowl. Stir in the sugar and vanilla essence, then slowly add the milk and mix with your hands to a sticky dough. Place the dough on a floured board and knead for 1 minute until soft.

Dust the board with flour again, put the dough in the centre and roll out to a 12 × 7 inch/30 × 18 cm rectangle. Brush off the excess flour and lift the dough onto the floured tray. If not already slightly torn, make a small tear near the corner. Place on the bottom shelf of the oven and bake for 20 minutes. Reduce the heat to 250°F/130°C/gas mark ½ and bake for a further 1¼ hours or until the bread is completely dry and can be lifted with one hand. Store in an airtight tin.

THE MUSICAL SHEPHERD

When we lived in Manshad, our favourite walk was along the slopes of the mountains where we could see the stream pouring down to the reservoir, glistening in the reflection of the sun. Numerous almond trees, their branches laden with nuts, would overshadow the stream and we often came across the old shepherd under one of the largest of these trees, shaded under the branches and his old felt hat. His small batique cloth (*sofreh*) was spread out beside him and he would be looking straight ahead as if deep in thought. His rough, working hands broke off pieces of thick *nan* and chunks of homemade cheese (*panir*), and he took large bites of homegrown onion, pointing out the sheep and goats to us as they spread out along the mountain slope.

He used to take a drink from the crystal clear stream and wipe his mouth clean with the back of his hand when he had finished eating, then he would fold up the empty *sofreh*, place it behind his head and rest back against the trunk of the tree. Stretching out his legs, he took his homemade flute out of his pocket and played the most hypno-tic tune, the sound of the animal bells acting as a kind of background music. The combination of these sounds echoed magically around the moun-tains and brought us to a standstill. We would sit ourselves down and listen to this free wild concert and it was very difficult to leave. But we had to get to our destination and eventually we resumed our walk, waving to him with the sign of Khodahafez, which means 'God be with you'. He would answer back with a nod of the head, and the sweet sound of his flute would follow us for a long way along the mountain path.

꧁꧂

Cinnamon Loaf

Nan-e-darchin

¼ oz/10 g dried yeast or ½ oz fresh
1 teaspoon sugar preferably brown
1½ lb/685 g plain wholemeal flour
1 teaspoon salt
2 tablespoons oil
1 heaped teaspoon brown sugar
1½ teaspoons ground cinnamon
1 teaspoon milk, to glaze
1 teaspoon sesame seeds

Dissolve the yeast and sugar in 2 fl oz/50 ml warm water and leave in a warm place for 5–10 minutes until frothy. Mix the flour and salt together in a large bowl. Stir in the oil and cinnamon. Make a well in the centre, add the frothing yeast and slowly add 16–18 fl oz/475–500 ml warm water to form a soft dough. Knead the dough in the bowl for 10 minutes, then cover with a damp cloth and leave in a warm place until doubled in bulk, about 1–1½ hours. Transfer the dough to a board and knead hard for 5 minutes.

Grease a 1½ lb/685 g loaf tin and dust with flour. Place the dough in the tin and brush with the milk to glaze. Sprinkle with the sesame seeds and leave in a warm place again until doubled in bulk.

Preheat the oven to 400°F/200°C/gas mark 6. Bake the loaf for 20 minutes at this temperature, then reduce the heat to 350°F/180°C/gas mark 4 and bake for a further 35 minutes. Turn the bread out of the tin onto a wire rack and leave to cool.

꧁꧂

Zoroastrian Nan

Hushva nan

This was one of my mother's specialities and there was always some in the house: to satisfy her large family she sometimes had to make it three times a week. As a little girl it was a great treat when she allowed me to spread my own small piece of dough in the corner of the *tabeh*, the large frying pan used for making HUSHVA.

¼ oz dried yeast or ½ oz fresh
1 teaspoon sugar
1 lb/455 g plain wholemeal flour
1 teaspoon salt
1 tablespoon oil

Dissolve the yeast and sugar in 2 fl oz/50 ml warm water. Leave in a warm place for 5–10 minutes until frothy. Mix the flour and salt together in a large bowl. Make a well in the centre, add the frothing yeast, oil, and slowly add 12 fl oz/350 ml warm water. Gather the flour into a dough with your hands, knead in the bowl for 4–5 minutes, then cover with a damp cloth and leave in a warm place until doubled in bulk. As this dough is looser than most it can rise very high so check frequently – it will take between 15 minutes and 1 hour depending on the warmth of the room.

Dampen your hands with warm water, knead the dough again, adding up to 2 fl oz/50 ml warm water until the dough becomes fairly loose but not runny. Cover with a damp cloth and leave in a warm place again until doubled in bulk.

Preheat the grill to hot. Heat a lightly greased 12 inch/30 cm cast iron frying pan on the hob. Using both hands, remove one-third of the dough and gently form into a ball the size of a large orange. Place in the middle of the hot pan. Dampen your hands with water and pat the dough up and down with your fingers to spread the dough out. With one hand only, pat the dough into a circle to fill the pan. Reduce the heat and cook for 2–3 minutes. Place the pan under the grill, about 4 inches/10 cm from the heat, and cook for 3–4 minutes. With a fish slice, transfer to a wire rack and leave to cool. Divide the remaining dough and repeat twice more, remembering to wet your hands each time before handling the dough. Eat fresh, or freeze for up to 1 month.

Makes 3 *nan*.

EARLY MORNING BAKE

A scene I often recall is the men on their bicycles riding through Tehran first thing in the morning, BARBARY NAN tied on behind their seats. I also remember the long queues of people waiting to collect the hot *nan* from the *tanoor* at nearby shops. Some of their children still looked sleepy, but they were hungry, and awaited their turn with eagerness. They could then enjoy a piece on the way home, eating it just as it was. Split open and stuffed, BARBARY NAN makes a very convenient 'sandwich'.

ᘓᘍᕁᘓᕁ

Barbary Nan

Barbary nan

This recipe makes enough dough to make three *nan*. You can bake them one at a time or two together, remembering to get the oven as hot as it can possibly be before starting each bake. BARBARY NAN freezes well, for up to 1 month.

¼ oz/10 g dried yeast or ½ oz fresh
1 teaspoon sugar
1 lb/455 g plain wholemeal flour
1 teaspoon salt
1 tablespoon milk, to glaze
1 tablespoon sesame seeds, to decorate (optional)
1 fl oz/25 ml oil, plus 1 tablespoon

Dissolve the yeast and sugar in 2 fl oz/50 ml warm water and leave in a warm place for 5–10 minutes until frothy. Mix the flour and salt together in a large bowl. Make a well in the centre, add the frothing yeast and slowly mix in 9–10 fl oz/250–300 ml warm water with one hand. Dampen your hands with warm water, knead with the extra tablespoon of oil in the bowl for 10 minutes, then cover with a damp cloth and leave in a warm place until doubled in bulk.

Knead the dough again vigorously. Place the dough in the middle of a floured board and divide into three equal parts. Form each piece into an oval and roll out on the floured board to ¼ inch/5 mm thickness. Transfer to a well–floured baking tray. Dab the milk all over the *nan* with your fingers and sprinkle with the sesame seeds, if using. Leave in a warm place again until doubled in bulk.

Pour the oil onto a heavy, flat baking tray and place on the shelf just below the centre of the oven. Preheat the oven to its highest temperature. Gently lift the *nan* on to the hot tray, return to the oven and reduce the temperature to 475°F/240°C/gas mark 9. Bake for 13 minutes until the bread has risen and is light golden. Transfer to a wire rack and leave to cool before serving.

ᘓᘍᕁᘓᕁ

Turmeric and Cumin Nan

Nan-e-zardchoobeh

TURMERIC AND CUMIN NAN gives an interesting change of taste and colour to the table. It makes an unusual snack on its own; served with cheese or salad, it makes a filling lunch.

2 fl oz/50 ml oil
1 medium onion, peeled and finely chopped
1 heaped teaspoon turmeric
¼ oz/10 g dried yeast or ½ oz fresh
1 heaped teaspoon sugar
1½ lb/685 g plain wholemeal flour
1½ teaspoons baking powder
1 teaspoon cumin seeds
1 heaped teaspoon salt
10 fl oz/300 ml plain yoghurt

Heat the oil in a heavy frying pan, add the onion and fry gently until golden. Add the turmeric and stir for 1 minute, then remove from the heat and leave to cool.

Dissolve the yeast and sugar in 2 fl oz/50 ml of warm water and leave in a warm place for 10–15 minutes until frothy. Mix the flour, baking powder, cumin seeds and salt together in a large bowl. Make a well in the centre, add the frothing yeast and 8 fl oz/225 ml yoghurt. Knead in the bowl, gradually working in the cooled onion and turmeric and mixing in about 7 fl oz/200 ml warm water and the remaining yoghurt to form a soft dough. Knead in the bowl for a further 10 minutes, then dust the dough lightly with flour and cover with a damp cloth. Leave in a warm place until doubled in bulk.

Preheat the grill to hot. Heat a lightly greased 12 inch/30 cm cast iron frying pan on the hob. Turn the dough out onto a lightly floured surface and knead for 3 minutes. Divide into 6 equal balls and dust with a little more flour if too sticky. Roll each ball of dough to an 11 inch/28 cm round and brush off any excess flour.

Place the *nan* in the hot pan, reduce the heat to very low and cook for about 3 minutes. Place the pan under the grill about 4 inches/10 cm from the heat, and cook for 4 minutes until bubbles rise. With a fish slice, transfer to a wire rack and leave to cool. Repeat with the remaining dough, remembering to increase the heat between each cooking so that the pan is very hot when the *nan* is first put into it.

Makes 6 *nan*.

꧁꧂

Sesame Nan

Nan-e-khaskhkosh

Once a month we were visited by a specialist baker and the old man would spend the whole day making *nan* in the clay oven (*tanoor*). Afterwards, a whole lamb was put into the oven and friends and relations would come to share the feast.

1 lb/455 g plain flour
1 heaped teaspoon baking powder
½ teaspoon salt
1 teaspoon sugar
14–15 fl oz/400–450 ml plain yoghurt
1 tablespoon sesame seeds

Sift the flour, baking powder and salt into a large bowl. Stir in the sugar, then slowly add the yoghurt a little at a time and knead to form a soft dough that is not too loose. If more yoghurt is necessary, carefully add a little more. Knead in the bowl for 10 minutes, then cover and leave in a warm place for about 1 hour.

Preheat the grill to hot. Heat a lightly greased 12 inch/30 cm cast iron frying pan on the hob. Turn the dough out on to a well-floured surface and knead for 3 minutes. Divide into 3 equal balls and roll each into an 11 inch/28 cm round. Sprinkle with the sesame seeds and press them in with the rolling pin. Place the *nan* in the hot pan, reduce the heat to low and cook for about 3 minutes. Place the pan under the grill, about 4 inches/10 cm from the heat, and cook for 4 minutes until bubbles rise. With a fish slice, transfer to a wire rack and leave to cool. Repeat with the remaining dough, remembering to increase the heat between each cooking so that the pan is very hot when the *nan* is first put into it.

Makes 3 *nan*.

LAVASH ON FRIDAYS

Friday was a general holiday, like Sunday in the West, and this was the day we had our family gathering. I remember waking up from my nap on summer afternoons to the sound of my brother Firooz watering the persimmon trees and the creeping rose trellis in the garden.

Our house in Tehran was of modern design with floor to ceiling picture windows. The kitchen was extremely modern, with both electricity and gas laid on. The everyday electric samovar was always on the kitchen table, with the teapot (*ghoori*) on top brewing away for most of the day. We also had a traditional brass samovar which was lit by coal, but this was only brought out on very special occasions.

The hall in the centre of the house acted as the family dining room and I remember how beautiful it looked when the family was due to arrive, with its dark, highly polished walnut table covered with a hand-embroidered white cloth. On Fridays it was laden with different dishes such as savoury cake (*kuku*), savoury meat balls (*shami*), small dishes of natural yoghurt (*mast*) sprinkled decoratively with mint, homemade cheese (*panir*) and fresh salad (*sabsi khordan*) of mint, tarragon, spring onions and basil. Radishes made a colourful garnish for all of these dishes. Paper-thin LAVASH bread was cut into triangular or square shapes and placed all around the table for everyone to help themselves. We would fill the LAVASH with some of the cooked dishes and salad, then roll it into a kind of sandwich. To drink we had sweet black tea sprinkled with cinnamon, and the room was filled with soft Persian music. The family took it in turns to entertain like this on Fridays, and often a new dish would be tried out. It was almost like a competition to see who could cook the most interesting new dish.

Lavash Nan

Nan-e-lavash

8 oz/230 g plain flour
½ teaspoon salt
1 tablespoon oil
about 5 fl oz/150 ml plain yoghurt

Sift the flour and salt into a large bowl. Add the oil and slowly add the yoghurt, mixing with your hands until a soft dough is formed. If more yoghurt is needed, add it very gradually, a little at a time.

Turn the dough out onto a floured board and knead for about 4–5 minutes. Divide into 8 equal balls, then roll each ball of dough to an 11 inch/ 28 cm round.

Preheat the grill to hot. Lightly grease a 12 inch/ 30 cm cast iron frying pan and place under the preheated grill until hot. Remove the pan from the grill, brush off any excess flour from the *nan* and place in the pan. Return to the hot grill and cook for 35–40 seconds, or until bubbles rise. Turn the *nan* over and grill the other side in the same way.

Remove the *nan* from the pan and immediately wrap in a large sheet of foil (to prevent steam escaping). Repeat with the remaining 7 pieces of *nan*, piling them all up in the foil parcel. Leave to cool, then overwrap the foil in a polythene bag. Store in the refrigerator for up to 2 weeks.

Makes 8 *nan*.

Basic Nan

Nan-e-sadeh

¼ oz dried or ½ oz fresh yeast
1 pound wholemeal flour
½ teaspoon salt
1 teaspoon sugar
1 tablespoon oil and a little extra for greasing the pan

Dissolve the yeast and sugar in 3 oz warm water and place in a warm place to rise which takes approx 10 minutes. Place the flour and the salt into a large mixing bowl and add in the frothy yeast. Slowly add approx 8/9 oz water and knead until a soft dough is formed. Knead for at least five minutes. Cover with a damp cloth and allow to rise in a warm and draught free place. Remove the bowl add in a tablespoon of the oil and knead again. Return back in the warm place to rise, which takes approx one hour. Divide the dough into 9/10 equal balls, and roll out each to approx 5/6 inch circles on a floured work surface. Remove the excess flour, put a lightly greased 12 inch round frying pan on high heat and turn the grill fully on. Place the nan into the frying pan, lower the heat and leave for one or two minutes until the bubbles appear. Place the nan under the hot grill 4 inches away from the heat and cook for about 2/3 minutes until risen and golden. Remove to wire tray to cool repeat until completed.

8

Jams, Pickles and Drinks

Jams are traditionally made at home, with recipes handed down in families from one generation to another. There is no such thing as 'tea-time' as in the West, so jam is usually served for breakfast.

Spicy Cherry Jam

Moraba-ye-alubalu

8 oz/230 g pitted fresh black cherries
2 tablespoons lemon juice
8 oz/230 g preserving sugar
1 teaspoon ground cinnamon

Put the cherries in a heavy saucepan (preferably a preserving pan), add the lemon juice and 3 table-spoons cold water and bring to the boil. Reduce the heat, cover and simmer for 15 minutes.

Remove the pan from the heat, add the sugar and cinnamon and stir well to mix with a wooden spoon. Return to the heat and boil vigorously for 3–4 minutes or until the ingredients are soft and setting point is reached. Pour into warm sterilised jars, leave to cool, then cover and store.

Makes about 12 oz/350 g.

Carrot Jam

Moraba-ye-havij

8 oz/230 g grated carrots, or carrot pulp (chopped in a food processor)
10 oz/285 g preserving sugar
4 tablespoons lemon juice
2 oz/60 g blanched almonds or other nuts, finely chopped
3 tablespoons rosewater

Put the carrots in a heavy saucepan (preferably a preserving pan), add 4 fl oz/120 ml cold water and bring to the boil. Reduce the heat, cover and simmer for 10–15 minutes or until the carrots are soft.

Remove the pan from the heat, add the remaining ingredients and stir well to mix with a wooden spoon. Return to the heat and boil vigorously for about 12 minutes or until setting point is reached. Pour into warm sterilised jars, leave to cool, then cover and store.

Makes about 1 lb/455 g.

Apple Jam

Moraba-ye-sib

8 oz/230 g finely grated eating apples
8 oz/230 g preserving sugar
2 tablespoons lemon juice
2 tablespoons rosewater
¼ teaspoon ground cardamom

Put the apples in a heavy saucepan (preferably a preserving pan), add 4 fl oz/120 ml cold water and bring to the boil. Reduce the heat, cover and simmer for 10–12 minutes or until the apples are stewed.

Remove the pan from the heat, add the remaining ingredients and stir well to mix with a wooden spoon. Return to the heat and boil vigorously for 10–15 minutes or until setting point is reached. Pour into warm sterilised jars, leave to cool, then cover and store.

Makes about 10 oz/285 g.

Pumpkin Jam

Moraba-ye-kadu zard

8 oz/230 g finely grated pumpkin flesh, or pumpkin pulp (chopped in a food processor)
8 oz/230 g preserving sugar

2 tablespoons rosewater

finely grated rind and juice of 1 large lemon

1 teaspoon ground cinnamon

Put all the ingredients in a heavy saucepan (preferably a preserving pan) and heat gently until the sugar has dissolved. Bring to the boil, then reduce the heat and cook moderately for 25–30 minutes or until setting point is reached. Pour into warm sterilised jars, leave to cool, then cover and store.

Makes about 12 oz/350 g.

Cucumber Jam

Moraba-ye-khiyar

8 oz/230 g thinly sliced peeled cucumber

6 oz/175 g preserving sugar

2 fl oz/50 ml rosewater

3 tablespoons lemon juice

Put the cucumber in a heavy saucepan (preferably a preserving pan), cover with about ½ pint/300 ml cold water and bring to the boil. Reduce the heat, cover and simmer for about 10 minutes or until the cucumber is soft.

Drain the cucumber then return to the rinsed-out pan and mash with a potato masher or fork. Add the sugar, rosewater and lemon juice and stir over moderate heat for about 5 minutes. Bring to the boil and boil vigorously for about 8–10 minutes or until setting point is reached. Pour the jam into warm sterilised jars, leave to cool, then cover and store.

Makes 6–7 oz/175–200 g.

Aubergine Rosewater Jam

Moraba-ye-badimjam
ba golab

14 oz/400 g aubergines

8 oz/230 g preserving sugar

2 fl oz/50 ml rosewater

3 tablespoons lemon juice

Bring a heavy saucepan (preferably a preserving pan) of water to the boil. Peel the aubergines and slice thinly. Drop them immediately into the boiling water (to prevent them turning black) and simmer for 8–10 minutes until soft. Drain, then return to the rinsed-out pan and mash with a potato masher or fork. Add the sugar, rosewater and lemon juice and stir over moderate heat for about 5 minutes. Bring to the boil and boil vigorously for 8–10 minutes or until setting point is reached. Pour into warm sterilized jars, leave to cool, then cover and store.

Makes about 13 oz/375 g.

Quince Jam

Moraba-ye-beh

5–6 oz/140–175 g quinces, chopped to a pulp (preferably in a food processor)

5 oz/150 g preserving sugar

juice of 1 large lemon

2 fl oz/50 ml rosewater

¼ teaspoon ground cardamom

Put the quince pulp in a heavy saucepan (preferably a preserving pan), cover with about 11 fl oz/325 ml cold water and bring to the boil. Reduce the heat, cover (if the pan is not covered the quince will lose colour) and simmer for 30–35 minutes or until soft.

Add the sugar, lemon juice, rosewater and cardamom. Cover and boil vigorously for 2–3 minutes or until setting point is reached. Pour the jam into warm sterilised jars, leave to cool, then cover and store.

Makes about 6–7 oz/175–200 g.

Orange and Carrot Marmalade

Moraba-ye-porteghal va havij

8 oz/230 g coarsely grated carrots
10 oz/285 g sugar, preferably brown
2 small oranges
2 tablespoons lemon juice

Put the carrots in a heavy saucepan (preferably a preserving pan), cover with 3–4 fl oz/50–85 ml cold water and bring to the boil. Reduce the heat, cover and simmer for 8–10 minutes or until the carrots are soft.

Remove the pan from the heat and stir in the sugar. Remove the rind from the oranges with a zester or canelle knife. Rinse under hot running water, then halve the oranges and squeeze the juice (there should be 3 fl oz/85 ml). Add to the pan with the lemon juice. Bring to the boil and boil vigorously for about 12–15 minutes or until setting point is reached. Pour the marmalade into warm sterilised jars, leave to cool, then cover and store.

Makes 13–14 oz/375–400 g.

PICKLES/TORSHI

Persian pickles are uncomplicated, mostly made with just a few ounces of vinegar and fresh seasonal fruit or vegetables. They give a wonderful lift to even the most humble of dishes, and in some Middle Eastern countries even the liquid is kept after the pickle has been eaten so that it can be used to give extra flavour to plain dishes.

The longer you keep Persian pickles, the tastier they become.

Pickled Onions

Torshi-ye-piaz

12 oz/345 g pickling onions, peeled
12 fl oz/350 ml malt vinegar
3 garlic cloves, peeled and crushed
1 teaspoon crushed dried mint
1 teaspoon salt

Put all the ingredients in a heavy saucepan and bring to the boil over high heat. Boil vigorously for 1 minute, then remove from the heat and set aside to cool. Store in airtight jars.

Orange Relish

Torshi-ye-pust-e-porteghal

8 oz/230 g thinly pared orange peel
7 garlic cloves, peeled and crushed
2 oz/60 g preserving sugar
1 teaspoon salt
10–12 fl oz/300–350 ml malt vinegar

Put the orange peel in a small heavy saucepan, cover with cold water and bring to the boil. Reduce the heat and simmer uncovered for 2 minutes. Drain, cover with cold water and repeat. Drain again, place on kitchen paper and leave overnight.

The next day, grind the orange peel in an electric grinder, then place in a heavy saucepan (preferably a preserving pan) with the garlic, sugar and salt, and enough vinegar to cover. Bring to the boil and boil vigorously for 2 minutes, then remove from the heat and set aside to cool. Store in airtight jars.

Makes about 1¼ lb.

Pickled Aubergines

Torshi-ye-badimjan

---
1 lb/455 g very tiny pickling aubergines, stems removed
---
3 teaspoons salt

½ pint/300 ml malt vinegar
---
1 head of garlic, divided into cloves, peeled and crushed
---
4 teaspoons raw cane sugar

4–5 sprigs each fresh mint and tarragon, finely chopped, or 1 teaspoon each dried
---
a little pepper, to taste

Cut a small lengthways slit in the centre of each aubergine. Simmer in water with 2 teaspoons of the salt for 5–6 minutes, then drain well.

Put the aubergines in a heavy saucepan (preferably a preserving pan) with the remaining ingredients. Bring to the boil and boil vigorously for 4–5 minutes, then remove from the heat and set aside to cool. Store in warm airtight jars.

Pickled Aubergine with Herbs

Torshi-ye-badimjan va sabsi

---
10 oz/285 g aubergines
---
salt
---
4 oz/115 g chopped mixed fresh herbs (basil, coriander, dill, mint and tarragon)
---
1 head of garlic, divided into cloves, peeled and crushed
---
1 teaspoon cumin seeds

4–5 fl oz/120–150 ml malt vinegar

Put the aubergines under a preheated hot grill for about 15 minutes, turning them about every 3 minutes, until softened and wrinkled. Leave until cool enough to handle, then peel, place on kitchen paper and sprinkle with a little salt. Leave to dégorge for 2–3 hours.

Chop the aubergine, then place in a heavy saucepan (preferably a preserving pan). Add the herbs, garlic, cumin seeds and 1 teaspoon salt, and enough vinegar to cover. Bring to the boil and boil vigorously for 3–4 minutes, then remove from the heat and set aside to cool. Store in airtight jars.

Pickled Garlic

Torshi-ye-sir

---
1 lb/455 g garlic cloves, peeled

10–12 fl oz/300–350 ml malt vinegar
---
1 teaspoon salt

Put the garlic cloves in a heavy saucepan (preferably a preserving pan) with enough vinegar to cover. Add the salt and bring to the boil, then remove from the heat and set aside to cool. Store in airtight jars.

Date and Tamarind Chutney

Torshi-ye-khorma

---
8 oz/230 g pitted dates

½ pint/300 ml TAMARIND LIQUID (page 149)
---
2 fl oz/50 ml lemon juice
---
1 head of garlic, divided into cloves, peeled and crushed
---
2 oz/50 g sultanas
---
1 oz/30 g ground mixed spice

⅛ teaspoon cayenne pepper
---
a little salt

Grind the dates to a paste in an electric grinder or food processor. Place in a heavy saucepan (preferably a preserving pan) with the tamarind liquid and bring to the boil. Reduce the heat, add the remaining ingredients and simmer uncovered for 30 minutes, stirring occasionally until thick and soft. Pour into warm sterilised jars, leave to cool, then cover and store.

Makes about 1¼ lb/565 g.

૪ૹ૪ૹ

Pickled Grapes

Torshi-ye-angoor

1 lb/455 g large white grapes
12 fl oz/350 ml malt vinegar
1–2 garlic cloves, peeled and crushed
1 teaspoon crushed dried mint
½ teaspoon salt

Wash the grapes and pat dry with kitchen paper. Put all the ingredients in a heavy saucepan (preferably a preserving pan) and stir once or twice, taking care not to crush the grapes. Bring to the boil and boil vigorously for 2 minutes, then remove from the heat and set aside to cool. Store in airtight jars.

૪ૹ૪ૹ

Pickled Cherries

Torshi-ye-gilas

1 lb/455 g black cherries, pitted
½ teaspoon salt
about 6 fl oz/175 ml malt vinegar

Wash the cherries and pat dry with kitchen paper. Spread them out on a clean cloth and leave to dry, in a safe place, for 2 days. It is important that they have dried out completely before the next step. Put the cherries in a warm jar, sprinkling the salt in between the layers. Heat the vinegar gently, then pour over the cherries to cover. Seal and store.

DRINKS NOOSHABEH

Whenever you visit someone in summertime in Persia the hostess will greet you with a tray of iced drinks – whatever flavour she happens to have in the house. These drinks are refreshing and cooling, the perfect drinks for daytime entertaining, especially in the midday heat.

FERDOWSI

You could hear Uncle Shari's footsteps on the cobbled streets approaching the house. Even as a little girl of only five I knew his routine well. On hot summer days his favourite place was in the cool cellar, where he would wait impatiently to begin his game of chess with my father. They would sit on the Persian carpet, leaning against the long bolsters placed around the creamy coloured brick walls. All along the walls were many shelves filled with clear glass bottles containing home-made drinks (*sharbats*). After a game of chess, Uncle Shari would take the heavy book of Shah-nameh (Epic of Kings), which contained several thousand pages, and read the legendary stories to me in his soft musical voice. Many of the stories written by Ferdowsi were about Zoroastrian relig-ion and history, and during my stay in Mashhad I visited nearby Tus where I saw his tomb. It took me back to my childhood days in the cool cellar in Yazd. I could almost hear Uncle Shari reading out the legendary Shahnameh to me all over again.

૪ૹ૪ૹ

Yoghurt Drink

Doogh

10–12 fl oz/300–350 ml plain yoghurt, preferably sharp in flavour
salt
ice cubes and a little crushed dried mint, to serve

Put the yoghurt in a bowl and beat with a fork.

Add a little salt to taste, then slowly beat in about 1 pint/600 ml iced water.

Pour into individual glasses, add ice cubes and sprinkle with mint.

Serve chilled, with any meat and rice.

HAMMAM

Hygiene played an important part in daily life, and an everyday wash was not considered sufficient! A tradition throughout the country was to attend Hammam, a custom which goes back to Roman times. There were three or four 'Hammam' buildings in every district and as you approached you were met by the distinctive smell of steam. The low flat roof had numerous domes built with frosted green and blue coloured glass, for the sun to reflect into the building. Hammam was either public or private. If public, the day was divided into mornings for men and afternoons for ladies. I remember entering the large steam room in the afternoons. It had many taps and a heated floor and several ladies (*kisehkesh*) who rubbed you down and gave you a good massage. The area was filled with ladies and small children and the washing procedure could be as long as three or four hours. Everyone was lazing around in the hot, steamy atmosphere, chatting and gossiping while they waited in the queue to be rubbed and massaged on the mosaic stone platform bed. The hours passed quickly because we enjoyed ourselves so much. In a private Hammam there were individual rooms which men and women could hire by the hour. I used to love going with my mother and sister Sarvar because we turned the changing room into a refreshment room and *memeh* would always come up with a surprise of a refreshing drink or her special mixed fruit.

Cucumber and Mint Drink

Nooshabeh-e-sekanjabin va khiyar

4–6 tablespoons MINT DRINK (page 147) to taste

10 oz/285 g finely grated peeled cucumber

ice cubes, to serve

Put the MINT DRINK in a bowl with about 1 pint/600 ml iced water. Mix well, then add the cucumber. Taste for sweetness, then pour into individual glasses and add ice cubes.

Serve chilled, with a spoon.

Cucumber and Rosewater Drink

Nooshabeh-e-khiyar ba golab

10 oz/285 g finely grated peeled cucumber

4–6 tablespoons rosewater, to taste

4 teaspoons granulated sugar

Put the rosewater and sugar in a bowl and stir in about 1 pint/600 ml iced water. Slowly stir in the cucumber, then pour into individual glasses and add ice cubes.

Serve chilled, with a spoon.

Variations

Melon and Rosewater Drink

Nooshabeh-e-Kharbozeh ba golab

Make as for CUCUMBER AND ROSEWATER DRINK above, with 5–6 tablespoons rosewater or to taste and 2–3 teaspoons granulated sugar. With a spoon, scrape the flesh from ½ large ogen melon (discarding the seeds). Stir the melon flesh into the drink.

Apple and Rosewater Drink

Nooshabeh-e-sib ba golab

Make as for CUCUMBER AND ROSEWATER
DRINK above, with 4–5 tablespoons rosewater or
to taste, 2–3 teaspoons granulated sugar, 4 eating
apples, peeled, cored and finely grated, and the
juice of ½ small lemon.

༄༅

Watermelon Drink

Nooshabeh hendevaneh

½ ripe sweet watermelon
sugar (optional)
ice cubes, to serve

Work the watermelon flesh in a Mouli-légumes to
extract the juice. Discard the flesh. Add sugar to
taste if necessary (the watermelon may be sweet
enough), then place in individual glasses and add
ice cubes.
   Serve chilled.

IMAM-REZA IN MASHHAD

During my childhood in Yazd, Malog my Muslim
nanny could often be heard calling to Imam-Resa.
She always promised that one day she would take
me to Mashhad, to see the tomb of Ali Reza, the
eighth *Imam* (holy man), but it was much later in
life that I finally did travel to the holy city, some
540 miles east of Tehran – 1½ hours by plane. I
remember seeing the golden dome of the 200-
metre-high mosque glistening in the distance as
the plane was banking to land.
   I was met by my friend Shahnaz who took me to
her home in the suburbs. Soon after arriving she
suggested a visit to the shrine during midday, as
many would prefer the cooler part of the day and
there would be fewer pilgrims about.
   Shahnaz gave me the choice of several *chadors* –
the long cloth worn by orthodox Muslim women to
cover their clothes. I recalled the colour of Malog's
chador and chose brown with white spots, remembering how she had taught me to wear it as a little
girl. I wrapped the long shawl over my clothes,
making sure that my hair and face were completely covered, with only one eye showing.
   It was exciting arriving on the wide avenues of
the city centre, with bustling people and heavy
traffic, but as we approached the mosque I felt
quite relaxed. On entering the anti-chamber in the
forecourt of the mosque, we were asked to remove
our shoes, as it is the custom to enter the mosque
in bare feet.
   The mosque was made up of several high-
ceilinged rooms, some of which were highly ornate
with mirror-mosaic patterns set into plaster or
woodwork. Gold leaf was much in evidence, deco-
rating walls and ceilings, and numerous chande-
liers hung from the ceilings, giving the place an
almost fairy-tale atmosphere. There were several
thousand pilgrims, and hardly enough room for
anyone to move about, but I was determined to
touch the famous Zary near the tomb and make a
wish. I found my way amongst the thousands.
Some who had already reached the tomb held on
to their gold jewellery – bangles, rings, chains and
necklaces – as they thronged through the decorative iron lattice work which covered the actual
tomb. Some cried out to Imam-Resa, urging him
to make their wishes come true. The atmosphere
was highly charged with emotion and every
moment added to the numbers of pilgrims.
   Back home, Shahnaz served chilled Rosewater
Drink and showed me around her modern house.
Dinner was served in the garden, after which my
hosts allowed me to sleep on the flat roof of their
house so that I could enjoy the spectacular scenery
of this holy city under the stars.

༄༅

Rosewater Drink

Sharbat-e-golab

This Zoroastrian drink is traditionally served at
weddings and New Year (*nov rooz*) celebrations.

| 8 sugar cubes or 5–6 teaspoons granulated sugar |
| 2 fl oz/50 ml rosewater |
| 1 teaspoon white basil seeds, washed and soaked for about 10 minutes in cold water |
| ice cubes, to serve |

Put the sugar in a large bowl, add about 1 pint/600 ml iced water and the rosewater and stir to dissolve. Add the basil seeds and their soaking water, pour into individual glasses and add ice cubes.

Serve chilled.

Mint Drink

Sekanjabin

| 6 oz/175 g granulated sugar |
| 3 fl oz/85 ml malt vinegar |
| 6–8 large sprigs of fresh mint |

Put the sugar in a heavy saucepan, pour in 8 fl oz/225 ml cold water and bring slowly to the boil. Reduce the heat and simmer for 10–15 minutes, then add the vinegar and simmer for a further 20 minutes or until a syrup is formed (drop a little onto a cold plate – it should barely spread). Add the mint, then remove the pan from the heat. Leave to cool uncovered (do not leave the lid on the pan or the condensation will spoil the syrup), then remove and discard the mint sprigs. Store in airtight bottles or jars.

Serve diluted with iced water.

Orange Drink

Sharbat-e-porteghal

| ½ pint/300 ml orange juice, freshly squeezed |

| thinly pared rind of 2 medium oranges |
| 4 tablespoons lemon juice |
| 3–4 oz/90–115 g granulated sugar, to taste |

Put all the ingredients in a small heavy saucepan, heat gently until the sugar has dissolved, then bring to the boil. Reduce the heat and simmer for about 30 minutes until thick, then pour through a sieve into a bowl and leave until cold. Store in airtight bottles or jars.

Serve diluted with iced water.

Variation

Cherry Drink

Sharbat-e-alubalu

Make as for ORANGE DRINK above, with ½ pint/300 ml cherry juice, 4 tablespoons lemon juice, 3 oz/90 g granulated sugar and a few drops of vanilla essence.

Quince and Lemon Drink

Sharbat-e-beh-limoo

Make as for ORANGE DRINK above, with 4 fl oz/120 ml quince juice (made in a juice extractor), 2 tablespoons lemon juice, 5 oz/140 g granulated sugar and ¼ teaspoon ground cardamom.

EAT AND DRINK AT NOV ROOZ TIME

One of the sweetest memories of Nov Rooz in Yazd was *Didani*, the custom of visiting relations and friends. Guests would be offered sweet after sweet until their plates were piled high. If uneaten, they would be wrapped in a serviette to take home. A carrier bag was always appreciated as this was one of my favourite customs, and somehow my plate always seemed fuller than the others!

Living in Tehran, I was introduced to another custom associated with *Didani*. Before lunch, a drink made of dried fruit was offered to guests. During Nov Rooz one generally overeats, and this special drink was supposed to clear the system! The drink is offered today as an appetiser during Nov Rooz time, and in England my Aunt Lal makes one of the best Dried Fruit Drinks I have ever tasted, from a recipe which was passed down to her from her mother.

Dried Fruit Drink

Ab-e-miveh

2½ lb/685 g mixed dried fruit (including
   cherries)

Wash the fruit and place in a bowl. Pour over 2 pints/1.2 litres cold water, cover and leave to stand in a cool place for 2–3 days. Turn the fruit in the water every day, to help extract the flavour. Ladle the liquid into individual glasses, with a few pieces of fruit for each glass.

Serve at room temperature with a spoon.

9

Basic Recipes

Pomegranate Puree

Robb-e-anar

If the pomegranate juice is sweet rather than sour, add the juice of 1 large lemon to sharpen the flavour of the purée.

2 pints/1.2 litres sweet and sour or sour pomegranate juice (made in a juice extractor)
1 medium uncooked beetroot, peeled and diced
1 teaspoon ground cinnamon

Put all the ingredients in a heavy saucepan (preferably a preserving pan) and bring to the boil. Reduce the heat and simmer uncovered for 1½–2 hours, stirring occasionally, until thick. Remove from the heat and set aside to cool. Store in airtight jars in a cool place.

Makes about 8 oz/230 g.

Hot Mint

Naana dagh

2 teaspoons oil
1 teaspoon crushed dried mint
2 garlic cloves, peeled and crushed

Heat the oil in a small heavy frying pan, add the garlic and stir quickly once or twice, then add the mint. Immediately remove from the heat to prevent the mint burning.

Use sparingly.

Tamarind Liquid

Ab-e-tambr

Tamarind pods are available from Indian and oriental shops. The liquid which is produced by soaking them is dark and rich, with a sweet-sour flavour. If you prefer, you can use concentrated tamarind liquid. Dilute it with water in the proportion of 1 fl oz/25 ml to 6 fl oz/175 ml cold water.

10 oz/285 g tamarind pods
2¼ pints/1.25 litres cold water

Wash the tamarind pods, place in a bowl and cover with 2 pints/1.2 litres of the water. Leave to soak overnight.

The next day, crush the pods with a fork, then place in a large saucepan with the soaking liquid and bring to the boil. Reduce the heat and simmer for 2–3 minutes until fairly soft.

Place a colander over a bowl and pour the contents of the pan into it. Stir with a spoon and let the liquid drain through into the bowl, then return the pods to the pan and add the remaining cold water. Stir and, if cool enough, squash the pods with your hands to extract as much liquid as possible. Drain into the colander again. If necessary, repeat with cold water to extract more dark liquid until only the pulp remains. Then discard the pulp.

Makes about 2½–2¾ pints/1.5–1.6 litres.

Yoghurt

Mast

Yoghurt is traditionally used a lot in Persian cooking to give a delicious creamy sauce to many dishes without the high cholesterol of cream. Although it is now readily available in your local shops, the homemade variety is much better in flavour and texture, and it is more economical too. Electric yoghurt-making machines can be used, so too can a vacuum flask, but this is how I make yoghurt, without any special equipment. First of all you will need a starter – purchased natural yoghurt or some held back from a previous batch.

1¾ pints/1 litre milk
1 generous tablespoon plain yoghurt

Bring the milk to the boil. As soon as froth rises to the top of the pan, remove it from the heat and pour into an ovenproof earthenware or glass dish. Leave for about 35 minutes, depending on room temperature, until tepid. Put the yoghurt in a separate small bowl and mix with 2 tablespoons of the tepid milk. Beat vigorously, then add to the remainder of the milk. Agitate with a fork from the edge inwards.

Put a warmed plate over the bowl to reduce condensation and place in a warm place. Put a thick cover such as a towel over the plate and bowl and leave for 5–8 hours (no longer, or the yoghurt will turn sour). Very gently tilt the bowl to see that it is set. If a slight coating of liquid does remain, carefully spoon it off into a glass – this is delicious to drink!

To avoid curdling when adding yoghurt to a hot liquid during cooking, beat 2 pints/1.2 litres yoghurt with 1 egg white, lightly broken up with a fork, and about 2 fl oz/50 ml milk or water. Slowly bring this mixture almost to the boil, then slowly add it to the hot liquid by stirring with a wooden spoon in one direction only. Lower the heat to barely simmer and as soon as thick sauce forms, remove from the heat.

An alternative method to prevent curdling is to whisk plain flour into the yoghurt in the proportion of 1 teaspoon plain flour to ¼ pint/150 ml yoghurt. Gently stir over low heat until it just comes to the boil and is a creamy consistency. Immediately remove from heat and add to hot liquid.

Persian Cheese

Panir

Panir is eaten in every Persian house from morning until night – for breakfast, lunch, dinner and supper! In summer it is delicious with *nan*, watermelon or other melons; in autumn with *nan* and white grapes, and in winter it is eaten with *nan*, dates and walnuts. It is both nourishing and satisfying. Here are two recipes for *panir*: the first uses yoghurt and is so quick that it can be made in minutes; the second has a creamier texture and softer taste which is acquired by using rennet rather than yoghurt. Traditionally, *panir* is made with goat's milk, but nowadays it is equally often made with cow's milk. Only use pasteurised milk, not homogenised or skimmed.

Panir I

2 pints/1.2 litres pasteurised milk

½ pint/300 ml plain yoghurt

Bring the milk to the boil. Beat the yoghurt and pour it into the milk, which will curdle. Stir once and remove from the heat. Line a colander or sieve with a large piece of muslin. Ladle in the curdled milk, tie the ends of the muslin tightly to make a bag, then place on a tilted kitchen board by the sink. Place a heavy object on it and leave for 30 minutes or until the excess water has drained away.

If the *panir* is not to be eaten straight away, dissolve 2 teaspoons salt in 1 pint/600 ml boiling water. Leave until cold, then gently drop in the *panir*. Keep in the refrigerator for up to 2 days.

Makes 7–8 oz/200–230 g.

Panir II

2 pints/1.2 litres pasteurised milk

2 tablespoons rennet essence

Warm the milk in a heavy saucepan to 98°F/37°C (or just warm to the finger if hot it will curdle). Add the rennet essence, stir once or twice, then immediately remove from the heat. Pour into a dish and cover with a warmed lid to reduce condensation. Put in a warm place, such as an airing cupboard or by a central heating unit. Leave to stand for 3–5 hours according to temperature, until set.

Gently pour off the excess whey and discard, then leave until really cool. Line a colander or sieve with a large piece of muslin. Ladle in the set milk,-tie the end of the muslin tightly to make a bag, then hang over the sink for 3½–4 hours or until the *panir* stops dripping. Gently squeeze the bag to check. This cheese can be stored in the refrigerator for 1–2 days; for longer storage, keep in salted water as for PANIR I above.

Makes about 6 oz/175 g.

Noodles

Reshteh

2 oz/50 g plain white flour
pinch of salt

Sift the flour and salt into a bowl. Slowly add 2 tablespoons warm water and knead for 2–3 minutes to make a soft dough. Cover and leave to rest in a warm place for about 20 minutes.

Roll out the dough on a floured surface to a 14–15 inch circle. Fold in half to make a semicircle, then fold again. Cut into very thin matchstick strips. Dust with flour to prevent the strips sticking together.

WATER IN THE GARDEN BEFORE WATER IN THE POT

All our family appreciated the taste of good, natural food and we were very proud of our figs, apricots, peaches and pomegranates, which could only be grown with the aid of purchased irrigation water from the mountains. I always looked forward to the visit of the irrigation team. One man would shout over the wall that he was releasing the flow of water, and another man would stand by the pipe with a stop watch to make sure we didn't get a drop more than we'd paid for.

It was lovely to see all the trees fresh with water and the ground so soaked that we could not step into the sodden garden for several days. All around the trees, the peas and beans interspersed with herbs were a brilliant green. I enjoyed eating the peas and beans straight from their pods, but even more so when *memeh* added the art of cooking to that of growing them!

MINT

Even though hot mint (*Naana Dagh*) is generally very popular throughout Persia, my family were quite fanatical about it – one terrace of our garden was planted with nothing but mint. Every few weeks the mint would be cut, a job which I enjoyed helping with, but I used to try to get out of the washing and spreading, as there was so much of it and it was not easy. My mother, my sister and I had to clean the mint, then spread it well apart on the *sofreh* (a very large white cloth), where it would be left to dry for 2–3 days. Then we would crush it and put it into jars for winter use. The house would be filled with the lovely smell of mint for days.

Index

INDEX OF MAIN INGREDIENTS